SURVIVING INSIDE
CONGRESS

◆●▶

A guide for prospective, new and not-so-new
Congressional staff – and a guided tour for those
who just want to learn how it all works

Mark Strand
Michael S. Johnson
and **Jerome F. Climer**

Founded in 1987, the Congressional Institute, Inc. is a not-for-profit 501(c)(4) corporation dedicated to helping Congress better serve its constituents and helping their constituents better understand the operations of the national legislature. The Institute sponsors major conferences for the benefit of Members of the U.S. Congress as well as a number of smaller gatherings, all devoted to an examination of important policy issues and strategic planning. The Institute conducts important research projects consistent with its mission, develops resources such as a House Floor Procedures Manual and this book and sponsors Oxford-style bipartisan Congressional debates.

A volunteer Board of Directors chaired by Michael S. Johnson governs the Institute. Mark Strand is the Institute's President. Jerry Climer is the former president.

The Congressional Institute
1001 North Fairfax St., STE 410
Alexandria, VA 22314
Phone: 703-837-8812
Email: info@conginst.org
Website: http://www.conginst.org

Table of Contents

Table of Contents

Introduction

The 21st Century finds leaders at all levels of government challenged by increasingly complex issues. International terrorism, worldwide economic uncertainty, natural disasters and the nation's crumbling infrastructure are just a few of the challenges demanding we do more with less. Ideological rigidity and tough partisan tactics have become the norm in the struggle for political domination, testing the ability of the elected to govern and to do so with civility. Low public confidence in government and its leaders has made it all but impossible for the elected to communicate effectively with those who elected them.

Their unelected professional staff members, who meet the diverse, sometimes critical needs of elected officials and their constituents, also face these challenges. Most new members of Congressional staffs are ill equipped to handle such demands. There are no comprehensive training programs, no curriculum that adequately addresses the multiple roles they will play and functions they will perform. This is due in large measure to the uniqueness of the roles they will play and the environment in which their work will be done. As a result, the academic credentials and professional experience they bring with them will have little relevance to the tasks they're about to undertake.

Many of those tasks will be defined by the elected officials they serve, elected officials who for the most part have little training for the positions they hold, let alone the supervisory experience required to guide subordinates to the level of professional efficiency and effectiveness that is demanded of those working in the private sector.

This handbook explores what professional staff in the public arena can do to prepare themselves for the challenges facing them and those they work for. Although it focuses primarily on work within the United States Congress, what is written here may be of value to everyone interested or involved in government, whether as a student, an elected official, a member of a government agency or a constituency hoping to influence an elected official's actions.

The authors owe a debt of gratitude to a number of experienced public policy experts – particularly Art Rynearson and Billy Pitts – who contributed to this volume as well as the many elected officials with whom the authors once worked. The extent to which their comments and suggestions were taken to heart is reflected in the number of places where they will recognize their thoughts woven into the fabric of the text – often without attribution.

We are deeply grateful to the contributions of the Congressional Institute staff: Amy Mertzeis, Patrick Deitz and Carolyn Bolls. Finally, the authors would like to acknowledge the research performed by interns Natalie Warrick and Robert Kelly on generational differences on Congressional staffs.

Chapter One
In the Beginning

When philosopher and poet Georges Santayana observed that those who don't study history are doomed to repeat it, he wasn't talking just about students attending summer school. Many recent political scandals, for example, could have been avoided if those who initiated them had paid closer attention to the lessons provided by the scandals of the past. But it's not just notoriety that can be avoided by familiarity with the lessons of history – bad policy and bad politics, too. The past is where we get the knowledge that propels us into the future – if every generation reinvented the wheel, mankind would still be dreaming of flights to the moon on gossamer wings. And if that's not reason enough to invest a few minutes exploring the heritage of the Congress, do it out of respect for the traditions that have made the institution a beacon in mankind's search for government of and by the people.

It began in 1789 when the 65 Members of the House of Representatives and the 26 Senators of the 1st Congress convened in the nation's capital – New York City. No personal staff members were provided in those days. House Members didn't need much help. They represented districts that included a mere 30,000 or so people, many of whom couldn't read or write, thus limiting the volume of correspondence Congressmen had to deal with.

Senators were chosen by the legislatures in the states they represented. They too operated without the benefit of staff.

Although 48 percent of House Members and 56 percent of Senators had college degrees, those without degrees were far more representative of the overall population at the time.

"There are few shining geniuses," wrote Fisher Ames of Massachusetts, who described his colleagues as sober, solid folks. "There are many who have experience, the virtues of the heart and the habits of business. It will be quite a republican assembly."

Not by today's standards: All 91 Members were white, male landowners. The average age in the House was 43, and in the Senate, 46. They were paid $6 a day for their efforts.

Like many who would follow in his footsteps, Ames discovered soon into the 2nd Congress that familiarity could breed contempt – especially in the Halls of Congress, where he complained about the yawning listlessness of many who served there.

One of the original Members of the House of Representatives, Fisher Ames kept an extensive diary during the first Congresses.

"Their state prejudices, their over-refining spirit in relation to trifles, their attachment to some very distressing formalities in doing business," he said in tallying the reasons for his growing disenchantment. "The objects now before us require more information, though less of the heroic qualities than those of the 1st Congress."

Whether heroism was uppermost among the goals of the Constitutional Convention of 1787 is debatable, but it was very much in evidence. Those in attendance had been tasked with rewriting the Articles of Confederation. Instead, they closed the doors and windows, and under the cloak of secrecy, wrote a new Constitution.

They drew upon the experiences of the Continental Congress and the Congress of the Confederation, both of which had been unicameral, consisting of a single legislative chamber rather than two separate houses. They drew upon the political philosophers and parliaments of Britain and other European nations. They even drew upon the governing documents of Pennsylvania and Virginia. And in the process, they evolved a clear and definite role for the Congress to play: It would be the first branch of government, the one that was truly representative of the people.

"The grand depository of the democratic principles of government," is how George Mason of Virginia envisioned it. "The requisites in actual representation are that the Representatives should sympathize with their constituents, should think as they think and feel as they feel and that for these purposes should even be residents among them."

Among the most important of the 18 Congressional powers enumerated in the Constitution is the power of the purse – the authority to tax and the authority to spend. The authors of the Constitution insisted that this power reside in the House of Representatives. It also gave the Congress the power to impeach and to the Senate, the power to confirm or deny presidential appointments, and ratify treaties.

There can be no confusion as to the intent of the Founders. They established the Legislative branch as the seat of the government and the font from which the nation's newly won independence would flow. Its importance is reflected in the fact that Article One of the Constitution, the one creating the Legislature, is twice as long as Article Two, which establishes the Executive branch, and four times as long as Article Three, which defines the Judiciary.

(Sometimes, it seems, the Founders thought of everything – including term limits, which had been among the provisions of the Articles of Confederation. The Constitutional Convention considered weaving term limits into its document. Instead it limited Members of the House of Representatives to two-year terms, naively assuming that would guarantee a constant flow of new blood into the Congress.)

Throughout the history of what the Founders referred to as the Republic, the balance of power has shifted back and forth among the Executive, Legislative and Judicial branches. Factors such as the leadership abilities of those in charge, the political alliances they formed and events throughout the nation and the world have contributed to changes in the power structure that drives the three branches.

Several presidents have exercised substantial influence over the Congress, usually in times of national emergency, but the Congress has exercised substantial influence over Chief Executives, as well. Sometimes both occur in a single administration, as was the case with President Bill Clinton, a Democrat, who at times dominated, and in turn was dominated by a Republican-controlled Congress.

The relationship between the Legislative and Executive branches was less tempestuous in the early days of the Republic, particularly when the Legislature was dominated by supporters of the Executive du jour. George Washington, for example, is said to have been significantly influenced in the writing of his first inaugural address by James Madison, who at the time represented the State of Virginia in the U.S. Congress. The day following Washington's address, Madison was appointed to head a committee of the House to prepare a response to the President's message he wrote.

Madison exemplified what influence a true leader can have whether legislator or President. As legislator, Madison headed a panel that drafted the first rules of the House and was a driving force behind the Bill of Rights, originally introduced as 12 amendments to the Constitution. Individuals from both the Federalist and Anti-Federalist factions opposed Madison's amendments. Anti-Federalist Aedanus Burke of South Carolina captured the spirit of the debate when he called the amendments "little better than whipsyllabub, frothy and full of wind, formed only to please the palate."

But Madison prevailed and the 12 amendments were submitted to the States for ratification on the last day of the 1st Congress. Ten were ratified.

One of the two that were not adopted would have prohibited Congress from giving itself a pay raise while in session, which meant a raise could not take effect until after the next election. It was resurrected in 1992 when it became the 27th and most recent amendment to the Constitution. The non-ratified amendment is discussed below.

Without Madison's commitment, the Constitution might never have been ratified since the faction demanding the protections contained in the Bill of Rights carried enough weight to permanently table the entire document. His success cleared the way for the 1st Congress to flex its oversight muscle early, instructing the Executive departments it had just created to report back to it on various matters under the Executive's jurisdiction. The House also appointed a committee on Ways and Means to advise it on fiscal matters but dissolved it eight weeks later in favor of relying on advice from Secretary of the Treasury Alexander Hamilton – a reflection of the still-unresolved ambiguity in the roles played by the branches of our federal government.

The 1st Congress apparently had more confidence in other actions it took. It created three federal departments – Treasury, War, and Foreign Affairs. It established the nation's court system, passed laws dealing with trade, patents, crime, mail, the military and bankruptcies, and deliberated over slavery and relations with the native peoples they called Indians.

The Congress also established rules governing its internal operations. And the House and Senate devised ways to communicate with each other and set salaries. The House also created the first permanent committee – the Committee on Elections to judge the qualification of its elected Members.

The first time President Washington visited the Congress, he witnessed events that made it clear once and for all that, just as the Founders had intended, the Legislative, Executive and Judicial branches of government are equals – but the Legislative is more equal than the others. Washington and Secretary of War Henry Knox went to Federal Hall in New York City, which at the time was the nation's capital, to seek the Senate's advice – but more importantly, its consent. At issue was creation of a commission to negotiate a treaty with the Creek Indians, who at the time laid claim to much of what eventually would become Florida, Georgia and Alabama. If Washington and Knox expected a rubber stamp, they were sadly mistaken. Several Senators indicated that they wanted to see documents related to the plan and since no such documents were available, it was agreed that the issue ought to be referred to committee. There ensued an uncomfortable period of silence and muttering, during which Senator William McClay of Pennsylvania observed that Washington was visibly irritated. When Washington and Knox retreated from the chamber a short time later, the President vowed never to return. But he did – two days later, when the Senate approved the commission. The incident established the independence of the Senate in regard to meeting that Constitutional responsibility – and marked the last time a President has shown up in person to petition for that body's advice and consent.

Despite President Washington's disappointment, harmony, civility and willingness to compromise stood as hallmarks of decision-making in the 1st Congress. It considered 168 bills, of which 108, or 64 percent, were enacted. Its accomplishments were recorded in a little more than 500 days, with almost no incidents of partisanship.

"There is less party spirit, less of the acrimony of pride when disappointed of success, less personality, less intrigue, cabal, management, or cunning than I ever saw in a public assembly," wrote Fisher Ames. "There was the most punctual attendance of the Members at the hour of meeting. Three or four have had leave of absence, but every other Member actually attends daily, till the hour of adjourning."

"Small wonder they completed so much in such a short time," historian Robert V. Rimini writes in *The House: The History of the House of Representatives*, "and all this without a staff of assistants to aid them."

They got away with it because despite the contentiousness surrounding various issues, life was simpler then – if only because there weren't as many people looking over the shoulders of those in the Congress and making demands upon their time and energy.

The addition of staff in the intervening years reflected the nation's growing population.

Today, elected officials and their staffs represent most every segment of society and U.S. geography, most every religious belief, professional pursuit, education and political persuasion. Critics point out, however, that the proportion of lawyers far exceeds the ratio of lawyers to the rest of the nation's population and that women and minority representation is

The Upper House – Literally!

It was at Federal Hall in New York City that the terms upper house and lower house were first used in reference to the Senate and the House of Representatives. It is commonly assumed that these designations refer to the power vested in these governing bodies, but in fact, they are the result of the building's architecture. The Senate could be accommodated within the comparatively modest confines of the structure's second floor, but the House required the more spacious first floor. Thus the Senate was referred to as the upper house and the House of Representatives the lower house.

11

nowhere near their proportion in the population as a whole. Yet, the Congress is more representative than it ever has been or is obligated to be. The fact is that Congress was never intended to be a microcosm of its multitudinous constituencies.

Consider the characteristics of a single resident of the United States: age, ethnicity, religion, gender, education, regional concerns, professional concerns and the list goes on. The electorate is so fractionalized that there's no way to identify, let alone represent, the idiosyncrasies of every citizen.

In our nation's earliest days, this fact of life didn't represent a significant problem. The Congress and the people it represented subscribed to the philosophy of political theorist John Locke, who believed government ought to have as little influence as possible on the lives of the governed.

By the time the 2nd Congress convened in 1791, the Legislative branch was well on its way to abandoning the Locke model. The influence of the federal government has been ever more palpable ever since.

Abraham Lincoln enunciated it well: "The legitimate object of government is to do for a community of people whatever they need to have done, but cannot do at all, or cannot do so well, for themselves, in their separate and individual capacities."

Finding things the community of people could not do at all or not very well has become one of the driving *raisons d'être* of the federal government. Its search has been very successful. Journalist Saul Pett points out that during the Civil War the offices of all the people who worked for the federal government would have fit comfortably in a building the size of the modern Pentagon. But it was growing at a hectic pace even then. The cork was out of the bottle, so to speak.

Yet it wasn't until 1884 that Senators were finally authorized to employ staff, and even then it was only for the period when the Congress was in session. The Legislative Appropriations Act of 1891 cleared up the fact that the enabling legislation failed to specify how many staff members a senator could have. It stated that Senators who were not chairmen of committees would be provided with one clerk – that's it, a clerk, singular, just one – to handle administrative duties and free up the Senator to focus on the work he was elected to perform.

In 1893, the House of Representatives followed suit, allocating funds enough to employ a clerk for each Congressman. Representatives were earning $7,500 a year by this point – it was their clerks who were being paid just $6 a day.

To avoid confusion, we'll pause here to explain that even though Senators are Members of the Congress, the term Congressman is generally reserved for Members of the House, unless, of course, they're women, but at the time we're talking about there wouldn't be any Congresswomen for another 23 years. Individual Senators, by the way, are always referred to as Senator. Congressional staff, on the other hand, refers to employees of either the House or the Senate – or both.

It was also in 1893 that the Senate extended its authorization for clerical help from the period when the Congress was in session to year-round status, and in 1910, Senators were allowed to hire an additional staff member. Four years after that, they were authorized to increase their staff size to three.

It is worth noting that by the time the Congress got around to providing lawmakers with clerical help, many already had support staff on their payrolls and paid them out of their own pockets. The decision to pay these employees with tax dollars did more than just relieve these lawmakers' financial burden. It signaled the realization that the role of government and the demands that were being placed upon it were changing.

Members of the House of Representatives didn't get three staff members until 1940, but they saw that number rise to six less than a decade later.

By the time Senate staff allotments reached eight in 1947, the ranks of federal agencies under the auspices of the Executive branch were increasing at such a rapid clip that tongue-in-cheek prognosticators predicted that by the year 2025, every resident of the United States would be working for the government.

Even if that prediction comes to pass, however, it is unlikely they'll be working for the Congress. Membership in the Senate is limited to two representatives from each state. Unless new states are admitted to the Union, the size of the Senate is not going to increase. The size of the House of Representatives is only slightly more likely to change if legislation is enacted to provide Washington D.C. with representation in the House.

Between 1790 and 1910, the number of Representatives grew almost every decade to reflect increases in the nation's population. That process came to an abrupt halt in 1913, when Congress capped House membership at 435.

Some observers claim the Founders never intended the population of a Congressional district to exceed 50,000, let alone, nearly 700,000 – which is about the size of the districts today. The one amendment proposed by Madison in the Bill of Rights that was not eventually ratified specifically limited the size of Congressional Districts to 50,000. Yet, if districts had only 50,000 constituents the House would have 6,000 Members today.

"Consequently, the principle of proportionally equitable representation has been abandoned," observes one group interested in apportionment.

Tell that to the overworked Congressional staff members whose job it is to accommodate the needs of the ever-increasing number of constituents represented by each Member. Yet the need to increase in the size of Legislative staffs is not predicated solely on increases in the number of people they serve. The Congress simply cannot maintain oversight of countless federal bureaucracies nor serve its own constituents without adequate personnel.

The need for oversight is one reason Senate staff allotments increased to eight in 1947. A year later, limits on how many people a Senator could employ were abandoned altogether. Instead each Senator would be provided with an allowance, which since 1951 has been based on the population of the state the Senator represents, and it would be up to each Senator to decide how to spend it.

Comparatively speaking, staff sizes exploded in the 1960s, when the number of staff in the House of Representatives reached 12 per office before increasing to 18 in 1975. Four years later, each office was allowed to hire four additional temporary, part-time or shared employees.

House Members are not required to spend all the funds allotted to them, which is why in 2003 expenditures ranged from a low of $700,000 for salaries to a high of $1.6 million. Staff sizes averaged close to 18 but fluctuated as staff moved on to jobs outside of government or were transferred to committee assignments – and to committee budgets – creating temporary vacancies that lasted until replacements could be found. That same year, Senate allowances ranged from $2.2 million to $3.7 million and covered wages and benefits for an average staff size of 40 per office.

Not everyone considers tax dollars well spent when they are used to provide the Congress with staff. Even the Congress sometimes expresses doubts, as it did in 1993 when Congressional staffing became the focus of a Joint Committee inquiry.

The only significant cut in staff ever made occurred after the Republican takeover in 1994 when the new majority cut all committee staffs by one-third.

Those who help Congress serve the needs of its various constituencies and help shape laws that serve the changing needs of the nation probably would argue that they're anything but bloated.

Ambitious?

Yes!

Idealistic?

Obviously!

Overworked?

Always!

But bloated?

Not likely. The salaries paid on Capitol Hill may seem exorbitant to people in Peoria but not to those trying to make ends meet in one of the world's most expensive cities. Congress remains the branch of government that is truly representative of the people it serves, but it doesn't protect those who are elected to serve there or those who work for them from the constant barrage of complaints, criticisms and second-guessing from the media, from interest groups and the people it represents.

It's easy to become defensive when you're on the receiving end of this sort of carping – but it's a fact of life that comes with the job.

If being misunderstood hurts your feelings, find another line of work. Those who benefit most from the experience of working for Congress are the ones who develop a thick skin, the ones who are undaunted by the slights of those at whose pleasure they serve, and the ones with enough self-confidence to believe that what they're doing makes a difference.

Chapter One Summary

- The 1st Congress convened in 1789 when the 65 Members of the House of Representatives and the 26 Senators met in the nation's capital – New York City. Today there are 435 Members of the House and 100 Senators. Neither the House nor the Senate had personal staff support.

- At the time of the nation's founding, only white, land-owning citizens were allowed to vote and they, for the most part, fell into just a few occupational classes: merchants, farmers and ranchers. Most were not formally educated, communications were poor and Congress received little advice or feedback from the governed. Today, the education level of the constituents almost equals that of Members, communications are instantaneous and citizens frequently know more about specific topics than the Members.

- Of the 12 original amendments to the US Constitution, ten of which are known as the Bill of Rights, only one has not been adopted. That amendment would have established a constitutional process for limiting the size of congressional districts that have grown from their original 30,000 citizens to the current 700,000. That growth has significantly changed the nature of being a Member of Congress and both dictated the number and duties of congressional staff.

- The principle of Congressional oversight was established when President Washington visited the Senate for what he assumed would be quick advise and consent of his commission to negotiate a treaty with the Creek Indians. Washington sat in dismay as the proposal was questioned and documents sought by an ad hoc committee to study the treaty.

- Congressional staff was unheard of in the early days of the republic. Not until 1891 did the Senate authorize the hiring of one staff member for each Senator. The House followed suit and authorized the payment of $6 per day for one staff person per Member in 1893.

- The need for oversight is one reason Senate staff allotments increased to eight in 1947. A year later, limits on how many people a Senator could employ were abandoned altogether. Instead each Senator would be provided with an allowance, which since 1951 has been based on the population of the state the Senator represents, and it would be up to each Senator to decide how to spend it.

- Comparatively speaking, staff sizes exploded in the 1960s, when the number of staff in the House of Representatives reached 12 per office before increasing to 18 in 1975. Four years later, each office was allowed to hire four additional temporary, part-time or shared employees. The Senate now averages around 40 staff members per personal office while House Members are limited to 18.

- The only significant cut in staff ever made occurred after the Republican takeover in 1994 when the new majority cut all committee staffs by one-third.

A Job or a Career?

There's no shame in using an appointment to the Congressional staff as a stepping-stone. Nearly everyone who works for the Congress is a temp, most of all the elected officials who run the show but whose futures are as uncertain as the next election. If the boss is defeated, the entire staff is fired – though some might catch on with another Member. What little job security there is usually derives from a staff member's dedication, talent and experience – not to mention the gerrymandering of congressional districts to protect Members from opposition and keep them in office.

Despite these harsh realities, Congressional offices have little problem filling vacancies. They typically receive anywhere from several hundred to several thousand applications a year from people intent on serving the public by serving the institution and those elected to it. Although patronage no longer is the surest means to a job in government, elected officials still put a premium on ideological compatibility and familiarity within the district or state they represent – especially among those in their inner circle. Yet, education, professional skills and the ability to produce results are in greater demand than ever before, and there are lots of people with those skills eager to fill any slot that comes open.

People start their careers in different ways. They can start at the bottom as an intern or at the top as chief of staff. For most, however, the advice aspirants hear most often from veterans is: "just get your foot in the door."

This is good advice. The problem with Hill jobs is that they are rarely advertised. You have to be in the right place at the right time – you dropped by an office the day the front desk staffer walked out, for example – or you have to work your way into the informal grapevine that spreads the word when there's a vacancy.

For individuals in college or just out of one, the best avenue is an internship or entry-level staff assistant job. Prepare a resume that lists your education and experience – include summer jobs and volunteer activities that demonstrate a willingness to work hard and make sacrifices for others. For heaven's sake, use spell-check and grammar review software – it is amazing how many people do not and wonder why they never get called.

Hill offices are always looking for interns – especially in the non-summer months. A summer internship is a great thing – in the Senate it even pays enough to cover your expenses in DC – but the time when offices most need interns is during the spring and fall. Most colleges have internship programs, and often offer college credit for a semester in the nation's capital. Take advantage of them.

Hill veterans will quickly sort interns into three categories:

1) Offspring of a friend of the Congressman or FOC's.

2) Nice kid, but not cut out for the Hill.

3) Potential staff material.

Every moment an intern is in a Congressional office they are auditioning for a permanent job – whether they understand that or not. Offices typically promote from within first.

Coming to work with a hangover one day or even having an inappropriate picture show up on a Facebook page can irreparably damage a reputation. Blowing off a request for help from a permanent staff member will also earn a permanent mark against you. Saying something offensive to a constituent that a senior staff member has to apologize for will probably get an intern sent home.

Working hard, lending a hand wherever it's needed and taking every opportunity to learn something new will get an intern noticed. A good attitude and great manners – especially around constituents – also go far.

When an entry-level opening does occur – usually at the staff assistant or legislative correspondent level – an intern who caught the eye of superiors will be on the short list of candidates. That's because an internship provides far better evidence of an applicant's talents and abilities than a thirty-minute job interview and comments from former employers.

If you can't relocate to Washington D.C., look into the possibility of interning in a district or state office. Sometimes an internship at that level can be even more advantageous than one in D.C. – when Members are in their home offices, their schedules are typically less intense and provide opportunities to get to know the intern driving them from one town to another to meet with constituents.

Another popular method of attracting attention is to work on a campaign. Campaigns are incredibly intense but at the same time fun. The camaraderie between campaign workers is similar to the bond between soldiers. As Winston Churchill once observed with tongue firmly in cheek: "Politics is just like war, except in war you can only die once – in politics many times."

There are key differences between working on a campaign and working in a congressional office – some of which are discussed later in the book – but a smart, hard-charging staffer will always be noticed, appreciated and rewarded.

Politics is really the last of the great meritocracies. Academic credentials are nice – but they don't mean all that much in a Hill office. It doesn't matter where you came from, what your background is or your gender, religion or race. If you help a Member succeed they are going to find a way to keep you in the political family.

People who come to Washington without a job often are unable to land one right away. Don't be discouraged. Sometimes the timing is just wrong. The next best thing is to get into the orbit that revolves around the Hill – political party organizations, think tanks, and lobbying and consulting groups, as well as the thousands of associations and non-profit groups headquartered in Washington, are always looking for research assistants. Many of these organizations work directly with the Hill and offer the opportunity to develop contacts, friendships and networks that form the Capitol Hill job grapevine.

Some will take a more direct route to the Hill – but these are people who for the most part will occupy senior level positions. A campaign manager, for example, might be hired as chief of staff – but it's not as common as you might assume – or a campaign spokesman might become press secretary, which is a far more natural fit. Someone with expertise in a topic near and dear to a Member's heart might be hired into a policy position or onto a committee staff. Almost every situation is unique.

The greatest challenge facing those fortunate enough to be hired lies in fulfilling expectations. The public's demand for efficient, cost-effective government often exceeds what mere humans can produce. That's why it's a good idea to bring more than altruism to a job on the Hill.

Typically, staff members share motivations such as a desire to:

- Immerse oneself in public-policy issues and the art of governing.
- Make more money than they've been earning.

Hill veterans often make
reference to hacks and wonks.
Both terms are pejorative – but
hack is considerably more
pejorative than wonk.

Hacks are often despised
for their perceived lack of
convictions. They're considered
mercenaries, great campaigners
who possess no belief system
to guide their activities if their
candidate gets elected and
they wind up with a job in
government. They are the inside
equivalent of outsider Jack
Abramoff, the misguided lobbyist
who took down a number of
Members and staff as a result of
illegal activities.

Hacks are objects of scorn even
when they're on your side.

If you call someone a hack, it is
an insult.

If you find yourself being unfairly
characterized as a hack,
chances are you're projecting the
wrong image.

Being called a wonk is far less
devastating. A wonk is the
political equivalent of a nerd.
You might hear the term used to
describe someone who is very
bright but not politically astute.

- Follow in the footsteps of a relative or mentor.

- Acquire celebrity, fame or notoriety.

- Amass and exercise power.

- Promote a partisan or philosophical agenda.

Some new staff members consider themselves devotees of the art of politics – there to advance a party or ideology.

Others consider themselves issue specialists or policy experts and advocates – there to promote issue-related outcomes.

The most successful Congressional staff members possess the best qualities of both – political and policy savvy and the intelligence to use it productively. Such staff members are essential to the successful operation of the Congress and make it possible for the elected to legislate.

Yet circumstances dictate that the vast majority of those working at any one time in a Congressional office will take the experience and contacts they've accumulated to other jobs. They may find themselves employed in the Executive branch, in academia, in the private sector or perhaps even fulfilling their own political ambitions.

Bob Michel of Illinois, who was the House's GOP leader before his retirement, and former Senate Republican Whip Trent Lott of Mississippi began their careers on Congressional staffs. Fred Thompson worked on the Hill as a junior counsel for the House Judiciary Committee. So did Democrats Tom Harkin and Hillary Clinton. All in all, according to the Congressional Research Service (CRS) there were 101 Members of the 110th Congress that had been Congressional staffers or pages earlier in their careers.

Congressional staff anticipating they'd be there until retirement are often lured away by industry, other branches of government or the vast range of agencies that benefit from the skills and knowledge of those who've been intimately involved in the lawmaking process. Those who stay, though fewer in number than those who moved on, may have arrived on Capitol Hill with plans of cutting their teeth there, then moving to the higher-paying, high-visibility jobs, discovered themselves better suited to working behind the scenes and stayed on.

Most people helping make policy seem to fall into this category. Their ideas see the light of day only when adopted and articulated by elected or appointed officials. They prefer it that way even though they often must subjugate their views to those of their bosses. They are not paid to be independent actors. They are agents of the elected official for whom they work.

They are obligated to share their opinions, but once a decision is made by the man or woman who will carry responsibility for it, they are required to give it their enthusiastic support or find work elsewhere. Their job satisfaction derives from the fact that their opinions are considered and sometimes their ideas are implemented, even if someone else gets the credit.

These career professionals are the nucleus of Capitol Hill. They are the glue that holds the Congress together, the unseen, unheard, unsung heroes of federal government. They know the ins and outs of the legislative process, as well as the history of almost every federal policy, from environmental issues to tax laws. Like all professions, theirs has distinctive cultural aspects, and archaic codes unique to the Hill.

For example, among Congress' archaic codes is an antiquated system of bells, buzzers and lights that is used to summon Members of the Congress for a vote on the chamber floor. In the old days, it was the only means anyone could come up with to guarantee that every Member within earshot knew his or her presence was required. Today, most Members carry pagers and get word via a clearly articulated message.

Since voting is the one task a Member may not delegate, each Member must make his or her way to the Floor when summoned there. In order to cast their votes, Members must get there before the voting concludes – usually within 15 minutes.

Members learn quickly how long it will take them to get to the chamber from anywhere on the Congressional campus and often cut their departure as close as humanly possible to give them time to finish whatever they were doing when summoned. There was a time when staff members were expected to be experts on the system of bells, lights and buzzers so they could remind the boss in case he or she lost track of time. Modern staffs rely on emails, portable electronic devices and closed-circuit telecasts of what's taking place on the Floor.

The system of bells, buzzers and lights, the Mace, the bowing protocols and other pomp and circumstance surrounding the House and Senate are what distinguishes the institution and preserves its unique and revered place in our national body politic. Some of these may seem anachronistic to the uninitiated – they definitely can prove mind numbing to master and downright disturbing when they unexpectedly shatter your concentration – but they aren't likely to be abandoned just to make life easier for newcomers. Eventually, they'll contribute to the richness of the memories you take with you, whether your stay on a Congressional staff proves to be a temporary oasis or the last job you ever have.

Career professionals do more than merely maintain such traditions. The good ones are experts in parliamentary procedure and communication within the Congress; between the Congress and the rest of the federal government; between the Congress, on the one hand, and state and local governments, on the other; between the Congress and the people; and between the House and the Senate, as well as their committees and personal offices, each of which has a unique personality and a language all its own. It is their knowledge and skills that enable them to survive the winds of change that blow through the nation every decade or so.

New Members bring with them new staffs, but invariably they rely on the veterans to help them navigate through unfamiliar rules, procedures and protocols, to say nothing of the small fiefdoms and principalities that dot the landscape. Newcomers also find a universe that bears little resemblance to their expectations. They come to the nation's capital with dreams of conquering the panoply of complex issues facing America, from globalization's cultural and economic ramifications to educational needs in a rapidly changing scientific and technological environment. They quickly learn that answering constituent mail can be their most urgent priority on any given day.

The Balancing Act

Legislative staff members must learn to balance political awareness, sensitivity to voter attitudes, the legislative process and constituent service. They must accept, for example, that:

- All power is situational and temporary. Members of the House and Senate get to the Congress by a variety of routes and for a variety of reasons. The same holds true for their staffs. The positions they hold are not necessarily based on skill, experience or knowledge. Their duration is subject to the whim of the electorate.

- Decisions made in the Congress are based on consensus. Because power there is transient, there are no accepted rules for how a Member should decide whether to support or oppose a measure. It should come as no surprise then that when a Member is forced to take a position, it is as much shaped by outside pressures and the imperative to compromise as by principle or logic.

- There is a never-ending tension between following the people and leading them – and often conflicting obligations, as well. Members of Congress are forever being challenged to weigh their beliefs against public opinion. Some Members vote their perception of how constituents view the issue at hand, believing it is the safest course and the reason they were sent to Congress. Others act on their own beliefs, even when they believe a majority of their constituents might disagree with them then go home and explain why the course they've chosen is the right one. Others venture further into their Constitutional responsibilities and engage in activities and issues with a national or international impact that may not be of interest to constituents back home. A good many Members blend all three patterns of behavior.

Among the reasons it's hard to decide whether a Member should vote his or her conscience or his or her constituency is the leeway provided by the Founding Fathers when they took what they considered the best qualities of a republic and best qualities of a democracy and created our democratic republic.

- A democracy is governed by majority rule – in our case, the ballot box.

- A republic is governed by a charter – in our case, the U.S. Constitution – which puts the burden on those elevated to positions of authority to make decisions based on their best judgment within the framework of the charter.

Reflecting both forms is not easy, particularly when a representative knows more about an issue than the constituents. The fate of many elected officials and their staffs has been doomed when a strongly held belief or principle conflicted with the strongly held opinions of voters back home.

Former Senate Majority Leader Lyndon Johnson experienced that conflict when as President he tried to convince his fellow Southern Democrats to support the Civil Rights Act of 1964. Despite the fact that Johnson previously had resisted such change in the Senate and despite their assurances that they would support the measure when it came to a vote, many of those Democrats voted nay. Had it not been for former Senate adversaries like Republican Everett Dirksen of Illinois, Johnson might never have mustered the votes he needed to turn civil rights into the law of the land.

Less daunting is the need to review the lessons you learned in high school civics:

- The entire House of Representatives must be elected every two years, forming a completely new Congress that must elect (or re-elect) its party leaders, adopt its own rules and appoint its officers; Members of the Senate serve six-year terms, but the terms are staggered so that only one-third of the Senate changes every election – making the Senate an ongoing body.

- Senators represent entire states; House Members represent districts within each state – districts that are a fraction the size of the states and whose inhabitants tend to be more cohesive in their attitudes (with the obvious exception of single-Member states – Alaska, Montana, North Dakota, Rhode Island, South Dakota, Vermont, Wyoming).

- Senators serve on a larger number of committees and have larger staffs to support their efforts; House Members typically don't even have committee specialists on their staffs until they achieve seniority – nor are they required to develop expertise in as broad a range of committee topics.

- It is believed by some that all House Members want to be Senators and all Senators want to be President. Ironically, the election of 2008 was the first in nearly half a century to elect a Senator as President.

The Culture of the House and Senate

Staff is expected to know whether appropriation bills can be initiated in the Senate, whether the House can ratify treaties, whether House Members vote to confirm nominees to the federal court system, whether a supermajority of the Senate and House can amend the Constitution. Does a simple majority vote of both houses override a veto?

(The answer to all of these questions is no, by the way.)

Most of your peers will assume you understand such basics and will

---

Three Perspectives on Representation

- "A portrait is excellent in proportion to its being a good likeness – the legislature ought to be a most exact transcript of the whole society." – James Wilson (Signer of Declaration and Constitution and one of the original Supreme Court justices)

- "Your representative owes you, not his industry only, but his judgment; and he betrays instead of serving you if he sacrifices it to your opinion." – Edmund Burke, Member of Parliament

- "Members of Congress need to be at least as clear on the reasons why they would risk losing as they are on the reasons why they wanted to come here in the first place." – The late Rep. Henry Hyde

not take time to explain them. This assumption is so firmly entrenched, in fact, that it has led to conversational shorthand to describe congressional actions. Were a House colleague to say, for example, that a bill has gone to Rules, he or she would mean the legislation has been approved at the committee level and submitted to the Rules Committee where it will be scheduled for debate on the Floor.

The same expression will not be heard in the Senate, which does not rely on a committee to control the flow of work on the Senate Floor or determine how long debate will be. In most cases, the rules of the Senate do not vary from one bill to the next, and the Senate Majority Leader handles scheduling.

Keep in mind as well that the Constitution says that members of Congress answer only to their constituents, including how they manage their offices, unless their behavior leads the chamber in which they serve to judge the ethics or morality of their activities.

Become familiar with the culture of the Legislative branch as a whole, as well as distinctions between the culture of the Senate and the culture of the House.

The House consists of 435 independent players representing all of the people in all 435 congressional districts in the nation. There are an additional 5 non-voting delegates.

The 100 U.S. Senators are equally independent.

It is the stature of the offices these men and women hold that affords them a semblance of respect among their colleagues and staff. Maintaining appearances is essential and part of the culture. Congressional employees may be on a first-name basis with the boss in the office but should always address him or her formally in the presence of outsiders: Congressman Smith or Congresswoman Applegate, for example, when speaking to a constituent, other Members or the media. Always address other Members formally unless invited to do otherwise – and even then, follow the same rules that apply in your relationship with your boss.

Familiarize yourself with the roles of other staff in your congressional office, as well as personnel in other offices, committees and the leadership. Employees of the Legislative branch are much more interdependent than those in the Department of Agriculture, which has somewhere in the neighborhood of 100,000 employees with a range of specialties and a measure of autonomy working in offices scattered around the world. A Congressional employee, on the other hand, might oversee her office's computer operations while the staffer sitting next to her might manage scheduling and another neighbor might be a central player in legislation or constituent services. Mutual respect is vital to peaceful and prosperous co-existence.

Successful staffers respect the history of the Congress. They become sensitive to its ebb and flow. They recognize it as a living part of the body politic, one with muscles and nerves that give it elasticity and ever-changing form. Successful staffers understand the goals and aspirations of the Member they serve and how those goals and aspirations affect the behavior of not only the Member but his or her staff and everyone else working on the Hill.

Learn to recognize formal and informal power structures and the relationships among the staffs of Members, between the staffs of Members and those of Leadership. Leaders in both parties may do their best to persuade Members to march in lock step, for example, but they have little leverage with which to do so. It's why Former Senator Trent Lott titled his book on leadership *Herding Cats*.

Be aware most of all that the Congress is a well-lighted fishbowl that is monitored 24-hours a day by mainstream media, independent bloggers, political adversaries and dozens of non-profit organizations whose livelihood is dependent upon their self-appointed role as overseers of the body politic. Those in government are often painted with broad strokes and harsh tones. Sometimes it seems that as far as these watchdogs are concerned, whatever public servants are doing is never enough and usually wrong.

You'll find that the work can be mundane, seemingly counterproductive, and sometimes counter-intuitive, with conclusions and outcomes often elusive. Bringing home the bacon – providing public benefit to the district or state, more often in the form of federal tax dollars earmarked for district or state projects – can become so all-encompassing that it completely distracts – and at the same time, detracts – from what you set out to accomplish. Egos, political ambitions and jealousies are magnified in this environment, usually at the expense of staff relationships and office efficiency.

And yet it is these quirks that contribute to the human dynamic that is the U.S. Congress, that make it an unparalleled gathering of Americans trying to assure that self-government lives up to its ever expanding potential. And it is this institution of Congress that has shaped the greatest governmental system in history for the richest country and blessed people.

Chapter Two Summary

- The majority of congressional staff do not remain with the Congress for a life-long career.

- Those that do form the nucleus of Capitol Hill. They are the glue that holds the Congress together. They know the ins and outs of the legislative process, as well as the history of almost every federal policy, from environmental issues to tax laws. Like all professions, theirs has distinctive cultural aspects, and archaic codes unique to the Hill.

- According to the CRS there were 101 Members of the 110th Congress that had been Congressional staffers or pages earlier in their careers.

- Job openings in the congressional world are rarely advertised; it pays to be at the right place at the right time and to know Members of the House, Senators or other staff. Internships and campaign work (voluntary or paid) are great avenues to entry.

- Politics is really the last of the great meritocracies. Academic credentials are nice – but they don't mean all that much in a Hill office.

- Staff must become familiar with the culture of the Legislative branch as a whole, as well as distinctions between the culture of the Senate and the culture of the House. Successful staffers respect the history of the Congress.

- Be aware most of all that the Congress is a well-lighted fishbowl that is monitored 24-hours a day by mainstream media, independent bloggers, political adversaries and dozens of non-profit organizations whose livelihood is dependent upon their self-appointed role as overseers of the body politic.

Every enterprise has a hierarchy, whether it is Microsoft or the PTA. Understanding such hierarchies can mean the difference between succeeding or merely surviving – particularly in Washington, D.C.

Just as no Member of Congress owes allegiance to any other, neither is there uniformity in staff titles and their meaning or function. While each office has great autonomy, Members must respond to a maze of obligations ranging from committee assignments and party loyalties to constituent demands. Each office has its own unique hierarchy.

A Member's interests typically reflect his or her personal background and concerns of his constituents. A district from Kansas or Iowa, for instance, is likely to elect a representative interested in farm policy. Those representing western states are likely to seek appointment to the Interior or Natural Resources committee. A lawyer or a doctor prior to election may want to serve on the Judiciary Committee or a committee involved in health issues such as Ways and Means or Energy and Commerce.

When first elected most Members don't get their first choice or even a committee that addresses their home district's most pressing concerns. They're more likely to be appointed to second-choice committees, where they await opportunity to move up should someone retire or be unseated. There are instances, however, when a candidate campaigns on a pledge to seek appointment to a committee important to the home district and gets party leadership to guarantee the appointment if the candidate is elected.

Staff also tends to reflect the Member's background, interests and district while the organizational structure typically mimics that of his or her predecessor. Obviously the new Member brings a new direction and needs, but there's so much to deal with that it's usually beneficial to look to the predecessor's staff and approach to office needs and constituent services. This is particularly true when the Member is representing a district that was formerly held by a member of his or her party.

Unless the new Member is replacing someone from the opposition party, it's likely some of the predecessor's staff will even be retained, in the short term, at least, providing the continuity and experience that will enable the newcomer to focus on more urgent matters. At a minimum, however, the newcomer is likely to bring along a couple of trusted allies – people from the district and the campaign.

Once in Washington the Member-elect, particularly those replacing a political rival, looks for experienced staffers who can get the office running, handle committee chores and deal with the federal and state agencies on behalf of constituent needs.

Personal Staff

Despite the fact that Senate offices typically have more than twice the staff of their counterparts in the House, the organization charts of the two chambers are very similar.

Not surprisingly, the Member occupies the pinnacle of the power structure, but who's next in line?

That depends. In a few cases, someone may have the chief of staff title but it will be the Member as micromanager who really runs the show, and in increasingly rare cases a staff member may carry the title but the Member's spouse actually exercises informal but real authority.

In the vast majority of offices, however, the chief of staff is the Member's strong right-arm, the most important hiring decision the Member makes – sometimes, the only one. An effective chief influences every aspect of the Member's political and professional life. It is on this, the most common types of chief that we'll focus our attention.

You'll sometimes hear the position referred to as an administrative assistant. Don't be misled. In non-Congressional parlance, Administrative Assistant may be a euphemism for *executive secretary*, which is an important position, but an effective chief of staff carries considerably more responsibility.

In the absence of the Member, the chief is the boss. Even in the Member's presence, the chief makes decisions affecting how things get done. On one level, the chief functions very much like a Chief Operating Officer (COO), holding everyone else within his or her domain accountable to the Member's mission and goals, supervising every aspect of the Congressional office. The chief oversees the legislative and communication operations and helps coordinate relations between the Member's personal office, on the one hand, and committees and leadership, on the other. The chief also coordinates the activities of the D.C. office with the Member's district or state office. Sometimes the chief even coordinates interaction between the office and the Member's family.

In addition, the chief has a hand in policy initiatives and even re-election efforts. Although the chief is legally prohibited from participating in campaign activities during working hours, he or she is usually the liaison between the Congressional office and the Member's campaign staff – particularly if the chief played a role in getting the Member elected in the first place.

Some chiefs are former campaign managers but the nature of a government office and a campaign are quite different. Conventional wisdom suggests that individuals that have experience on the Hill or previously served on the Member's senior staff at another level of government may be better suited for the task.

Despite the responsibilities heaped on the chief, there are no legally mandated qualifications for the job. No experience or age requirements, no degree or certification requirement, nothing. As a result, it's not uncommon for a Harvard Law School graduate to be working the phones in the front office under the supervision of a chief of staff whose academic achievements stopped at graduation from high school. Far more important than degrees are a chief's personal qualities – primarily competence and loyalty.

Regardless of what sort of relationship exists between the Member and the chief at the time of the appointment, they are likely to become life-long friends and confidants.

The Member will usually be less involved in the hiring of staff that will serve under the chief, taking a collaborative role in the selection of senior positions but pretty much leaving others to his or her top aide. The Member is likely to be involved in selecting a legislative director or communications director, for example, but far less involved, if at all, in hiring a staff assistant or receptionist.

The focus of staff members who report to the chief fall into four basic categories:

Legislative

Communication

Outreach and Constituent Services

Support and Administrative Staff

The legislative team deals with what many think of as the main job of Congress – the making and amending of laws. These staff members manage the legislative process from the early development of policy positions to research into legislative and political options to drafting bills and amendments to shepherding them through the legislative thicket. They review incoming constituent mail that expresses views on policy issues and conduct specialized research on key measures being advanced by the Member. They meet with individuals, constituent groups and lobbyists who have an interest in issues of importance to the Member's constituents or the committees on which he or she serves.

Legislative staff must be knowledgeable in the rules, procedures, processes and peculiarities of the Congress, its history and traditions, including myriad rules and precedents, and the jurisdiction of committees and leadership. They must possess near-encyclopedic knowledge of issues for which they are responsible and be able to respond swiftly to questions from the Member or constituents.

B may be a passing grade in college, but a legislative staff member who gives the boss a memo on an issue that is only 90 percent accurate and balanced will soon feel the sting of rebuke. The legislative staff must earn and maintain a level of trust that assures any information it provides will be accepted and acted upon.

The legislative team is usually a three-tiered hierarchy that consists of the legislative director or LD, legislative assistants or LA's and several legislative correspondents or LC's.

The **legislative director** oversees the day-to-day activities of the legislative staff – four or five people in the House and more than 10 in the Senate – and is responsible for developing a strategy for pursuing the Member's legislative agenda. The LD also reviews all legislative staff work done within the office to assure it is consistent and reflects the Member's point of view. In addition, he or she works with the Member to map out support or opposition to efforts endorsed by the leadership or the Executive branch. The LD also has the task of keeping the Member abreast of key provisions in legislation being debated on the Floor or under consideration within committees and subcommittees.

Although some chiefs of staff have deputies, the LD is second only to the chief in most offices.

Legislative assistants commonly have several committees or topics for which they are responsible. It is their job to audit the work going on in committees and advance the Member's interest on specific legislation. In the House, they also draft answers to constituent, agency or committee inquiries associated with their areas of specialty.

An LA in the Senate doesn't usually draft correspondence but works closely with staff that does.

Legislative correspondent is the entry-level position in the legislative hierarchy, but LC's often are the best-informed team members when it comes to specific bills or amendments. Their survival depends on it. They are the ones who coordinate responses to all kinds of inquiries regarding questions on which a position has already been taken.

Such responses usually start with a pre-approved text that requires research to be sure its contents are still current. That's why the LC position is considered the best place to learn about legislation and its impact.

There are ample opportunities for LC's to learn. More than 10,000 pieces of legislation are introduced during each Congress – and each of them is the most important measure in the world to somebody. The ability to quickly research issues and reduce complex issues into easy to understand language is among the most valuable skills in any Congressional office.

The demand for such skills adds to the challenges facing the legislative director, who must teach and mentor a new LC, one fresh out of law school, perhaps, to abandon precise legalistic writing that may be accurate but far too complex in favor of communicating in a manner that constituents find straightforward, accurate and reassuring.

Constituent Mail

The biggest challenge for legislative staff is constituent mail. Every office gets lots of it. Some House office receives up to 100,000 communications per year from their constituents. Senate offices can receive many times that. As a new legislative correspondent or legislative assistant in the House, answering constituent mail may very well take up 50 to 75 percent of your day.

Communications take many forms. There is the written letter – or what you will learn to call "snail mail." This is the traditional handwritten or typed letter from an individual constituent on an issue of great importance to them. It has always been as good as gold in a Congressional office because someone went to a great deal of effort to exercise one of his or her prerogatives as a citizen – almost akin to a sacrament in a civil religion.

Today, the personally written letter is just as valuable, though shrinking as the main form of constituent communication. First, the ease with which people can communicate with email, has supplanted the handwritten letter. Second, the September 11, 2001 attacks, and the subsequent anthrax attack on Capitol Hill a month later resulted in all letters and packages being sent to an outside facility for irradiation. This terrorism protection measure has dramatically slowed the mail process on Capitol Hill since it takes 10-14 days to process mail through this facility. By the time an office receives a letter to the time it can answer and turn it around, a month has usually passed before the constituent gets a response. And that's the best-case scenario.

Finally, there are professional firms that are now counterfeiting personal letters from constituents. When Jeff Birnbaum was at the *Washington Post* he reported that there are now companies that compose letters on behalf of people for their signature for special interests campaigns. As if to prove the market value of these letters, these operators receive $75 to $125 for each letter they are able to get a constituent to sign. If this continues it will dilute the value of authentic letters since Congressional offices won't know which ones are from constituents and which ones are from hired writers.

Another variation of this is the postcard campaign, where organizations generate postcards on behalf of their members. The cards are usually identical and unsigned. The silver lining is that when these postcards bombard you, an organization is essentially giving you their mailing lists that an office can harvest and then use to communicate their own message to the constituent.

A second source of communication is constituent phone calls. Most offices will respond in writing to phone calls on an issue. Phone calls are personal and require a constituent to take action and verbally state an opinion. A smart office will promptly write to the caller and store the name, phone, address and issue in a database.

The highest volume of constituent communication is now email.

According to the Congressional Management Foundation, Congress received 313 million emails in 2006. Offices need to respond to emails just as they would a letter. Don't make the mistake of responding to an email with snail mail – the constituent has already shown his or her preferred means of communication.

Once again, professional companies are generating large volumes of email on behalf of various organizations. There are companies that sell, as a service, web modules that allow an organization to automatically generate emails from their membership to congressional offices. While some of these efforts may be legitimate liaisons between advocates and their supporters, these emails are often generated by slick campaigns that only reveal a small portion of the information available on an issue. For instance, in 2005 a major cancer organization contracted with one of these organizations. They whipped their membership into a frenzy by telling them that Congress was trying to pass a law that would outlaw breast cancer screenings. Nothing, of course, could have been further from the truth – the underlying legislation was a small business health care bill that would have allowed any small association of people to form a group for health insurance purposes, and operate under the same federal law that governed the health care plans of labor unions and large corporations. By operating under federal law it might have evaded state mandates – but all of the union and corporate plans covered under federal law had coverage for breast cancer screenings. These email-generating campaigns are often thinly disguised fundraising efforts by the organization originating the letter designed to create lots of smoke with a minimum amount of fire.

That doesn't mean an office can avoid answering these emails. The more inaccurate the information being received by the constituent the more important it is to generate a response that sets the record straight. And, like the postcard campaigns discussed earlier – an office can harvest the email addresses of constituents who you know care about a certain issue.

How does an office answer this massive volume of mail? It does so with enormous amounts of time, effort and technology. In the House, every legislative person writes or reviews mail.

Generally, all messages are "logged into" a computer database. That database allows an office to identify the constituent's name, address and email address. The software also allows the user to attach an "issue code" which identifies issues that are important to a constituent. Finally, a record of previous letters and responses by that constituent is kept in the database.

The letter drafting process is different in each office – but generally speaking, offices try to answer as many letters as possible with a form response. This is essentially an identical letter written to people who have identical concerns. If an office can answer 80% of its messages with a form letter or email, it still would have some 20,000 letters – 400 per week – that require original text.

The degree to which the Member directly participates in this process varies. The best offices have the Member review all major new text. For instance, a legislative assistant may notice that a lot of letters and emails are beginning to come in regarding an upcoming tax bill. The legislative assistant will likely want to brief the Member, explain the issue, and seek his or her guidance as to how they would like to respond. The legislative assistant will then go back and draft a response based on the Member's position. The legislative director and the chief of staff will review the letter. In most offices the Member will make a final review – especially on a major issue. Once the letter is complete it is usually mailed to letter writers and callers, and emailed to people who prefer email.

It sounds redundant, and it is. That is because the written word lasts forever. A junior staffer writing an inaccurate or offensive response could cost the Member votes in the next election. There is a guiding principle about letters – never write anything you are not prepared to defend if your worse enemy gets a hold of it – because they will.

Additionally, all of these letters make up a library of "approved text" that can be used by other staff to write portions of other individual responses.

Most importantly, once the letter has gone out, a permanent computer record is made. This can be used to generate proactive email newsletters that keep constituents informed on issues you know are important to them. How do you know? Because they told you so themselves when they wrote their letter.

Other Staff

The **communications director**, who's sometimes called a press secretary, handles communications of a different sort but is involved in more than just public relations. The position has evolved into one of the most significant in any Congressional office. These days, the communications director is involved in every aspect of the office. He or she has to be. Effective communication is essential to political and legislative success – no function in a congressional office can be performed well without consideration of the others.

Like Caesar's wife, it is important for the communications director to be above reproach. Members must be able to trust that their communications directors will accurately express their thoughts, opinions and positions to the media. And the media must be able to trust that when a communications director speaks, it is with the Member's voice and that the information imparted is reliable. A seemingly innocuous misstep can prove fatal to a lawmaker's career. That's why most Congressional offices prohibit staff other than those responsible for communications from talking to the media – even casually.

Communications directors also help manage the Members' public appearances, prepare materials for public distribution, write newspaper columns and speak on radio shows, help coordinate state or district scheduling, and sometimes act as a legislative assistant, overseeing activities surrounding measures such as those involving media regulation. We write a great deal more about communication later in the book.

Outreach and Constituent Services may seem to describe many of the activities that have been ascribed to members of the Legislative team, but legislative activities are centered in Washington, D.C., while Outreach and Constituent Services are more localized.

Outreach is primarily a communications function directed by the district or state director and carried out by key staff members, who attend countless meetings of Rotary and other service clubs, farm groups and veterans' organizations and visit senior centers, churches and schools on behalf of the Member. They also work closely with the communications director to assure press coverage for local events that will be attended by the Member. For many constituents, outreach staff is tantamount to speaking with the Member since they are immediately accessible and presumably provide a direct conduit to the Member.

They listen to questions, concerns and needs and, when appropriate, pass them along to the constituent service staff. Constituent service has become increasingly important as government has grown in size and complexity, making it difficult for the average citizen to find their way through the federal bureaucracy.

Efforts on behalf of constituents are referred to as casework. Most involve immigration law, social security, small business issues, the military and veterans' benefits, but there are literally hundreds of situations that might lead to the Member or his staff being called upon for assistance.

Although the majority of casework is handled at the district or state level, there are Congressional offices that prefer to run constituent services out of Washington D.C.

There is no right or wrong place to do it – as long as it gets results.

Obviously, staff can generate considerable good will for their boss by serving as ombudsmen for constituents in dealings with federal agencies, but they have to know precisely how far they can go. Some of the biggest scandals in recent Congressional history have resulted when Members were asked to help convince agencies to bend the rules. Past examples include ABSCAM, the Keating Five, and a most recent case where a Senator called a U.S. Attorney to inquire about the status of a legal investigation (offices should never intervene in legal matters).

To help avoid such pitfalls, most district offices employ a **director of constituent services** to set parameters, but in some cases these activities are overseen by a district or state director or even the chief of staff. As a further safeguard, all employees are now required to take ethics training within a few months of joining a congressional staff.

The **district director** in the House and the **state director** in the Senate perform the role of the chief of staff at the local level. Most supervise the activities of five or so people in a Congressional District and as many as 20 in a Senator's state office. It is up to the district director to track political developments at the grassroots level and build relationships with elected officials. When a Member wants to know what constituents are thinking or how they will react to an issue, a bill or an action, it is usually the state or district director who is called.

On a day-to-day basis, however, these local directors usually report to the chief of staff.

There has always been interdependence among staff at the local office as well as in D.C. The Internet and other means of enhanced communications have made it possible for those who handle what are commonly referred to as the functional needs of the Congressional office – the legislative and communication teams in D.C. and the outreach and constituent services teams at the local level – to work even more closely. **Cross-functional teams** have been credited with making these offices more efficient and more effective

Websites represent one example. In most cases, these are designed by the communications director and maintained by the computer systems administrator. Legislative staff contributes by constantly updating issue and policy information and the local outreach and constituent services personnel share noteworthy activity occurring on the home front or on issues of broad concern.

Legislative directors, meanwhile, have developed a close working relationship with computer systems administrators in an effort to track correspondence and response times and keep the Member informed of the volume of communication on hot issues, as well as the opinions such correspondence contains.

Just a few short years ago, all it took to become a computer systems administrator – or IT (Information Technology) manager, as they're called in some offices – was to attend a class and perform data entry to support the correspondence program. No longer. Technology tools have become essential to the successful operation of every Congressional office and require specialized knowledge.

Most offices have a staff member whose specialty is technological tools and is responsible for the storage and protection of highly confidential data requiring sophisticated backup and redundancy systems. The systems manager also must meet the challenges presented by a network that may include work stations in five or more state offices, as well as those used by 18 staff members in the House and an average of 40 in the Senate, not to mention a host of laptops and other high-tech devices.

Handheld communications devices such as the Blackberry, which was introduced into the market in 1999, have proliferated on the Hill like rabbits, making the old bells-buzzer-lights system of communication obsolete while at that same time all but guaranteeing that like the old system, they'll still be around long after the next wave of technology has swept through the country.

The systems manager is not part of the so-called functional staff. He or she belongs to the support team, which does what support staff in any office do – they facilitate the efforts of everyone else, make it possible for other teams to do their jobs, keep the wheels oiled and turning. In a Congressional office, the duties of support staff vary from filing to the tasks performed by what's affectionately known as the **scheduler**.

The scheduler, who is referred to in some offices as the *executive assistant*, is usually the gatekeeper to the Member's inner office and, not surprisingly, maintains the Member's schedule. This itinerary not only identifies where the Member is going but where he or she has been. Keeping such a schedule is not an easy task, given the fact that plans often change several times a day as unforeseen events create detours and changes of plans.

The fact that the scheduler typically is responsible for the Member's personal correspondence and phone calls adds to the need for discretion and loyalty on the part of the person who holds that position. The scheduler usually knows more about the Member's activities than anyone except the Member and chief of staff. If the Member is thinking about a bid for higher office, chances are the scheduler knows about it. If the Member is having family problems, chances are the scheduler knows about it. If the Member is avoiding the party whip, the scheduler definitely knows about it.

Among the challenges the scheduler faces is figuring out what events the Member can and should attend. Members receive hundreds of invitations to events in Washington, D.C., and the home district or state. Almost all are worthwhile, but it's humanly impossible to be at every one. In ages past, such invitations were accepted or rejected more on the basis of expediency and personal taste than strategic planning. These days, however, activities, including sporting events, are weighed against the Member's goals – and in some instances, events are actually created to help fulfill strategic goals.

When the Medicare Prescription Drug bill was signed into law, for example, some Members made it a priority to get to every senior center in their state or district to explain the new plan and help people with the complex enrollment process. Instead of waiting for an invitation, the staff called each senior center and asked if the Member could stop by and talk to a gathering of seniors. This sort of aggressive, well-thought-out scheduling maximizes the effectiveness of the Congressional office's most finite resource – the Member's time.

It has been suggested that the scheduler's duties have such an impact on the operation that the position should be a *functional* category unto itself. But in the House, at least, many of the scheduler's other duties fall into the support category – and include maintaining supplies, contracting for package delivery and handling expense and payroll records. (Since 1995, Congress has been subject to most of the same labor laws as any other employer and must keep track of compensatory time, overtime, distinctions between salaried and hourly employees and mandatory leave schedules.)

In the Senate, where staff sizes make support functions a full-time job, the duties handled in the House by the scheduler are usually divided between two employees.

The **staff assistant** is another member of the support team. It's a position most people would call a receptionist, but he or she is not a receptionist in the traditional sense. The receptionist's job in a Congressional office has a lot more facets. Besides being the point person on the phones and the individual who greets guests as they enter the office, providing in the process that all-important positive first impression, the staff assistant frequently manages office interns, arranges and coordinates tours of numerous D.C. sites – particularly the White House – that require tickets and fields requests for flags to be flown over the Capitol.

Staff assistant is typically an entry-level position taken by people hoping to work their way into a legislative, communication or administrative position. Most are successful. That's because they're completely over-qualified for the job. Don't be surprised if you learn that the first person you meet when you walk into a Congressional office holds an advanced degree from a highly rated college or university.

For obvious reasons, staff assistant is a high-turnover position. Those who hold that job typically move up in a year or they move on.

Chapter Three Summary

- Each office has great autonomy and its own unique hierarchy. Staff tends to reflect the Member's background, interests and district.

- Senate offices typically have more than twice the staff of their counterparts in the House but the organization charts are very similar.

- In the vast majority of offices the chief of staff is the Member's strong right-arm and the most important hiring decision the Member makes.

- The focus of staff members who report to the chief fall into four basic categories: Legislative, Communication, Outreach and Constituent Services, Support and Administrative Staff.

- Legislative staff must be knowledgeable in the rules, procedures, processes and peculiarities of the Congress, its history and traditions. The legislative team is usually a three-tiered hierarchy that consists of the legislative director, legislative assistants and legislative correspondents.

- The biggest challenge for legislative staff is constituent mail. Congress receives nearly a million constituent communications every day. To answer this massive volume of mail requires enormous amounts of time, effort and technology.

- The communications director is involved in every aspect of the office. Effective communication is essential to political and legislative success.

- Outreach is primarily a communications function carried out by key staff members who attend countless meetings on behalf of the Member.

- Constituent service has become increasingly important as government has grown in size and complexity, making it difficult for the average citizen to find their way through the federal bureaucracy. The district director in the House and the state director in the Senate perform the role of the chief of staff at the local level.

- Technology tools have become essential to the successful operation of every Congressional office and require specialized knowledge.

- The scheduler is usually the gatekeeper to the Member's inner office and maintains the Member's schedule.

- The staff assistant answers phones, greets guests as they enter the office and frequently manages interns, arranges tours and fields requests for flags to be flown over the Capitol.

Among the aspirations shared by most members of Congressional staffs is to be around long enough and regarded highly enough to be named to the staff of one of the powerful House or Senate committees. Those who succeed are considered policy experts. They are among the best-paid Congressional employees because they handle the difficult, sometimes tedious nuts and bolts work of shaping legislation that moves through the Congress. If the House and Senate have bureaucracies, they most likely are composed of long-serving staff members on long-serving committees under long-serving chairmen.

(In order to avoid a deluge of angry emails, we'll pause here to explain Congressional nomenclature. It's impossible to discuss committees without mentioning their leadership. Many observers would contend that referring to those of the feminine gender who chair committees as *chairmen* is politically incorrect. Yet that is precisely what the vast majority of women who chair committees prefer to be called – not *chairwoman* or *chairperson* or *chair*, but *chairman* – and on formal occasions, *Madame Chairman*. So as a concession to Congressional tradition, we'll refer to those who chair as *chairmen* ... and hope for the best.)

Each committee divides staff positions based on which party is in power. In the House, the ratio in recent years can be as much as 2-to-1 in favor of the majority party. The Senate Republicans and Democrats negotiate staff ratios, so that when one party has a narrow overall majority, the disparity between the number of majority and minority staff members is typically far less than it would be in the House.

There are some notable exceptions, including the House Committee on Intelligence and the Committee on Standards of Official Conduct, which is better known as the House Ethics Committee. These committees split staffs equally.

The size of the staff allotted to each committee depends on the committee's jurisdiction and clout. The House Small Business Committee, for instance, has about 30 staff members, while the Appropriations Committee has around 90.

Regardless of how much clout a committee might have, the Chairman holds the bulk of the power.

The **Committee Chairman** is responsible for the payroll, office space and agenda. The ranking minority Member is, however, generally accorded the authority to oversee that portion of the payroll that affects his or her staff and to make personnel decisions without having to clear them with the Chairman.

Committees establish their own rules at the beginning of every session of Congress – the majority proposes the rules and expects its Members to support them. The proposed rules are usually approved, with everyone in the majority voting *yes*.

Most committees have subcommittees, which in turn have their own staffs, thus increasing the size of the staff available to do the committee's work. The Chairman of the full committee decides who will be hired to fill these positions but does so with varying degrees of consultation with subcommittee chairmen.

The hierarchy of committee staffs closely resembles the hierarchy of Members' personal staffs. But job titles are seldom the same. Among the exceptions are the **communications director** and the **systems manager.**

The chief of staff is typically called the **staff director** and usually comes to the job with a good deal of familiarity with the Chairman, familiarity with the Chairman's likes and dislikes and familiarity with his or her agenda. That's because the staff director may come from a variety of backgrounds, but they are first and foremost loyal to the Chairman. The staff director's responsibilities beyond making sure the Chairman's agenda is carried out include hiring and budget decisions, representing the committee at leadership meetings and coordinating the committee's activities with the Chairman's personal staff. (One of the surest ways for a Chairman to get into political hot water back home is to allow the committee's agenda to get out of sync with the constituents who elected him or her to office.)

The **chief counsel** plays a role similar to the legislative director's but is more likely to be called the committee's *policy director* or *deputy staff director.* In addition to experience, the chief counsel is expected to bring to the job expertise in the rules, history and traditions of the Committee, and a legal background as well as policy expertise relating to the issues before it. It usually is the chief counsel who assigns the committee's senior legislative staff to organize hearings, generate lists of potential witnesses, develop lines of questioning and brief their party's committee members. He or she is usually the one you see whispering in the Chairman's ear in videos shot during such hearings.

It's not unusual for tension to exist between the staff director and the chief counsel. The staff director is interested in advancing the Chairman's agenda, putting the Chairman's mark on the Committee and making sure the political ramifications benefit the boss. Chief counsels, on the other hand, sometimes see themselves as guardians of tradition. They are the ones most likely to say, "This is the way we have always done things..."

The minority party generally puts together a legislative staff of its own that mirrors the majority's but typically is somewhat smaller.

Most committees have an abundance of legislative staff positions. Committee Members rely on those who fill these positions for instant recall of minute details relating to complex policy issues and to help manage the legislative process on the Floor of the House or Senate. Committee legislative staff serves as a resource for Members' personal staff as well, responding to questions concerning past and pending policies or legislation.

Providing information to non-committee Members helps foster positive relations by encouraging support for legislation being drafted by the Committee and more importantly, defining jurisdictional authority. A clear definition of authority over issue areas helps minimize turf wars between one committee and another, conflicts that could otherwise become nasty, intra-party struggles requiring the leadership of the House or Senate to referee.

Some committee legislative staffs are large enough to handle investigations. Investigative staff members spend months and sometimes years overseeing federal programs. Often recruited from the federal agencies they'll help oversee, they are typically young lawyers with a background in legal research.

In addition, each committee hires specialists in the area over which the committee has jurisdiction. The Ways and Means Committee, which is responsible for tax legislation and bills affecting Social Security, Medicare and other entitlement programs, lists "senior economist" among its staff titles. Other committees, such as the Armed Services Committee, have just as much specialization and expertise but refer to all senior legislative staff as "professional staff members" – a practice that often confuses outsiders trying to figure out who to talk to about a specific issue before that committee.

49

Don't be misled by staff-title roulette or the sometimes seemingly whimsical names that are given to committee staff positions. Often, the less pretentious the title, the more power the staff person actually has. The people who fill these posts are generally knowledgeable and experienced in what they do – though figuring out who's in charge may require the help of an experienced hand.

Legislative staff that serve simultaneously on a Member's personal staff and a committee's staff are known as **associate staff members**. The House Budget Committee, for instance, allows each of its members to appoint one personal staff person to serve on the Committee's legislative staff, from which subcommittee staff directors typically are chosen.

The **clerk** of each committee is the chief archivist, the keeper of committee records and the person responsible for the logistics of committee hearings. The clerk is usually a senior employee with several years of experience – and usually has an assistant if he or she is assigned to one of Congress's large standing committees. The clerk also maintains the calendar of committee activities and is responsible for everything from water and pencils for committee meetings to assuring that audio and video systems are available when needed.

Recordkeeping and archiving are more critical on a standing committee than in a Member office. That's because a standing committee has a life of its own – chances are it existed before today's Members were born and will continue to operate long after they've ended their careers. The clerk is among those who maintain continuity from one generation to the next.

A committee may also have a **printing clerk** whose primary responsibility is the publication of committee minutes and reports. Everything that is said in committee is transcribed and forwarded to committee staff for clarification (if there's uncertainty over precisely what words were uttered) then edited for grammar before being archived. All of this is necessary, not only because the House Rules require transcripts of hearings to be published, but because courts rely on these transcripts when considering a legal principle known as "legislative intent." Committee testimony also can be used in criminal and civil court cases, including those involving perjury for lying to a committee while under oath.

Once the transcript of a committee hearing has been corrected, proofed and formally released, the Committee will make it available on its website for use as a resource and reference, not only for the Congress but for anyone else in the world interested in the topic.

These tasks used to be handled by the Government Printing Office, but the era of desktop publishing has brought with it the ability to make printed and online copies available to more people more quickly and at less cost.

Most committees employ an **office manager** as well who is responsible for expenses, supplies and the payroll. In addition to serving much the same needs as an office manager in a Member office, a committee's office manager must be knowledgeable in the rules governing committees.

Leadership Staff

Staff also is provided to help shoulder the duties of those Members of Congress who are elected by their peers to serve in their party's Congressional leadership – and often find their jobs in even greater jeopardy than usual as a result of the honor.

Just like all other Members of the Congress, Leadership is elected first by constituents in their home districts or states. It is only then that colleagues in the House or Senate can elevate them to leadership positions. Leadership staff's primary responsibility, therefore, is to assure that Leadership meets its obligations to other Members – but like committee staff, they also must be sensitive to the demands of home constituencies, particularly when those demands conflict with Leadership obligations.

In 1994, the re-election campaigns of Speaker Tom Foley and several key Committee Chairs failed when constituents back home became convinced that their concerns had been sidelined or usurped by their elected representative's Leadership duties.

Adding to the pressures felt by Leadership staffs is the fact that both chambers give their bosses a great deal of power in decisions pertaining to which bills move to the floor and which don't. As a result, factions supporting and opposing various measures put a lot of importance on getting Leadership's ear. And there's never enough ear to go around.

Factions are undeterred, however. Experience has taught them that Leadership staff is the next best thing to a face-to-face with Leadership itself. Various journals go so far as to publish lists of those they perceive to be the most influential staffers. Though such publicity is flattering – and sometimes even accurate – it can be a burden to staff Members who must guard against appearing too responsive to outside forces lest the folks back home begin to think of their boss as a "Washington insider," which is not a flattering characterization no matter which side of the Beltway you're on.

Besides Speaker, elected Leadership offices in the House include:

- Majority and Minority Leaders
- Majority and Minority Whips
- Majority and Minority Chief Deputy Whips
- Chairman and Vice Chairman of the Democratic Caucus
- Chairman, Vice Chairman and Secretary of the Republican Conference
- House Democratic Steering and Policy Committee
- Chairman of the House Republican Policy Committee
- Chairman of the Democratic Congressional Campaign Committee (political arm)
- Chairman of the National Republican Congressional Committee (political arm)

The primary elected Leadership offices in the Senate are:

- President of the Senate (The Vice President)
- The President Pro Tempore
- Majority and Minority Leaders
- Majority and Minority Whips
- Chairman, Vice Chairman and Secretary of the Democratic Caucus
- Chairman, Vice Chairman and Secretary of the Republican Conference
- Chairman of the of the Democratic Policy Committee
- Chairman of the Republican Policy Committee
- Chairman of the Democratic Senatorial Campaign Committee (political arm)

- Chairman of the National Republican Senatorial Committee (political arm)

Most members of the Leadership are provided with budgets to cover the cost of staff dedicated to Leadership responsibilities, including Floor managers and other experts in House or Senate procedures, communication staff to handle the needs not only of journalists but also of congressional colleagues, and staff dedicated to the organizational responsibilities of the respective caucuses. In leadership offices that don't have dedicated staff, the Member will usually assign an individual from his or her personal staff to help carry out leadership responsibilities.

There's a reason tax dollars are appropriated to cover many leadership expenses. Each chamber is organized along party lines. Although leadership activities are partisan, however, they are not campaign organizations. The House Democratic Caucus and Republican Conference are organized along partisan lines and their leaders serve the needs of their Members.

The Speaker, the Majority and Minority Leaders and the respective party Whips have leadership staff positions assigned to them, as do the Conference and Caucus offices.

There are also sub-officers in each chamber. Officers of the House, such as The Clerk and the Chief Administrative Officer have staff assigned to them. The offices of the Sergeant at Arms of the House and Senate (the chief law enforcement officers of each house) are financed through the Legislative Branch Appropriations bill. These positions are elected at the beginning of each Congress by the full membership in the House and Senate. Officers traditionally do their best to avoid any overt appearance of partisanship. The same holds true for the Chaplains of the respective houses.

After the Republicans attained the majority in the Congress in 1994, House Speaker Newt Gingrich created the Chief Administrative Officer in an attempt to professionalize support functions in the House and eliminate the politicization and potential corruption associated with essential services. A year earlier, the House had been rocked by one of its most public scandals. A number of Members and several staff were found to have received preferential treatment in the form of non-interest bearing loans through the House Bank, which was managed by the Sergeant at Arms. It became clear that the Sergeant at Arms had personally benefited from some of these transactions. He and a number of Members ultimately resigned, decided not to seek re-election or lost their jobs, helping to lay the groundwork for the first Republican majority in 40 years.

The new Democratic majority kept the Gingrich reforms to the administrative processes of the House in place in 2006 though they eventually replaced the officers with their own appointees.

The role of Leadership staff members varies according to the role of the leader for whom they work. The Speaker and Minority Leader – and the staffs that assist them – have to balance the vast range of interests represented by Members of their party. When in the majority, they also must take on responsibility for crafting coalitions needed to actually pass legislation or frustrate efforts on the part of the opposition. The Whip, meanwhile, must understand the needs of individual Members and help them accomplish priorities that will benefit them back home, while at the same time pressing them to support important measures. Conference staff helps maintain party cohesion, shape a consistent message and provide support and direction to vulnerable or inexperienced Members.

Effective leadership staffs are servant-leaders. Their bosses are successful when the Members who benefit from the activities of Leadership staff are successful. This builds loyalty and cohesion within the party, which the leaders use as a form of collateral on the Hill when they need support for one of their priorities.

Some Leadership offices and those they lead are more successful than others. Poor leaders typically surround themselves with weak staffs – minions who reflect the worst qualities of their bosses. If the boss is "all about me," the staff will be, too. If the boss is a bully, the staff will tend to rule through intimidation. Such leaders and their followers may gain power. They may even hold it a while. But when things go sour, it becomes obvious that friends and supporters are few and far between, that these so-called leaders don't have the chits that accrue to leaders who help their colleagues succeed.

Finally, weak leaders sometimes appoint strong staff who, in the vacuum, assume roles and responsibilities they clearly should not, putting too much power and decision making in the hands of the unelected.

Congressional Support Agencies

There is yet another group of Hill employees – one that is seldom recognized as staff of the Legislative branch, in part because individual Members have comparatively little direct control over them. These are members of the staffs of support agencies such as the General Accountability Office (GAO), the Library of Congress (LOC), Congressional Research Service (CRS) and U.S. Capitol Police (USCP).

All told, the more than 20,000 members of agency staffs constitute the majority of employees working for the Congress. There was a time when their ranks were filled with patronage appointees, but no more. These days they're hired by professional managers and promoted based on merit. Their training, performance reviews and pay scales are administered much like any other governmental office's, without regard to partisan politics. Like the vast majority of their counterparts working within the Halls of Congress, they work for the people of the United States.

Chapter Four Summary

- Each committee divides staff positions based on which party is in power. The size of the staff allotted to each committee depends on the committee's jurisdiction and clout.

- The hierarchy of committee staffs closely resembles the hierarchy of Members' personal staffs. But job titles are seldom the same. Among the exceptions are the communications director and the systems manager.

- The staff director's responsibilities beyond making sure the Chairman's agenda is carried out include hiring and budget decisions, representing the committee at leadership meetings and coordinating the committee's activities with the Chairman's personal staff.

- The chief counsel is expected to bring expertise in the rules, history and traditions of the Committee, and a legal background as well as policy expertise relating to the issues before it.

- The minority party generally puts together a legislative staff of its own that mirrors the majority.

- Committee Members rely on legislative staff for instant recall of minute details relating to complex policy issues and to help manage the legislative process on the Floor of the House or Senate.

- Some committee legislative staffs are large enough to handle investigations.

- Don't be misled by staff-title roulette – a practice that often confuses outsiders trying to figure out whom to talk to about a specific issue before that committee.

- The clerk of each committee is the chief archivist, the keeper of committee records and the person responsible for the logistics of committee hearings.

- Leadership staff's primary responsibility is to assure that Leadership meets its obligations to other Members – but like committee staff, they also must be sensitive to the demands of home constituencies, particularly when those demands conflict with Leadership obligations.

- Most members of the Leadership are provided with budgets to cover the cost of staff dedicated to Leadership responsibilities, including Floor managers and other experts in House or Senate procedures, communication staff to handle the needs not only of journalists but also of congressional colleagues, and staff dedicated to the organizational responsibilities of the respective caucuses.

- Officers of the House, such as The Clerk, the Chief Administrative Officer as well as the offices of the Sergeant at Arms of the House and Senate are financed through the Legislative Branch Appropriations bill.

- House Speaker Newt Gingrich created the Chief Administrative Officer in an attempt to professionalize support functions in the House and eliminate the politicization.

- There are 20,000 nonpartisan Hill employees of the Legislative branch at the General Accountability Office (GAO), the Library of Congress (LOC), Congressional Research Service (CRS) and U.S. Capitol Police (USCP).

Question: How does a bill become law?

Answer: Any way it can.

Legislation doesn't always follow the route they taught us back in high school. An idea can become law as a stand-alone bill, an amendment, an appropriations rider or any of a number of other alternatives. In fact, most legislation becomes law by being attached to one of the few so-called must-pass bills that go through the entire process required of a stand-alone bill.

What counts is getting it done.

It is impossible to provide an exhaustive explanation of the legislative process – think of this chapter as the foundation upon which you can build an understanding, an introduction, if you will, to the challenges you are likely to face and to the first faltering steps that will be required on your journey. Come to grips with the fact that most legislative proposals never become law. Take heart from the fact that some are approved every week that Congress is in session.

Someone has figured out the system: If you hope to become a professional legislative staffer, make sure you figure it out too – and in a hurry. As for those of you who aren't on the legislative staff and figure this chapter has nothing for you, think again. Everything you'll be doing will be affected in one way or another by the process.

A Congressional staff member must know the basics of legislation, beginning with the steps necessary to transforming an idea into a law – framing the issue, writing the language, promoting the cause, mastering the process and following the procedures. Staff must understand the role the Rules Committee plays in the House, how things get to the Senate Floor, how parliamentary procedure can be used to help a bill succeed or guarantee that it fails once it is there, the importance of precedence and the ways a Member can advance an idea and even an agenda.

When the framers were writing the Constitution, they spent little time defining how the Congress should function. They made the House of Representatives the only directly elected governing body – the President was to be chosen by the Electoral College, Senators by their State legislatures and the Supreme Court justices nominated by the President and approved by the Senate. Fear of excessive power in the hands of the President occupied the bulk of their attention – how could they keep the balance of power from tipping in the chief executive's favor at the expense of the other two branches of government? They were less concerned with excesses by the Legislative branch and therefore gave both chambers discretion to establish their own rules and procedures.

As a result, the House and the Senate looked for role models and found one in the British Parliament, upon whose rules then-Vice President Thomas Jefferson drew heavily in drafting his *Manual of Parliamentary Practice*, a volume that continues to be provided to every new Member. Though the *Manual* serves as a guideline for the conduct of business in both chambers, its significance has diminished in the Senate, which used it as a starting point but quickly established its own rules and customs.

The Senate is the only legislative body in the world, for instance, that considers itself as constant as the seasons. Since only a third of its seats are up for grabs in any general election, the Senate functions as though there is never a break in its activities. As a result, it has become traditional for rules and precedents established in one session to be perpetuated by those that follow.

Unanimous Consent and tradition are the two most important factors in determining how the Senate operates. But to understand the daily flow of legislation in the modern Senate, it is important to understand what the filibuster is and what the filibuster is not: no longer is it latching onto the microphone and refusing to let go like Jimmy Stewart in the movie *Mr. Smith Goes to Washington* when he talked himself hoarse to defend himself against false charges.

That filibuster tactic was among the tools used in the Senate half a century ago to block passage of civil rights legislation until the Senate leadership countered by establishing *cloture*. Cloture sets a time limit on consideration of a bill or other matter. If activated by a three-fifths vote of the full membership (it had been a two-thirds vote before the reforms of the 1970s), it invokes a 30-hour time limit on debates with a vote finally made in order.

Cloture seemed like a good idea at the time – in fact, it deserves at least some of the credit for passage of the Civil Rights Act of 1964. But it has had the unintended consequence of requiring 60 votes to cut off debate on virtually all legislation before the Senate and all but rendered the one-man filibuster made famous by *Mr. Smith* extinct.

The onus previously was on Senators conducting filibusters to find creative ways to keep control of the floor. Cloture has taken the work and the embarrassment out of the practice, reducing filibuster to a parliamentary tactic and the *de facto* starting point for all legislation. It enables a minority party with more than 41 seats to effectively control much of the Senate agenda without being perceived by the public as obstructionist. Debate on legislation continues until the majority gets 60 votes for passage or until everyone wearies of the debate and gives up on the measure under consideration.

Increased partisan polarization has resulted in a sharp rise in the use of the filibuster. The amount of legislation in the Senate subject to the filibuster went from 8% of the bills brought to the Senate Floor in 1960 to an average of nearly 50% over the last decade.

It is axiomatic in the Senate that the majority determines what comes to the floor and the minority determines what leaves. The 60 vote super majority required for cloture is the main reason.

Cloture may be unique to the Senate, but for our purposes it illustrates why Members and staff in both chambers need to understand the rules and how these rules can be manipulated to prevent laws and appointments from being made, for both defensive and offensive purposes.

Hulton Archives, Getty Images

Not your father's filibuster.

Cloture reform has dramatically changed the filibuster from the tactic used by the character played by Jimmy Stewart in *Mr. Smith Goes to Washington,* when he refused to surrender the floor until he collapsed.

House procedures not only limit debate, but they restrict as well the number of amendments that can be offered and permit consolidation of those amendments that are accepted. There are two primary means by which legislation can be considered on the Floor of the House.

The least controversial bills are placed on what is referred to as the Suspension Calendar. Debate on these is limited to 20 minutes per side. A two-thirds vote is required to suspend the rules and pass the bill. Often the House will consider multiple bills under this procedure, conduct the debates and postpone the votes until all are completed, then vote them up or down in rapid succession. It is rare that the Speaker miscalculates and a measure on the Suspension Calendar fails to win the two-thirds vote required for approval.

Other measures, including most major appropriation, authorization and tax bills, are considered under regular order. After legislation is approved in committee, it is referred to the Rules Committee, which will adopt a *special rule* that defines how long the bill will be debated, how long

Members will be allowed to speak, what amendments may be added and how long amendments will be debated, as well as whether points of order under the rules of the House will be waived to accommodate immediate consideration.

The Rules Committee is the House's traffic cop. The majority party, which dominates the Rules Committee, can refuse to forward to the Floor any measure the party in power opposes. At one time, the Rules Committee was an independent force, but over time it became a tool the Speaker uses to control how legislation is considered by the full House.

The Rules Committee may conduct a hearing on any measure that comes before it but isn't required to. If it does, the Chairman and Ranking Member of the committee putting forth the measure will offer testimony on how it should be considered. The Rules Committee will then assign one of three possible designations:

1. An *open rule* means that all germane amendments to the measure will be allowed but only if they are presented within an allotted period of time.

2. A *closed rule* means no amendments will be considered.

3. A *restricted* or *modified open rule* or *modified closed rule* means that amendments aimed at specified portions of the underlying bill will not be considered, but that other portions of the bill will be fair game.

As with most activity that occurs in legislative bodies, there are varying degrees of formality to the process. The Chairmen of the Rules Committee and committees putting forth legislation generally work closely since they are members of the same party. Members who want to offer amendments usually try to reach out informally to these Chairmen. Whether they win their support typically depends less on the persuasiveness of the amendment's sponsors than on how controversial the amendment is and whether a deal can be struck between the Speaker and the Minority Leader.

Once the Rules Committee has approved a special rule defining how long the underlying bill will be debated and other issues affecting the measure, the special rule resolution is referred along with any proposed amendments to the full House. There, the special rule must be adopted by a majority vote before the bill can be considered.

The majority party controls the Rules Committee, so special rules put forward by that committee are almost guaranteed approval when voted on in the full House, where the same party is in the majority. Yet in every Congress, there typically is at least one incident in which party cohesion breaks down and a rules resolution is defeated.

House rules, like filibusters in the Senate, have been dramatically changed by partisan polarization since the late 1970s. In 1970 only 12% of special rule resolutions were modified or closed. Over the last few Congresses an average of 70% of special rules affecting major legislation had modified or closed rules.

Although the *Rules of Procedure* for the House are very specific and govern all Floor actions, they are subject to change from one Congress to the next. The one constant is Jefferson's Manual, which continues to serve as the foundation for House rules and activities. Rules governing floor activities are, however, debated and often amended at the beginning of every Congress.

The rules and procedures in the Senate and House are akin to the keys to your house. They aren't designed to lock you out, but that's exactly what they do if you don't take the time to learn how they operate. Members and staff who master them know how to get measures approved and to keep measures they oppose from passing.

According to the official House *Legislative Digest*, 11,074 measures were introduced in the 109th Congress (2005-2006), generating 47,000 pages of Congressional Record. Of these 11,074 measures, 1,197 were advanced to the Floors of the Congress but only 417 were enacted into law.

Don't be misled by the statistics. There were thousands of amendments attached to the 417 measures that were enacted. Very few bills of any significance make it through the House and Senate without amendments of some kind being added. The practice is so common that a revenue or tax bill is often referred to as a "Christmas tree" because unrelated amendments are hung on them like so many holiday decorations. As a result, it's not unusual for the volume of an omnibus appropriations bill or a revenue measure, to approach 1,000 pages.

As the numbers for the 109th Congress suggest, most legislation that is introduced does not win passage. In fact, passage isn't always the objective. There are a number of reasons to introduce legislation that is doomed from the outset. The most common are:

Where to Learn More

You can start with the appendix in this book where you will find a Manual of Floor Procedure, published by the Congressional Institute at the beginning of every Congress. The staff of the House Rules Committee reviews it. Read it, and then keep it within reach until the next one comes out.

The classic pamphlet "How Our Laws are Made" is a more detailed version of what you probably learned in school. You can find it on the web at:

http://thomas.loc.gov/home/lawsmade.toc.html

Two excellent books that provide valuable historical overviews of each Chamber are: The House by Robert V. Remini and the first 100 pages of Master of the Senate, the Lyndon Johnson biography by Robert A Caro.

- To satisfy constituent interest in an issue.

- To establish a benchmark or ownership of an idea or issue in the current or a future Congress.

- To generate interest in or draw attention to an issue through its introduction and inclusion in a committee hearing.

- To establish a position that can be incorporated in or amended to legislation that is more likely to advance through the legislative process.

- To introduce an issue or an idea in an effort to attract criticism and expose its deficiencies.

Creating a Pathway to Passage

Committee Chairmen have a far greater influence than other Members over whether a measure makes it into law. They control committee agendas. They decide what gets voted on. Everyone else must create a legislative strategy for winning passage of a measure.

Every measure begins life as an idea. It might be original or it might originate with a constituent. It might be the result of a planning session with staff or with other Members. It might be a response to the lead story on the 6 o'clock news or it might be an issue that has been near and dear to a Member's heart for decades. It might even be a political imperative – an initiative designed to meet a need of his or her constituency. That's sometimes called pork, but it is always important to the Member's representation and ability to get re-elected. Whatever its derivation, success comes down to finding a way to get bills introduced and signed into law.

Coming up with a goal is the initial step in the legislative process. Only when you know where you want to go can you determine the tactics to get you there. While formulating strategy – and before drafting your proposal in legislative language – most Members test the waters by exposing the concept to various groups or individuals in their home district or state to gauge whether it will create political problems back home.

Many also try out the idea with interest groups that have a stake in what they are proposing. Such groups often have suggestions for how to increase the measure's effectiveness or suggest ways to build a coalition to support it. Interest groups with experience and expertise in the topic also can point out pitfalls and warn against approaches that will likely frustrate the Member's effort.

Pork Barrel

There has been lots of talk about legislative earmarks or "pork barrel." Both terms probably have their roots in agriculture. Earmarking refers to the branding of livestock to identify who owns what, as well as legislative provisions that specify projects on which appropriated funds must be spent.

Pork barrel originated in the 1800s when, before refrigeration, families stored their pork in a barrel filled with brine – how much was in that barrel was a sign of how well a family was doing. The term first was used on the floor of the House in 1909 when Members were accused of handing out pork to their constituents from the "Congressional Pork Barrel." From this came the term "bringing home the bacon."

"Pork," by the way, is only used in the third person – as in *their* pork barrel project. It is never used in the first person such as *our* district's pork – instead such earmarks are referred to as our district's vital road improvement.

Members also want to touch base with colleagues in Congress who have a personal or constituent interest or serve on committees with jurisdiction over the topic. The purpose of this exercise is essentially the same as communicating with outside interest groups: to identify strong and weak points, build support and interest in the initiative and determine the likelihood of success.

Generating interest and support among colleagues in Congress brings with it the bonus of potential cosponsors of a bill or, at very least, some idea of what it will take to recruit them. Perhaps equally important is the fact that it can help identify Members of the other body who might be willing to introduce a version of the bill in their chamber of the Congress. If, for example, you are a Member of the House, you'll need someone in the Senate to introduce your measure there – and vice versa.

The odds in favor of passage increase with every cosponsor a bill attracts because every cosponsor brings with him or her credibility with other colleagues and constituencies. The odds increase as well by having a measure introduced simultaneously in the House and Senate and the media attention it attracts as a result.

In addition, legislative proposals should be reviewed informally with the Executive branch. It is important to know at the outset whether the Administration intends to provide support or opposition – how strongly and in what form – or to be neutral on the issue.

Drafting a Legislative Vehicle

Lawyers within the Legislative Counsels' offices draft most legislation. Both the House and the Senate have them. These non-partisan, non-policymaking adjuncts are for all intents and purposes legislative ghostwriters. They help couch measures in the proper legal language and will often assist Congressional staff in understanding how a provision will affect laws and regulations already on the books.

Before drafting, you need to know what kind of legislative vehicle best serves your needs. Do you want your bill to be *free-standing* (an entirely new concept) or *amendatory* (a means of modifying an existing law)?

Next you need to decide how specific you want your legislation to be. There are three levels of specificity:

1. *Hortatory* or *precatory* language merely expresses an objective. (The Senate procedural manual refers to this as *a pious hope*.) For example:

   *It is the sense of the Congress that the Secretary **should** take steps to end homelessness in inner cities.*

2. *Authorizing* language empowers an individual to take action, but relies on that individual's use of discretion:

   *The Secretary **may** take steps to end homelessness in inner cities through discretionary funding of experimental programs.*

3. *Mandatory or obligatory* language is absolute:

   *The Secretary of the Department **shall** take the following steps to end homelessness in inner cities and shall report back to the Congress on his progress.*

The Legislative Counsel's office works with Members on a confidential basis to ensure that proposed legislation conforms to federal statutes and that the wording – and meaning – accurately reflects the intent of the sponsors. The Counsel's staff generally avoids making policy suggestions but will point out precedents and alternative means of accomplishing the stated goal.

They will explain that because only bills and joint resolutions become law through Presidential signature or veto override, only bills and joint resolutions can amend law and only they have the power to authorize or mandate actions by officials outside the Legislative branch.

Concurrent resolutions – concurrent budget resolutions, for example – express the intent of both chambers of Congress and have a binding effect on the Congress. A simple resolution, on the other hand, is adopted by only one chamber and therefore affects only the chamber that adopted it.

It doesn't take long to master such distinctions, but it takes years to become proficient at drafting legislation that applies them. That is why the Legislative Counsel was created. You may, however, find yourself called upon from time to time to contribute to the process. Here are some tips that will help you avoid embarrassing yourself and your boss:

1. Keep your terminology consistent. This is no time to be creative, colorful or exotic. Using different terms interchangeably will encourage judicial interpretation of the seeming distinction you are drawing

and the prospect of a law that is more honored in the breach than in the observance.

2. If you use a technical or legalistic term, define it.

3. Organize your thoughts by separating out phrases and sentences based on the legal function they serve within the legislation. Designate each thought by numbers or letters so they may be easily identified.

4. Avoid the use of Latinisms and legalisms. ("*Whereas...*" clauses are pre-ambles, which have no meaning in law. There should be only one "*Be it resolved...*" clause.

5. If you want either a delayed or a retroactive effect to your legislation you must say so. Otherwise, it will take effect upon enactment.

6. If what you're proposing will require funding, your bill should authorize it.

7. Be specific – avoid opportunities for interpretation wherever possible.

Following these guidelines will:

- Enable judges and lawyers to correctly interpret the meaning of the law.

- Minimize technical objections, help keep debate focused on policy questions and avoid unnecessary corrections that can introduce errors and ambiguity.

- Establish effective policies and avoid public embarrassment for those sponsoring the bill, enacting the law or implementing it.

NOTE: When submitting material to the Legislative Counsel, the goal is not to write the legislative language but to express what it is you want to accomplish. Be brief. Make it a memo explaining the intent and options you want considered. Often, a personal meeting with the counsel assigned to the bill makes sense – especially if an idea is particularly complicated.

Chapter Five Summary

- Most legislation that is introduced never gets enacted.

- Key elements of the legislative process are framing the issue, writing the language, promoting the cause, mastering the process and following the procedures.

- Unanimous consent and the traditions of the body are the mark of success in the Senate.

- The filibuster now affects 50 percent of legislation going through the Senate, making cloture a key to success.

- The Rules Committee is the traffic cop of legislation in the House.

- Jefferson's Manual is still the Bible for procedure.

- Getting legislation enacted isn't the only reason for introducing a bill. Sometimes there are other reasons for drawing attention to an issue.

- The term pork barrel dates back to the early 1800, when in the days before refrigeration, the amount of pork you had stored in a barrel was a sign of your prosperity. The term was used politically for the first time a hundred years later.

- Tactics for moving legislation include communicating with congressional colleagues, the Executive Branch and outside interest groups.

- The Legislative Counsel's Office is where legislation is written. They are professionals. You provide the blueprint.

At last the time has come to unveil the legislation, to tell the world what the Member is up to. The process is time-honored and almost ritualistic not so much because of tradition but because it usually works.

Introductions usually begin with a Dear Colleague letter, which will go to all targeted Members of Congress through the House or Senate mail system. This letter will explain the legislation, provide details and facts, and then ask Members of both parties to add their names to the list of cosponsors.

Although there's only one sponsor, a bill might have hundreds of cosponsors, adding to the bill's credibility among the leadership and committee chairs. Co-sponsorship is a form of endorsement. Theoretically, it's possible for every Member of the Congress to co-sponsor a single bill.

The sponsor's communications director, meanwhile, will earn his keep with a public information campaign that will target the broad range of local and national media – and invite counterparts in the offices of co-sponsors to do likewise.

Once the legislation is ready to be formally introduced, the House sponsor might seek to give a one-minute speech at the beginning of the legislative day or request time for a special order at the end of the day's business. In the Senate, a sponsor often gives a brief speech during "Morning Hour," which usually occurs before the start of legislative business.

Following this introduction process, the bill is dropped into what's known as the hopper in the House – a box on the clerk's desk. In the Senate it is handed to the bill clerk at the front desk of the chamber. It is then assigned a number and referred to the appropriate committee – or committees. The bill's subject matter usually defines the committee to which it will be assigned, but once in a while, legislation will be referred to several committees at once.

Bills can be referred jointly, which means that multiple committees will consider different aspects of the same bill, or sequentially, which means one committee will consider the measure. Then if – but only if – that committee gives its approval, another committee could possibly be permitted to claim jurisdiction and the right to hold hearings before deciding whether to add its endorsement. In the House, the Speaker makes the determination whether to refer a bill to more than one committee. In the Senate, multiple or sequential referrals require unanimous consent.

The Role of Committees

Committees are the backbone of the legislative process. They have been part of the legislative process almost from the outset. The first were *ad hoc* committees established by the House to address single issues that had been debated on the Floor but needed additional study before a final decision could be reached.

It wasn't until after the turn of the 19th Century that the House created standing committees to develop expertise in specific topics. The first of these was Ways and Means, followed closely by Revised Unfinished Business, Elections, Claims, and Commerce and Manufacturing. Then came the Foreign Affairs Committee and the Post Office and Post Roads Committee.

The Senate launched its first committee in 1807 and has pretty much kept pace with the House ever since.

Over the course of their history, committees and their Chairmen have assumed varying degrees of power and influence. Speakers of the House Henry Clay of Kentucky, Thomas Bracket "Czar" Reed of Maine and Joe Cannon of Illinois have been among that chamber's most powerful leaders, exerting almost absolute control over the legislative process, the House agenda and even the activities of committees. Since Joe Cannon gave up the reins in 1911, however, committees have more often than not dominated the agenda and the flow of legislation, in some cases to the consternation of the House leadership and the majority. Several southern, conservative Democratic chairmen retained such power, in fact, that it was not until the mid-1970s – over 20 years after Democrats had taken control of Congress – that a majority of their own party was able to unseat them and enact a set of caucus reforms that stripped their power.

Ranking committee Members – the highest-ranking minority Member on each committee – have seen their power ebb and flow depending upon the strength and weaknesses of their party's leadership and the willingness of the committee Chairmen to accommodate them.

There are three kinds of committees:

Standing Committees are permanent with specific legislative jurisdiction.

Special (or Select) Committees are, in theory, temporary or ad hoc panels that are given broad oversight and investigative authority over a particular problem – such as aging issues or narcotics.

Joint Committees consist of Members from both chambers and have very specific oversight responsibility but negligible legislative authority.

There are currently 16 standing committees in the Senate and three select committees. In the House there are 20 standing committees and two select committees. There are four House-Senate joint committees.

There typically are 17 or 18 Members per committee in the Senate and anywhere from 13 to 56 in the House, with an average of 10 Members per subcommittee in each.

Unless a committee Chairman decides the full committee should act on a measure immediately, it usually will be referred to a subcommittee for study. As a result, subcommittees bear the lion's share of the workload. It is generally at the subcommittee level that research is conducted into the measure's various components, where hearings are conducted to obtain expert testimony for and against it, and where fine-tuning occurs. If a majority of the subcommittee approves the measure, it is sent to the full committee for consideration.

Committee Hearings

The Congress is, by nature, reactive rather than proactive. It reacts to public pressure, to the media, to interest groups, to national emergencies, even to business left unfinished by the previous Congress. And, of course, to Administration requests – as the saying goes, "The President proposes and the Congress disposes."

And what is true of the Congress is true as well of its committees.

In addition to their role in the legislative process, the primary function of committees is oversight of federal programs. They authorize and re-authorize such programs, investigate them, bankroll them and craft policies that regulate them. It is the investigative phase of these activities that usually generates the most controversy. In the House of Representatives alone, there are about 3,000 subcommittee and committee hearings each year, mostly in the early months of March and April and mostly in off-election years. Such hearings are generally either fact-finding exercises or policy-reviews and fall into two categories:

- Field hearings highlight a specific issue in a region where it has the greatest relevance or highlight a committee member in a region where the Member is most relevant. Field hearings tend to be of little real consequence in and of themselves, but when properly applied may be one of the most valuable resources for developing the case for legislative action.

- Washington hearings are conducted in the nation's capital either because an issue is of national importance or is such a nuisance that a hearing is the only way to make it go away.

The purpose of hearings is to accumulate facts, information and opinion, while at the same time exposing issues or policy to Congressional or public scrutiny.

The most important individual at any hearing is the Chairman, who determines when it will be and how long it will last, as well as who will testify and for how long. In addition, the Chairman holds the gavel and controls most of the staff.

The Mark-Up

Following hearings that lead a committee to conclude that legislation is needed, the Chairman drafts a mark – or base bill. Committee members then proceed to the mark-up phase – a procedure in which they offer amendments they believe will improve the bill.

A similar mark-up precedes any action on legislation proposed by a member of the committee, a bill introduced by a Member not on the committee, a composite bill drafted by the committee staff and brought to the table as the Chairman's bill or any other measure that comes before the committee.

The Committee Report

Regardless of whether a measure originates in committee or elsewhere, it cannot be submitted for consideration by the House or the Senate as a whole without an official summary called a committee report that tells the House or the Senate what the committee did and why. Such a report contains:

- A description of the legislation and why it is needed, as well as the reasoning behind the committee's conclusion.

- Background on the issue being addressed by the measure.

- The administration's position on the measure.

- Pertinent information that is required by the Rules Committee or otherwise deemed significant, such as cost estimates, recorded votes, economic impact, oversight findings, recommendations and whether the measure will change existing law.

- Language of conciliation to opposing sides or language clarifying conditions that may be subject to litigation. (Litigants look to reports and Floor debate to determine Congressional intent.)

- Additional views – a Member may concur with the committee's action but not the reasoning behind it and choose to attach a local slant or provide further illumination of a particular viewpoint.

- Dissenting views – a Member who opposes the measure may opt to fully air his or her reasons for the benefit of future debate and deliberation.

- Minority views – statements by those who may have lost the debate in Committee but hope to sway opinion when the full Chamber acts the measure on. These will provide proponents with a picture of why opponents are against the measure and will help opponents expressing their dissent through the media.

Legislative staff will find the Committee Report one of the most valuable resources there is for the analysis of legislation. Member Views typically provide a quick means of identifying points of contention. There, explanations are usually expressed in persuasive rather than legislative language, making Committee's intent accessible and easy to understand.

Navigating the Committee Process

The majority of legislation initiated by Members is quietly euthanized through the committee process. Once a bill is referred to committee, it will die there unless the Chairman gives the green light for consideration. The bill also has a chance of survival if it has support from:

- A Member of the Committee who has a close personal and professional relationship with the chairperson – or something of value to offer, such as support for one of the chairperson's endangered initiatives.

- A Member who has the support of the majority leadership, which applies pressure on the chairperson to move the legislation.

- Important interest groups or the media.

Non-controversial legislation such as a bill commemorating a historical event or renaming a post office often – but not always – has a good chance of survival and may even be expedited through committee.

But getting a bill through committee doesn't guarantee the individual who originated it will get any credit. In most cases, it will be the Chairman who is identified as the sponsor of anything significant that comes out of the committee. Members can, however, help shape the Chairman's bill.

It is possible to offer an amendment that might have originated as a separate bill but been buried in the legislative graveyard. The caveat is that in the House, such an amendment must be germane to the bill that's carrying it. That means that in the judgment of the Parliamentarian, it must be directly related to the underlying bill.

Senate rules are far more lenient. There, even an amendment that's only tangentially related can often be added in committee. In 2006, for example, a Senate bill to regulate over-the-counter medical products used to make methamphetamines in home labs was attached to the Patriot Act, a measure that dealt with terrorism and intelligence services. The only thing the two had in common was that both had been referred to the Judiciary Committee and were under the jurisdiction of the Department of Justice.

An unspoken quid pro quo comes with action of this sort. The Chairman who allows such a pairing can expect the Member who originated the rider to support and even campaign in favor of the bill that's carrying it.

Although this same process is not duplicated in House committees, deals made in the Senate receive the House's stamp of approval when the House acts favorably on a conference report or by taking up a Senate bill rather than initiating legislation of its own.

Offering Amendments

If a Member has failed to get a legislative measure included on the committee agenda, he or she may still have an opportunity to get it considered on the Floor. In the House, several things must happen. First, the underlying legislation to which the Member is attempting to attach his or her measure must allow for amendments. Even if it does and the amendment is accepted for consideration, restrictions can be placed on its consideration. It must also be deemed germane by the House Parliamentarian, which means it must be consistent with the rules and precedents of the House. And if it gets past the House Parliamentarian, opponents can still challenge it, in which case the Speaker will have to resolve the conflict. All this assumes the Rules Committee has not passed a special rule excluding the amendment from consideration.

An essential House publication, Deschler's Precedents, is often called upon to settle such issues. This volume is named for the former House Parliamentarian Lewis Deschler, who served for 50 years after being appointed by Speaker Nicholas Longworth in 1925. His book contains rulings by the Chairmen of the Committee of the Whole and the Speakers who predated him and represent standards for Congressional activity much as court decisions serve as legal precedents. Deschler's Precedents is updated each time a new precedent is established or an old precedent modified or overturned. All precedent-setting action from the latest session of Congress is published in a new edition at the beginning of the next Congress.

If the Speaker rules that an amendment is out of order, there's at least one other option: Working with the Minority Leader and Ranking Member of the Committee, it might be possible for the source of the amendment to shape what is known as a Motion to Recommit, which would refer the bill back to committee with instructions to include the amendment attached. In reality, this process is a formality – the committee does not actually meet to consider the bill – instead it is deemed to have reported the bill with the amendment included in the Motion to Recommit. Thus, if the motion passes the amendment is included in the bill. Such a motion is entertained after completion of all other action involving the measure on whose coattails the amendment hopes to ride. The motion must be germane and the minority can only offer one Motion to Recommit on any bill.

The Motion to Recommit is a last-ditch parliamentary tactic reserved to the minority party. It provides the minority one opportunity to get a vote on one specific issue that the majority has otherwise blocked from consideration. It is often employed to score political points at the expense of the majority. Such measures can't win, of course, unless they garner a sufficient number of Members from the majority party.

Germaneness

Germaneness is among the Congress's most significant legislative principles. First adopted by the House of Representatives in 1789, the Rule of Germaneness limits considerations to one item at a time. Say for example a bill dealing with transportation safety is being considered and an amendment is proposed that, among other things, would require states to inspect and repair bridges on a regular basis. So far, so good.

Even if the amendment contains other provisions that have nothing to do with highway safety, the amendment can be considered. But, if a Member challenges any part of the amendment, the entire measure is jeopardized. Should even part of the amendment be ruled out of order, the entire amendment is disqualified.

An amendment can be challenged for any number of reasons. If it attempts to make a temporary measure permanent, for example, it could be ruled out of order. It is up to the Parliamentarian to rule on issues of germaneness. Because the burden of proof rests with the amendments' proponents, the Parliamentarian is typically consulted in advance for an opinion on whether an amendment is likely to be considered germane.

The Senate does not have a Rule of Germaneness as such. Senators may add unrelated riders to any legislation except appropriation bills and any measure for which cloture has been invoked – amendments to these exceptions must be demonstrably germane.

If the measure under consideration is an appropriations bill, there is at least one more arrow in the quiver. Although the rules prevent substantive amendments on such bills, a Member can strike or delete funding for a specific line item. One of the more famous examples was the Hyde Amendment that originated in the House and restricts federal funding of abortion. Because it was an amendment to a Labor/HHS (the Department of Labor and the Department of Health and Human Services) Appropriations bill, opponents could not add conditions or caveats. They were, however, able to temper the amendment when the Appropriations bill reached the Senate, where an exception was added to cover cases in which the life of the mother was threatened.

As with most other procedures, bringing an amendment to the Floor in the Senate is usually less tedious and less painful. The fact that a Senator must receive unanimous consent to offer an amendment doesn't mean all of his colleagues must support the amendment. It simply means all Senators agree to hear the measure.

The majority often is persuaded to give unanimous consent to a minority Member's amendment in exchange for unanimous consent for a majority Member's amendment, or for a pledge not to filibuster the bill at which the amendment is aimed.

The decision whether to consider an amendment through unanimous consent typically is made by Floor managers shepherding the underlying bill through the Senate – usually the chair and ranking Member of the committee from which the bill was reported. If they find the proposed amendment so odious that they refuse to accommodate it, there are legislative tricks they can pursue to block it. These include a practice known as filling the amendment tree. The Amendment tree is a metaphor for the chart that shows the Senate procedure for what amendments may be offered to a bill and in what order they will be considered. In recent times, the Senate Majority Leader, who has the right to be recognized first at the start of a debate, has increasingly filled the tree with extraneous or meaningless amendments to block the consideration of a legitimate amendment he opposes.

The Role of Leadership

A Member seeking to get a bill passed should bring it to the attention of the party leadership. In the House, Leadership involvement in the committee process has grown since 1994 when Newt Gingrich became Speaker. A simple reform eliminating seniority as the determining factor in who becomes committee chairman made chairmen accountable to their party in general and the Speaker in particular. If a chairman did not do what the Speaker or the party wanted, he or she could be replaced in the next Congress.

The Speaker of the House, on one hand, and the Minority Leader, on the other, as well as the Senate Majority and Minority Leaders, look for opportunities to help their party's Members succeed. So do party Whips in both chambers of Congress. Keep in mind that the assistance they provide isn't entirely altruistic.

A Minority Leader becomes a Majority Leader only if his colleagues succeed to the point that more Members of their party get elected. To retain that position, the Majority Leader must help other party Members succeed.

Everyone in a leadership position has skilled staff that works closely with Members and their staffs to win passage for their initiatives. When push comes to shove, they'll apply various forms of persuasion – some more pleasant than others – to get an amendment attached to a bill that has legs. In the Senate, whips of both parties will work with floor managers of bills to get riders added.

Not only do these efforts help consolidate leadership positions, but they earn the gratitude of the Members who benefit from them – gratitude that will pay bonuses in the long run.

Floor Procedure

The reason most Members seek election to the House and Senate is that they hope to one day shape legislation in Congress. In order to achieve this goal, they and their staffs must know what they're doing or know whom to ask.

An ill-prepared staff combined with an inexperienced boss, who has not worked closely with experts provided by the leadership, is likely to find themselves humbled before their colleagues and a nationwide audience watching on C-Span when they go head-to-head with someone who knows the rules and procedures better than they do.

No one expects you to know everything. They do expect you to recognize your limitations, work closely with allies who know where the landmines are and learn from them as the process unfolds.

When legislation is being considered on the Floor, every nuanced step has a purpose. The precedents and rules of the respective chambers choreograph every gesture. Occasionally, there are surprises that disrupt the proceedings, but these are rare and almost always the result of someone whose actions are inconsistent with the traditions of the body – such as when a Member's words are stricken following a verbal assault on another Member or the President.

Be conversant with the rules, regulations and precedents before going into the arena.

The Role of the Administration

The role the President, the Office of Management and Budget (OMB) and the cabinet play in the legislative process isn't always obvious to outsiders, but it can be pivotal. They're interested because the Executive branch will be responsible for implementing any new laws that are enacted. The leverage they apply is the President's veto power.

A committee Chairman will usually exhaust every other available means before risking a veto of one of his or her priorities. They are even less willing to spend their hard-earned political capital on someone else's initiative, by calling the President's bluff. There are times, however, when Congress or the President or both go out of their way to use the veto pen to make a point.

President Clinton twice vetoed welfare reform even though as a former governor he recognized how badly it was needed. He sent the measure back to the Congress twice to buy time and face-saving concessions sufficient enough to coax and coerce the left wing of his own party into accepting its reforms. The third time the bill came to his desk – with a few minor tweaks, but in substantially the same form as the measures Clinton had vetoed twice in succession – it had the endorsement of a good many Democrats and he signed it into law.

The Congress turned the tables on Clinton's successor. At the time, a united Democratic minority, along with a significant number of Republicans, sent President George W. Bush a bill that would have allowed federal

---

Congressional Ping-Pong

There are many instances where both chambers have passed separate measures and then taken up the bill passed by the other, attach their language as an amendment, and send the bill back with the hope that the amendment will be agreed to. In this case, it is hoped that the disagreements between the two chambers can be worked out through amendments that are called "messages" between the chambers. If this messaging continues back and forth, it is sometimes characterized as the legislation being "ping-ponged" between the House and Senate.

If the House gets an amendment from the Senate (or vice-versa), the measure is taken up and if they agree the bill goes to the President.

If the House disagrees they will send the bill back to the Senate with amendments of their own. The game of "ping-pong" can continue endlessly with no resolution and the measure would die at the end of the Congress.

If an important measure bounces back and forth, however, then a Conference Committee will be convened to resolve the differences.

funding of embryonic stem cell research knowing full well the President wouldn't sign it. The objective was to put the issue squarely in front of voters in districts and states that favored such research in hopes of persuading them to vote for Democrats in the next election.

The mere threat of a Presidential veto can and often does change the course of legislation, particularly if the Congressional majority is made up of Members of the same party as the President. All a Cabinet Secretary or a White House legislative staffer has to do is whisper in a committee Chairman's ear that the President will veto a bill if it includes a particular amendment the administration can't live with. If the Congressional majority is made up of Members of the same party as the President, the odds are that the amendment will never make it out of committee.

Among the reasons Chairmen are so gun shy is that the Congress's override of President Bush's 2007 veto of a $23 billion water resources bill was the first time Congress was able to muster an override in more than a decade. Getting two-thirds of each chamber to vote to override the President is a tall order.

If the Chairman and the President are affiliated with the same political party, they're likely to find an opportunity for compromise on a measure that has broad support beyond the Beltway, particularly if there is plenty of glory to go around. Besides, family fights are not good politics, so compromise instead of confrontation will likely result. Even a Member of the opposing party can benefit from compromise but isn't likely to be directly involved in the negotiations – that task will likely fall to the Leadership and a committee Chairman and have a greater chance of success if the administration fears being embarrassed in a public battle over the issue.

The bottom line: Even though the President has the power of the veto, his real influence in the legislative process tends to be the informal but substantial leverage he is able to exert.

Resolving Differences Between the House and Senate

If an amendment is successfully attached to a bill that is approved by one of the two chambers of the Congress, it's not out of the woods yet. It may have to survive the conference committee. A conference committee is an ad hoc group appointed solely for consideration of a specific piece of legislation. It is only convened if the House and Senate pass different versions of the same bill. Before a bill or joint resolution can be sent to the President for his signature (or disapproval), both the House and Senate must agree on one version of the measure.

This can happen in one of three ways: one chamber could pass a measure which is then taken up and passed with no changes; or take it up, adopt amendments and send it back to the originating house, which then agrees to the amendment(s); or each chamber could pass identical versions of the same legislation.

In those instances when one chamber takes up and passes a measure from the other body in its entirety, it is usually a relatively non-controversial measure or a simple extension of current law.

Conference Committees

If the differences between the House and Senate cannot be resolved, a "conference committee" made up of managers or conferees appointed by each chamber are appointed to reconcile the differences between the two chambers. The House Speaker and the Senate Majority Leader in consultation with the minority leaders in their chamber appoint the conferees. These two leaders determine how many Members will serve on the conference committee.

The rules and procedures for conference committees are choreographed as tightly as a ballet. It might seem excessively complicated, but since the most important legislation before the Congress must typically be resolved this way, the steps of this ballet must be learned.

The chamber literally in possession of the papers - the physical bill and the amendments passed by the other body - makes the request for a conference. This is usually done by unanimous consent, by motion in the Senate, or by adoption of a rule reported from the Rules Committee in the House. The chamber, receiving the request, may agree to the conference or disregard the request.

When a bill is sent to conference, there are limitations on the authority of the conferees regarding those issues that they may address - only those matters that are in disagreement between the House and the Senate.

The minority in House has the right to offer a motion to instruct conferees. However, any instructions to the conferees by the House are advisory and are not binding.

In contrast to the procedural ballet, the actual meeting of a conference committee can be the closest thing you'll find to the knife fight in the motion picture "Butch Cassidy and the Sundance Kid" – you know the scene, the one where Butch is facing off against a giant of a man and calls time out while they discuss the rules.

"Rules?" the giant demands and looks around at the ring of spectators for confirmation. "There are no rules in a knife fight."

"All right," Butch replies and kicks the giant squarely beneath his belt buckle.

While conference committees are often marked by some of Washington's best "horse trading," deliberations sometimes disintegrate into a clash of egos between Senate and House Chairmen. This is particularly true when different parties have control of the House and Senate. For the sake of decorum, all this takes place behind closed doors, and in some cases no one on the outside has any idea what the measure under consideration will look like until it is sent to the Floors of the two chambers for a vote.

Conference Reports

Once an agreement has been hammered out, the conference report needs to be agreed to and signed by a majority of the managers of both the House and Senate. A joint explanatory statement outlining the agreement is prepared by the conferees of the House and Senate, and is signed by the majority of the managers of each chamber.

The chamber that was invited to the conference is the first to call up a conference report for a vote. If it is agreed to, it is passed to the other chamber for approval. If the conference report is not agreed to by either chamber, the differences may be resolved by one chamber agreeing to an amendment by the other, or by requesting a further conference. Once both chambers agree the measure is enrolled and goes to the President for signature. A little trivia: by law the enrolled bill must be printed on parchment paper before being presented to the President.

It is essential that a Member interested in seeing a specific provision in the conference report find an advocate on the inside of the conference committee as quickly as possible. Otherwise, the Member is likely to find all the hard work that went into introducing the legislation, getting it included as an amendment, seeing it passed and sent to a conference committee along with the bill to which it was able to attach itself is all for naught because those involved in the negotiations used it as cannon fodder, swapped it into oblivion, made it a hostage of the debate, then gave it away as a concession to the other side.

It is prudent for a Member with an amendment in the bill to meet with the Committee staff director or general counsel. A meeting between a Member and the Chairman of the Conference Committee might even be arranged to finalize the deal. At the very least, the Member should expect to commit his or her support for the final conference report if it contains the Member's provision.

Follow-up and Oversight

The fat lady does not sing just because a measure is enacted into law, especially if it requires creation or changes in regulations. If the bureaucracy is not supportive, and often times even if it is, it can take months, perhaps even years to get the necessary regulations issued or refined.

It is important for the sponsor of any change in the rules to stay on top of the agency responsible for implementing it, to follow-up with letters, to demand that bureaucrats come in for face-to-face meetings to explain themselves and to use the oversight powers of whatever committee he or she serves on to make sure the will of the Congress is carried out by the Executive branch.

The Congress must jealously guard its prerogatives. Enforcement by the Executive branch of laws passed by the Congress goes to the heart of the Constitution's delegation of authority. Efforts to stall or obstruct – or outright refusal to enforce – those laws go to the heart of the Constitution as well, but bring with them dangerous consequences.

MPTV.net

A conference committee can be the closest thing you'll find to the knife fight in the motion picture "Butch Cassidy and the Sundance Kid."

Chapter Six Summary

- You introduce a bill by dropping it in the hopper. The hopper actually exists.

- When you introduce a bill, it is good to introduce it publicly with a speech on the Floor of the House or Senate.

- Bills are referred to committees. On rare occasions they are brought by the leadership directly to the Floor of the House or Senate.

- Committees are the backbone of the legislative process. The primary function of the committee is congressional oversight of Federal programs.

- Two important processes take place in committee, the hearing and the mark-up, followed by the preparation of a committee report.

- Germaneness is among the Congress's most significant legislative principles. It dates back to the 1st Congress and governs the ebb and flow of amendments.

- When a bill reaches the Floor of the House or Senate, the procedures established by each body govern the outcome.

- The House Rules are more restrictive than those of the Senate.

- The Leadership plays a critical role in the fate of legislation in both bodies.

- The Administration also plays an important role in its assessment of how future laws will be implemented and particularly in the use of the veto pen.

- It is in the conference committee where the last deliberations, often more secretive, occur on legislation.

Management is discussed in great detail in hundreds of books on the subject and in MBA courses the world over. None of them prepare a person for the job of running a congressional office. Chances are you'll never aspire to such a position, but perhaps some of the insights provided here will help you work effectively with the one who'll oversee your activities and perhaps even convince you it's a job you'd like to have some day.

An MBA degree is not a prerequisite. In fact, there are few MBAs on Capitol Hill – at least few serving in the chief of staff ranks. Most chiefs of staff have backgrounds in law, political science, history or communications. What they have in common is that very little of what they learned in the classroom or in previous jobs prepared them for the role they now play.

They learn by doing – and the good ones never stop.

At first glance, the challenges they face are similar to those confronted by anyone who manages a creative, highly skilled, overworked, underpaid staff toiling in offices whose amenities compare unfavorably with the mailrooms of most major corporations. But the chief of staff faces many challenges that are unique to the position. Among the greatest of these is coordination of activities at satellites scattered across a state or district where staffs are performing a range of different functions – that and the need to apply business principles within a uniquely political atmosphere. Responsibilities under the chief of staff's jurisdiction might include overseeing legislative initiatives, communicating effectively with friend and foe alike, solving problems with worldwide implications, and bartering support for another Member's effort to have May designated National Harmonica Month in exchange for endorsement of a bill your boss is sponsoring that would have a profound impact on child safety.

And security – let's not forget security. The chief is responsible for assuring that the workplace is safe and that there is a plan to help visitors in the event of an attack or other form of disaster, that all mail is screened, that restrictions are maintained on access to buildings and garages, and that emergency preparedness plans are updated and employees made aware of them.

All this within the confines of a comparatively miniscule operating budget – around $1 million a year for the typical Congressional office and about $3 million for each Senator's office.

Managing to Succeed

Perhaps most important of all, the effective chief of staff is a facilitator, clearing obstacles from the path of the Member and the staff alike, helping them remain focused on the tasks before them and keeping them apprised of changes in strategy and circumstance, making them aware of any shifts before rumors have a chance to distort reality, undermine confidence and distract from the shared mission.

Pitfalls to Avoid

Ineffective chiefs of staff operate on the theory that knowledge is power and do everything possible to conceal information from those who work under them – which is counterproductive, at best. In an age when knowledge flows like water around obstacles it might encounter, it is impossible to keep essential information secret. All that secrecy does is create distrust.

This sort of misguided approach to management is not unique to the chiefs of staff who employ it. It usually is a reflection of the temperament of the Members under whom they serve. These Members want their offices to be as disciplined as the political campaigns that brought them to D.C.

Political campaigns often require authoritarian management because they are structured on a military model: They have a defined objective, finite resources, limited time and usually are conducted in the face of enemy fire. When allowed to gain a foothold in a Congressional office, such a system generally limits access to the Member by funneling everything up through the top of the pyramid – the chief of staff, who exercises complete control over the flow of information.

The Member is isolated, usually by preference.

Staff has little decision-making authority and therefore little practical responsibility – unless something goes wrong. Authoritarian managers assume that no matter what the task, their subordinates aren't up to it. They assume staff will not take initiative unless pushed, that they will not recognize priorities unless those priorities are spelled out for them and that they will put self-interest ahead of the organization's well being.

Authoritarianism bottlenecks decisions and limits the options and perspectives available to the Member. It discourages initiative by staff and makes them less loyal to a boss with whom they have no interaction. That, in turn, undermines motivation and initiative. Staff develops slowly if at all. As a result, decisions affecting who gets hired have little significance.

Staff is expendable and easily cast off. Most don't wait for the axe to fall before beginning to look for opportunities elsewhere.

Some micromanaging Members actually aggravate the situation by acting as their own chief regardless of who holds the title on paper. It's not unlike Benjamin Franklin's admonition: "a man who acts as his own attorney has a fool for a client."

Members should lead – chiefs of staff should manage. These are two very different but equally important functions. There are certain things that only Members can do and that should be where they place their focus.

Only the Member can participate in Floor and committee proceedings.

Only a Member can appear at a press conference or do proactive interviews on television, radio, or for print and Internet.

Only a Member can meet with party and committee leaders to help pave the way for a legislative idea.

And only a Member can speak to organizations and coalitions to gather support and help build momentum for his or her ideas.

The Member should schedule his or her time doing those things that only a Member can do.

The Servant-Leader

At the opposite end of the management spectrum is what is known as the open system, which encourages professional behavior on the part of staff and increases the likelihood they will achieve desired goals. Under this system, the chief serves as a conduit rather than a faucet. He or she encourages communication and decision making that involves the Member and those affected by those decisions. The chief's role is to equip and enable staff to perform tasks for which they are suited.

There are 535 individual offices in the House and Senate. Most are run by very capable chiefs who recognize the synergistic aspects of what their staffs do – that the whole is greater than the sum of the parts. In politics as in most other endeavors, a team performs better than the best efforts of individuals operating on their own. Constituent-service personnel, for example, help provide direction for the legislative staff and the communications staffs, while legislative aides affect communicators, and communicators affect legislators.

Synergistic offices constantly seek ways to enable staff to interact with one another, for specialists in one aspect of the operation to contribute to the success of another. Interdependence built upon a common mission encourages an office-wide culture to which new staff finds it easy to adapt and learn. When everyone, from the receptionist at a district or state office to the chief of staff, feels he or she is contributing to fulfillment of a vision and that information flows freely between the Member and subordinates, negative influences such as office politics lose credibility and their sting.

The decision to encourage synergy must be deliberate.

And the Member and top staff must make it.

The open management system – which often is referred to as a flat organization – encourages staff to make decisions and take initiative. It results in greater productivity by spreading important, high-level tasks among more people. It provides the Member with a range of perspectives on important issues.

This system also has weaknesses. People lose focus and miss deadlines if there is not good accountability. Staff members burn out if they take on more responsibility than they can handle. Decision-making can become unclear with more people involved and often makes employees who need structure or dislike decision-making uncomfortable.

Most offices fall somewhere between a pure authoritarian approach and an absolutely flat or open system. Different personalities, circumstances and electoral security influence how an office will be managed. The more open an office tends to be, the more successful and innovative it is.

Marcus Buckingham, who has written several books on management, makes the point that effective management is essential to what he describes as a high-trust organization. In First Break All the Rules, he observes:

> "Great managers need to be recognized for what they do best: reaching inside a worker and encouraging exceptional performance. That is not the same as being a great leader.... Great managers look inward, inside the company, into the individual, into the differences in style, goals, needs and motivations of each person. Then they find the right way to release each person's unique talents into great performance."

This places a premium on chiefs developing their own management and motivational skills and on hiring people they can trust.

There are two essential components of trust: integrity and competence. Integrity is inherent. Competence can be taught.

At a time when unethical behavior by a few Members of the Congress has damaged the reputations of all Members, the need for integrity is as urgent as ever in the history of this nation. Acting with integrity means acting in a consistent and ethical manner – what you do must be consistent with what you say. Integrity matters in big things but also in seemingly little things. If, for example, a Member tells the staff that correspondence must be answered within two weeks, then takes a month to return drafts of letters, the staff quickly concludes that the Member's words and actions don't mesh.

Competence is equally essential. People trust those who accomplish what they say they will accomplish. Everyone from the Member to the newest staff assistant can learn to be better at what they do. One of the chief's jobs is to make sure staff has access to resources that will help them do just that. It is even more important to keep in mind that the shortest route to results is to establish clear goals and a compensation package that rewards performance.

The role of the chief of staff is to help everyone else succeed. The chief of staff's job is to accomplish the office's strategic goals by managing personnel and allocating finite resources such as time and money while fostering accountability. An effective chief of staff measures personal success by the success of those around him or her.

This chief of staff is the ultimate servant-leader.

Managing Between Generations

There are lots of factors that go into management on the Hill – geographic, academic, race, and gender to name a few. One the most dynamic demographic characteristics unique to the Hill is managing between generations.

A high percentage of those working in the Legislative branch are under the age of 30 – members of what's known as Millennials. Primarily those representing Generation X and the Baby Boom complement them. There are even a scattering of people serving in Congress and on staffs who were born between the beginning of the Great Depression and the end of World War II, a generation known as Veterans, Traditionalists and Silents.

Generation	Born
Veterans/Traditionalists	Early 20th Century to Mid-1920s
Silents	Mid-1920s to mid-1940s
Baby Boomers	Mid-1940s – Mid-1960s
Generation X/Xers	Mid-1960s to about 1980
Millennials	About 1980 to 2000
Cuspers are people who have qualities of two generations, usually born near the beginning or end of a generation's range.	

Tom Brokaw has declared the Veterans/Traditionalists "The Greatest Generation" because they not only survived the Depression but at least one of the two World Wars. That makes the *Veterans* reference obvious. They're called *Traditionalists* because they have a reputation for protecting traditional values such as civic pride, loyalty, respect for authority, a strong work ethic and living within one's means. Some researchers on the subject include a generation called *Silents* that falls between the Veterans/Traditionalist and the Baby Boomers. We won't spend too much time here because there are very few, if any, staffers left on the Hill from generations earlier than Baby Boomers.

On the Hill, it is the Baby Boomers who have been credited with inventing the 60-hour workweek.

"They have an almost Pavlovian tendency toward being driven," according to *Generations at Work* by Ron Zemke, Claire Raines and Bob Filipczak, whose conclusions are representative of the flurry of excellent books and articles that have been published in recent years on the need for managers to take into account differences between generations.

Boomers live to work.

Their sense of self is strongly connected to their job, which may help explain why they were so instrumental in winning many of the workplace rights and opportunities that are taken for granted today, particularly those affecting women. Theirs is a generation that has proven itself adept at navigating the political minefields that exist in most offices and are not bashful about voicing concerns when they feel an injustice has been done or they have not been treated fairly.

Many Members now serving in the House and Senate are Boomers. So are some senior staff serving on Congressional committees and in Member offices, who began arriving in numbers following the 1966 increase in employees each office was allowed. Boomers set the standard on the Capitol Hill with 12-hour days and frequent weekends at the office.

Generation X or Xers are the children of workaholic Boomers and perhaps the most over-analyzed and hyper-criticized sliver of society in history – mostly by their parents. Xers are the first generation of America's children to have arrived home after school to an empty house. Both parents were active members of the workforce and can't understand why their children aren't as dedicated to their jobs as they were – or any of their children's other attitudes, for the matter. As a result, Xers have been called lazy, self-focused and materialistic.

Xers contend that none of these harsh labels are fair, that they're simply more independent than their Boomer parents and even their Millennial offspring. They are intelligent but cynical and despise micromanagement. Evidence suggests that they actually are as hard working as the generation that preceded theirs and have perpetuated the 60-hour-plus workweek pioneered by the Boomers on the Hill. They simply prefer not to stay in the office unless there's something important to do.

Xers work to live.

Millennials, the most recent additions to the Capitol Hill workforce, are the most technologically savvy generation ever. They have grown up with computers and cell phones and know how to use the technology that's available to them more effectively than previous generations. It is their lifeline of sorts: They are inextricably *connected* to peers and family through technology.

Unlike Xers, who spent a great amount of time without parental supervision, Millennials consider what they refer to as their *helicopter* parents to have been almost too involved in their lives, having regulated everything from outdoor activities to dining choices. Millennials grew up on fields and in arenas where highly organized sports were played. As a result, they have no idea what stickball is but are enthusiastic collaborators and willing teammates.

They played well together, now they work well together.

They dislike rigid job descriptions, are achievement oriented and tend to be very confident in their ability to reach the goals that are set for them.

They differ from Boomers in that they don't see the need to pay dues and demand to be judged on the basis of merit, not seniority. Millennials may clash with Boomers on attitudes toward the workplace and scoff at Xers' emphasis on individualism, but they have almost reverential respect for Veterans/Traditionalists/Silents.

Though each generation has its own way of looking at the world and its own way of doing things, when allowed and encouraged to work together in an open system, they do so effectively. It's not unusual, for instance, to find a Millennial in a legislative director or a communications director's slot, a level of responsibility that's generally unheard of in the private sector unless your father owns the business. Soon it will not be unusual for Boomers and Xers to find themselves subordinate to Millennials.

Being aware of generational differences is essential to building effective organizations, especially in an environment where staff members are likely to move into positions of authority at much earlier ages and find themselves managing the activities of men and women who are older than they are. All managers must learn to be sensitive to the distinctions, appreciate the strengths of individuals, neutralize the weaknesses of each generation and mold those who work for them into an effective team.

When Xers and Millennials interact with Boomers, for instance, they would be wise to demonstrate respect, conduct face-to-face conversations rather than emailed exchanges, give such conversations their full attention since Boomers are uncomfortable with multi-tasking, understand that Boomers see the workplace in terms of office politics and maneuvering, and be conversant with the history of the Congress and the individual organization. The tendency of Millennials to ignore the past and focus almost exclusively on the present creates suspicion and even resentment among Boomers who contributed to that past and respect the lessons it has taught.

When dealing with Xers, other staff should say what's on their minds because Xers have a low tolerance for buzzwords and clichés. Realize as well that Xers function best when truly empowered. Give them the objective, offer support and let them determine the best way to get things done.

Make work fun.

Millennials, meanwhile, need to be challenged. They enjoy working with others as long as they are treated as an equal, a collaborator – often before their elders feels they have paid their dues. They want to be asked their opinions. Because Millennials benefit from mentoring, as opposed to instruction, managers need to take into account the fact that working with them is much more like a personal relationship than a transactional one.

Millennials need feedback. They are used to instantaneous responses from parents, teachers and the Internet. In many cases, these responses have always been excessively positive - and sometimes unwarranted - but there is nothing the manager can do to change their expectations. Channel those expectations with constructive criticism that is couched in positive terms.

One Senate chief of staff accomplishes the seemingly impossible task of behavior modification among Millennials through no-fault problem solving sessions during regular staff meetings. A situation a Millennial – or any other staff member, for that matter – may not have handled success- fully in the past or one that must be confronted in the near future will be described in general terms. Staff members will then take turns suggesting approaches they believe will work. Then the chief endorses those that are likely to provide the greatest return on investment.

Knowledge management

Another concern affecting the future of Congressional offices involves knowledge management – the way organizations generate, communicate and use their intellectual assets. A Congressional office is what the late Peter Drucker, a pioneer in management studies and author of numerous books including *Managing in the Next Society*, called an *information-based organization*.

In ages past, a Member and a few aides controlled most information and hired other people to support and carry out strategies based on that information. Today, a Congressional office is a collection of specialists who have knowledge that Members need but can't access on their own. For example, a typical Senate office will have a military expert with top-secret security clearance and detailed knowledge of highly technical procure- ment projects; an agriculture expert who knows the ins and outs of every support and loan subsidy program available for every size farm and crop; and an aide who knows transportation spending and has spent time talking with constituents, engineers, city managers and mayors, chambers of commerce and local citizen groups and businesses about specific road, rail, air, boat and bus needs.

All of this is highly specialized information that no one person can possibly acquire, let alone retain.

By default, every Congressional office has become what MBA's refer to as a cross-functional team. Generating a news release, for example, involves a team that typically consists of the Member, the Communications and Legislative staffs, the Scheduler and the Internet. It only makes sense then to develop information systems that allow for easy collaboration and knowledge sharing.

The most significant intellectual asset of any Congressional office is its people –but few Congressional offices take full advantage of it. Here's how forward thinking managers on the Hill perceive the situation:

- As a result of turnover, the research and development efforts of Legislative staff often go away when a staff member departs. A knowledge management system can capture and distribute information pertinent to legislation, scheduling, press, administration, IT training and other learning and educational resources.

- Collaboration involves working across function (Information Technology working with Legislative staff working with Communications, for example) as well as across space (integration of efforts by staff at the D.C. office and those in the home state). All staff members need access to information and the ability to compile and otherwise make use of it.

- Staff development demands access to learning, knowledge and experience. This includes new employee orientation, office manuals, ethics memos, streamlining financial and personnel reports – all of which are important in preserving continuity and office culture.

- Maintaining a history of the Member's Congressional career requires that critical knowledge be captured through carefully kept records and the ability to correlate the information they contain.

- An *electronic organization* enables continuity of operations in the event of a terrorist attack or other incident that forces staff out of their offices.

Too often, knowledge management systems in most Congressional offices consist of an inbox in the *Outlook* email program, an inbox whose contents disappear forever when the address of a departing staff member is eliminated. The technology needed to enable effective knowledge management programs is readily available off the shelf, including corporate mainstays such as *SharePoint* by Microsoft, which has been customized to serve the needs of Congressional offices.

If your office doesn't have the resources it needs to take advantage of what you and everyone else that works there knows long after you've moved on, you might want to suggest to your boss that such a system would be invaluable.

COOP planning

The 800-pound gorilla in every Congressional office is the ever-present threat of terrorist attack. The most important thing a chief of staff can do is be prepared. There are sources on the Hill to help offices design and implement a multi-faceted strategy called a COOP (Continuity of Operations Plan), but given security sensitivities, the less these strategies are written here, the better.

What you'll find readily apparent is that terrorism threats have already changed the way Members communicate with constituents – and vice versa. Paper mail, for instance, goes through a screening process that delays delivery for up to two weeks.

Other considerations range from knowing what to do in response to various types of threats to understanding the resources available and how they should be used, from designing a system to making sure visiting constituents, the entire staff – including interns – and the Member are secure and accounted for.

Plans need to include how the office will operate if forced out of its physical domain, including phone and email communication, redundant information systems and remote backups. A temporary base of operations should be identified, as well as an *order* or *battle* plan for bringing staff back to work. In addition, it should include an alternate means of communicating and coordinating with the district or state office staff.

Chiefs are responsible for the safety and security of staff. They are also responsible for cooperating with efforts aimed at making sure enemies are not able to shut down the Legislative branch of government, even in the wake of the most devastating attacks.

Chapter Seven Summary

- Very little of what chiefs of staff learned in the classroom or in previous jobs prepared them for the role they now play.

- A chief of staff must coordinate activities at satellite offices spread across a congressional district or state. A chief oversees legislative initiatives and external and internal communication. In general he or she is the "chief problem solver."

- Ineffective chiefs of staff operate on the theory that knowledge is power and do everything possible to conceal information from those who work under them.

- Members should lead – chiefs of staff should manage. These are two very different but equally important functions. There are certain things that only Members can do and that should be where they place their focus.

- Under an open or flat system, the chief serves as a conduit rather than a faucet. The chief's role is to equip and enable staff to perform tasks for which they are suited.

- Most offices fall somewhere between a pure authoritarian approach and an absolutely flat or open system.

- There are two essential components of trust: integrity and competence. Integrity means acting in a consistent and ethical manner – what you do must be consistent with what you say. Competence is equally essential. People trust those who accomplish what they say they will accomplish.

- The role of the chief of staff is to help everyone else succeed. The chief of staff's job is to accomplish the office's strategic goals by managing personnel and allocating finite resources such as time and money while fostering accountability.

- One the most dynamic demographic characteristics unique to the Hill is managing between generations.

- The majority of those working in the Legislative branch are members of a generation known as Millennials. Staff representing Generation X and the Baby Boom complement them.

- Another concern affecting the future of Congressional offices involves knowledge management – the way organizations generate, communicate and use their intellectual assets.

- The 800-pound gorilla in every Congressional office is the ever-present threat of terrorist attack.

You're talking on the phone trying to un-snag paper work for computer equipment your office has needed for the past three months when the staff assistant interrupts to say there's an emergency call from your district director. You lean forward in your seat anxiously waiting for the person at House Administration to finish his long-winded explanation for why you won't be getting any satisfaction soon and your elbow strikes one of several stacks of mail that have been accumulating on your desk. It scatters across the draft of a bill your newest legislative assistant just presented you with that would add five new depreciation schedules to the Internal Revenue Code. You glance at your wristwatch and realize you're missing a meeting on how to streamline your office's mail operations, which is probably just as well since your mail management software is down anyway. It's at this point that your boss walks in, orders you to drop everything and run down a rumor that an earmark for a badly needed highway project in your district was left out of an appropriation bill before the Senate.

"This," you reason, "is why the chief of staff gets paid the big bucks."

But you're not alone. Everyone in a management position on the Hill is heir to this sort of pandemonium – sometimes once a week, sometimes once a day, sometimes all day long. There are a seemingly infinite number of challenges vying for your attention. The only constraint is the finite volume of time available to address them. The situation might easily become impossible were it not for strategic planning.

Adrenalin may enable you to put out fire after fire, but inevitably there's a price to be paid – constituents don't get their mail answered, the advice that's given to the boss by your staff leads to a blunder on the Floor of the House or Senate, schedules become confused and staff begins to send out resumes.

The key is to know where you're going and how you intend to get there. Knowing, for example, what the Member's priorities are and building the entire operation around goals based on those priorities, as well as around commonly held values and issues that are important to the constituents you serve.

In short, a strategic vision.

If you're new to the staff of an incumbent, chances are one already exists.

Find it.

Read it.

Live it.

If you're new to the staff of a newly elected Member, whether you're the chief or an entry-level staff assistant, chances are you'll have an opportunity to contribute to the development of the office strategy.

If your office doesn't have one, doesn't have plans to come up with one, hasn't even given a thought to one, encourage your colleagues to do so. Without a strategic vision, a set of goals based on that vision and a plan for meeting the goals, the odds are against success.

How is it possible to make important decisions – any decisions at all, for that matter – without a common understanding of what you and other members of your staff are trying to accomplish?

How do you know what your website should contain?

What are your legislative priorities?

How do you know how much budget you need?

The term strategic planning has become ingrained in the business lexicon. It often means different things to different people, however. Don't over-complicate it.

The Planning Process

If you are in a position of authority and you expect everyone to work toward strategic goals, you must invite everyone whose job will be affected by them to have a hand in their development at an office wide strategic planning meeting. Only by getting the entire staff involved can you generate the sense of ownership necessary to produce a unified force, one whose activities reflect and benefit the office's strategic goals.

It may seem incongruous to suggest that the most effective way to create this unified force is to involve an outsider, but a dispassionate facilitator is essential – especially the first time you undertake an office-wide planning process. There are several reasons:

- An outside facilitator can be expected to bring to the task the skills necessary to engage everyone. It is almost impossible for a chief of staff or the Member, to participate as an equal among equals and serve as moderator and overseer too. An independent moderator brings no history, no personal agenda or other baggage to the process.

- A skillful facilitator can avoid a 2-day free for all by applying order, logic and experience to the process.

- An experienced facilitator will be more successful than an insider at flushing out areas of disagreement that must be resolved if the long-range plan is to succeed – even experienced staff have issues, some of which they may not even be aware of, that can have a negative impact somewhere down the road.

- A skillful facilitator can get staff to ask questions of them that they would not otherwise know to ask.

Choose a facilitator wisely. The characteristics that distinguish Congress from a business will have a significant impact on the planning process and its outcome. In business, the bottom line is measured by profits and stock prices. In the political world it is measured by job-approval ratings and votes. A legislature uses much different criteria in responding to public needs and demand. Choose a facilitator who is familiar with the qualities that make Congress unique.

The Mission Statement

One of the first things a facilitator will ask for is your mission statement. If the office doesn't have one, the facilitator will likely make its creation a priority.

A mission statement is the foundation of the strategic plan. It is the Member's credo, an encapsulation of values and aspirations. It provides staff with a sense of what their priorities should be and how they should focus their energies.

The statement must be brief but comprehensive, leaving little room for misunderstanding but plenty of flexibility for accomplishing the mission. It establishes firm ethical boundaries and demands the highest moral standards and level of performance.

In *The 7 Habits of Highly Effective People*, motivational author Stephen Covey describes an exercise that can kick start the process: *Imagine yourself a witness at your own funeral. Three people are going to speak – one from your family, one from your profession and one from your community. What do you want them to remember about you?*

Obviously, Covey is encouraging us to begin at the end by deciding what we want people to remember us for, then doing our best to assure it's what they do remember. Recognizing the desired result enables us to focus on figuring out how to get there.

It's important to know how long a mission statement needs to be. Most experts agree, the shorter the better. Consider one prepared by the House Committee on Small Business in the late 1990s:

> *Small businesses are essential to prosperity and community and create hope and economic opportunity. We will help them fulfill this role by working to minimize government intrusion, regulatory and fiscal, on small business and to assure that the government respects the worth of small business, the people they employ, and the principles of entrepreneurship.*

Here's how one Congressional office defined its mission:

- *In all things we will conduct ourselves with honesty, integrity and humility — insisting on accountability in our own actions and the actions of government.*

- *We will serve the people and protect their rights and interests against the abuses of power, whether local or national.*

- *We will fight to change the welfare/regulatory state in a way that advances the institutions and values of private society — such as life, faith, family, work, freedom, responsibility, community, enterprise, private property and national security.*

A mission statement should be based on principles rather than monumental self-interest.

Instead of focusing on specific legislation, it should address what that legislation will accomplish.

Instead of a specific form of constituent service, it should describe what constituent service will entail and what results it will provide.

Instead of specific committee action, it should define what people would remember the committee for having accomplished.

A mission statement should articulate core values that are to be translated into tangible results. It should set the standard by which an office will prioritize its time and resources. It is the office's *raison d'être*.

Logistics

Under existing Congressional Rules, there are many considerations that can affect the sort of planning session we're discussing here. It is therefore important to confer with your chamber's Rules Committee and the Federal Election Commission (FEC) to confirm that the session will not violate any codes or campaign laws. These rule-making bodies have constantly changing standards, so don't assume that what worked for a neighboring office or for your own office last year will work this time around.

Among the questions you'll want to get answered are:

- What options are available for covering costs associated with a planning session – can campaign funds or tax dollars be used?

- Is it possible for staff to attend such a session on the clock?

- Are expenses incurred by staff – transportation and meals, for example – reimbursable?

- Can related events such as a breakfast or a dinner be paid for by an outside source?

- Can space or other accommodations be donated?

As for where to conduct your session, schedule it in a location other than either the D.C. or the District office. The D.C. and District staffs should participate in a single event. If that is impossible a session for D.C. staff and another for District staff should be scheduled – but they will not be as productive as one for all.

It is important that everyone have an opportunity to contribute – and that the Member and chief be present when they do.

A retreat-type setting works best, one that is a substantial distance from office phones and routine work. Sessions typically are scheduled during a workweek in which there is little pressing business. Staff the office with a skeleton crew of interns or those staff members who are forced to beg off due to tasks that simply cannot wait.

The Member needs to understand going in that he or she will not be making a guest appearance but must be a full participant in the planning session and be there from beginning to end. Failure to make and live up to that commitment will be disruptive and downright counterproductive – if the Member doesn't take the process seriously, why should anyone else?

Preparations

Though secondary to the mission statement, goal planning provides the road map to the mission's fulfillment. The mission statement tells the world where the office's compass is pointing. The planning session determines the best way to get everyone moving in that direction. But in all likelihood, the planning will begin long before the session. The facilitator can be expected to require several weeks of phone conversations, face-to-face meetings and other fact-finding efforts in advance of the retreat.

With the help of appropriate office staff, the facilitator will gather information on office systems, the most recent polling data, statistical and demographic information on the home district or state, including major employers, federal installations and sensitive environmental sites. This information should be organized and presented to all personnel prior to the planning session. Among the topics that might be addressed are:

- What population shifts have occurred since the last census or redistricting?

- Is there an influx or outflow of specific ethnic groups?

- What is the unemployment percentage and how has it shifted over time?

- Who are the biggest employers?

- What is the per capita income and is it rising or falling?

- How is the population broken down in terms of educational attainment?

- How is the media changing?

- Which labor, agricultural or business groups are growing or shrinking in stature?

- What are the basic demographic ratios – male/female; black/Hispanic/white; under 18, 18-45, 45-65, over 65, etc. – and how are they changing?

The Session Itself

There are various ways to conduct strategic planning sessions. A good facilitator will lead subtly without seeming to impose his or her will. This will discourage staff from parroting what they think the facilitator wants to hear or become suspicious of the process.

Most planning efforts begin with some kind of team-building exercise. One favorite has participants introducing themselves, telling what they do and describing the accomplishment of the past year that they're most proud of. Participants also might be asked to share an amusing, office-related anecdote.

This gives everyone, particularly those from the D.C. and home offices who might not have much interaction, a chance to get to know each another. It also gets everyone talking and encourages him or her to be involved throughout the rest of the session.

If this is not the office's first planning session, the opening exercise can lay the groundwork with an assessment of past goals. This provides an element of accountability and emphasizes that the goals that come out of the current session will receive more than just lip service.

The Lay of the Land

As urgent as the need to know where you're going is the need to know precisely where you are now. In order to find out, you'll need to conduct what is known as a landscape analysis. It is important that the current operations and environment be carefully, fully and candidly scrutinized and discussed. Take inventory by applying the acronym SWOT:

Strengths. What are your strengths as an organization, politically, in the district or state and within the Congress?

Weaknesses. What are your weaknesses as an organization?

Opportunities. What unique opportunities exist?

Threats. What threats exist both from without and within?

Identifying Destinations

An office creates goals by synthesizing the strengths, weaknesses, opportunities and threats that can be identified by those who work there. It does so by determining which strengths and opportunities coincide, producing what can be characterized as offensive goals, and which weaknesses and threats coincide to produce defensive goals. Offensive goals capitalize on internal strengths and external opportunities, and should be aggressively pursued. Defensive goals attempt to correct internal weaknesses and mitigate outside threats.

Once you have a list of goals – and you will likely have 20 or more – you will filter out the unrealistic and the impractical. For instance, a goal of lowering the price of oil might be laudable, but it is not within an individual Member's capacity to attain.

Filtering the goals by means of Four Quadrants contained in the accompanying box (Fig. 5.1) is one way to accomplish this. Once you've gone through this process you should have a pretty good idea where to put your energies.

Filtering Goals

List factors that affect your office in the appropriate boxes of a chart patterned on the one below:

	Urgent	Not Urgent
Able to Affect	I	II
Less Able to Effect	III	IV

Quadrant I represents goals the office must achieve – these are both urgent and attainable.

Quadrant II is for goals that probably can't be fulfilled due to current limitations in time, budget or staff but that you'll work toward if you've got anything left after items in Quadrant I are achieved. (These are the stuff of legacies, the accomplishments that can produce a meaningful and lasting impact, such as solving energy shortfalls or developing a plan for Social Security reform.)

Quadrant III includes issues that affect you, your office, its constituents and perhaps even the entire nation but over which you have very limited control – yet goals in this category are more urgent than those in Quadrant II.

Quadrant IV consists of goals that are worth dreaming about but have almost no chance of ever coming true – don't waste your effort.

The next stage in narrowing the list of goals is referred to as a SMART analysis – another acronym. It judges each goal on the basis of the following criteria:

Is it Specific? No open-ended objectives, along the lines of "Improve communication between Washington and the District." Goals must include both an objective and a strategy: "Improve communication between Washington and the District office *by setting up regular conference calls and establishing an email system for disseminating important information such as votes, floor speeches and press releases to all staff.*"

Is it Measurable? It must be possible to gauge the success of goals – your action plan should actually create accountability: "Conference calls between the D.C. and District office will be made once a week. The effectiveness of these calls will be measured by a quarterly survey conducted by the Communications staff, which will encourage candor by guaranteeing the anonymity of participants."

Is it Appropriate? Goals must be consistent with the mission statement and the Member's vision – no goal will succeed if the Member isn't interested.

Is it Realistic? Goals that are not attainable waste time and resources. It might not be realistic to have all mail answered in 14 days, for instance – but it might be realistic to have 85 percent of it answered in that timeframe.

Is it Time limited? Goals must have a specified duration or a target date. A Congressional term only lasts two years. Otherwise, it's unattainable, unrealistic, immeasurable and entirely inappropriate. "The goal of answering 85 percent of mail in 14 days will be accomplished and sustainable within 90 days."

Goals that are SMART are more likely to be accomplished. Those that aren't, undermine the process. Worse yet, goals that aren't attainable undermine the credibility of future goal-planning efforts.

Only half a dozen or so goals are likely to make it through the SMART filter, but that is more than enough to provide your office with direction to keep it busy as long as everyone on the staff is able to feel or see the results.

Why Goals Fail

- The organization does not believe in the outcome — members do not believe that once the goal is reached it will be of any value.

- They don't believe the outcome is attainable — they think it is pie in the sky, either because the premise is flawed or it puts too much strain on resources.

- They can't figure out what outcome the boss really wants.

Turning Goals Into Action

Without an action plan, goal planning is little more than an academic exercise. The action plan is the strategy for accomplishing the goals, the tactics that will be used and the methods to assure accountability.

Each goal must have a project team and each team must have a project leader.

The success of the plan's implementation depends on accountability from the top down and from the bottom up. Each team needs support and resources, decision-making authority and the opportunity to succeed or fail. The chief of staff's main job is to provide the tools and demand accountability.

The teams' work begins at the end – a clear picture of what it hopes to achieve and what must happen to achieve it. Then, each project is divided into stages with benchmarks and timetables for completion. These action plans should be detailed and in writing. (Some people use sophisticated software to generate PERT or Gantt charts, but this is probably overkill.) The volume of time that's invested in the development of an action plan is directly proportionate to its likelihood for success. As a result, there's little likelihood an action plan will be finalized at the retreat.

Although mission statements should never be compromised, goals may be updated according to changing circumstances and reality. Action plans should be flexible enough to accommodate both – and should be reviewed regularly by the chief and the team to gauge the success of tactics that are being applied and consider alternatives where appropriate.

Both responsibility and initiative should be recognized and rewarded. Rewards, recognition and encouragement reinforce unity throughout the ranks. They also reinforce the importance of the planning process while at the same time creating measurable standards for promotion, pay raises and bonuses – a valuable byproduct of this approach to management since there are no secrets when it comes to compensation on Capitol Hill. (Staff salaries and office expenses are published quarterly in the House and biannually in the Senate.)

The Member's involvement is critical – so is determining precisely how involved he or she will be. On Capitol Hill at least, a successful action plan will be 90 percent the result of staff activity.

Action planning is a proven means of identifying and implementing goals – which are in turn, the practical expression of a Member's mission statement. In an environment of constant interruptions and non-stop demands, prioritizing goals and dedicating the resources of the office to carrying them out is the only way to make a positive difference, one that gives meaning to the trust placed in Members by their constituents.

Find out what your office's goals are, what action plans are in the works and where you fit in the process. If your office has none of the above, demonstrate your competence in your new job, and then begin quietly lobbying for a session where long-range planning can occur.

Chapter Eight Summary

- Everyone in a management position on the Hill is heir to pandemonium – sometimes once a week, sometimes once a day, sometimes all day long. The situation might easily become impossible were it not for strategic planning.

- If you are in a position of authority and you expect everyone to work toward strategic goals, you must invite everyone whose job will be affected by them to have a hand in their development at an office wide strategic planning meeting.

- Using an outside facilitator is a good idea for an office's first planning session.

- A mission statement is the foundation of the strategic plan. It provides staff with a sense of what their priorities should be and how they should focus their energies. A mission statement should articulate core values that are to be translated into tangible results.

- The Member needs to be a full participant in the planning session and be there from beginning to end.

- Goal planning provides the road map to the mission's fulfillment. The mission statement tells the world where the office's compass is pointing. The planning session determines the best way to get everyone moving in that direction.

- An office creates goals by synthesizing the strengths, weaknesses, opportunities and threats that can be identified by those who work there. Offensive goals capitalize on internal strengths and external opportunities. Defensive goals attempt to correct internal weaknesses and mitigate outside threats.

- Goals that are SMART (specific, measurable, appropriate, realistic and time-limited) are more likely to be accomplished. Goal that aren't attainable undermine the credibility of future goal-planning efforts.

- An action plan is the strategy for accomplishing the goals, the tactics that will be used and the methods to assure accountability.

- Although mission statements should never be compromised, goals may be updated according to changing circumstances and reality. Action plans should be flexible.

- Rewards, recognition and encouragement should reinforce the importance of the planning process while at the same time creating measurable standards for promotion, pay raises and bonuses.

Your title and your job description may not contain the word *communication* but it's what you do for a living. What you say and how you say it help determine you and your employer's success or failure in the political fishbowl.

Webster's defines *communication* as: *interchange of thoughts, opinions or information by speech, writing, etc.; information, thought or feeling that is satisfactorily received or understood; the act of imparting, participating; opening into each other; connecting; personal rapport.*

In other words, communication is more than mere information. It is more than just disseminating information. It demands that information be shared in such a way that it is understood, in a way that turns information into usable knowledge. It also demands rapport with those with whom you are communicating, the kind of trust and comfort level that makes the information credible, trustworthy and reliable. Perhaps most importantly, it demands a link that runs in two directions – he who shares knowledge gains it in return.

Listening is perhaps the least appreciated and most overlooked aspect of the communication process. "No man ever listened himself out of a job," said Calvin Coolidge.

A discussion of how those responsible for speaking to the media on behalf of your Member's office and how they can do their job effectively may not seem pertinent to the role you play, assuming you are not that person. But it is. Your office is a microcosm of the world into which your communication staff projects your efforts and aspirations.

A fundamental rule of communication is this: Be circumspect. It's all right to go on and on about where you took the kids over the weekend if you're having a casual conversation with a co-worker. But if the topic is work-related and the audience is potentially larger, be brief and to the point. Avoid thinking out loud. Remember, knowledge is power – and anything that can be held against you can be used to enslave you.

We aren't trying to make you paranoid; we are just emphasizing that even paranoid people have enemies.

Not everyone you encounter is your enemy, of course. Most aren't. But by the same token, not everyone is your friend – discretion isn't just the better part of valor, it's also the key to job security when friends and enemies alike hang on every word that is attributed to your boss and his staff.

Communication is a broad subject area. How you communicate inside an office may be more important than how you communicate outside. How you communicate with other offices and other staff members is critical to success. But for now we are going to concentrate on how you communicate with the outside world through the media. And the media is a pretty broad subject as well, stretching from news to entertainment and a morass of combinations thereof, all of which influence, to a greater degree than ever before, political thinking, political action and public policy decisions.

Let's focus on a broad definition of news media, or what used to be called the press, and those who dealt with them – press secretaries or press assistants, or administrative aides who served part time as the press connection.

Three decades ago media relations were simpler if only because there were fewer media outlets with which to contend. The communication staff dealt with newspapers, radio and television stations in the Member's home district or state and with the wire services. They were on a first-name basis with most of the journalists they encountered.

Unless a Member was part of the leadership, exposure to national media was usually restricted to instances where he or she was in trouble or was expert in a hot issue or from an area of the country that had been ravaged by disaster. Communication staffs produced press releases, and if the media considered those press releases newsworthy – or if the media were simply desperate for something to fill a few inches of space or a few moments of airtime – they passed the information on to the public.

Even deadlines were simpler: Television news was broadcast at 6 p.m., morning newspapers went to press at midnight, and afternoon papers went to press at noon.

Times and the volume of media that must be contended with have changed dramatically since then.

Traditional outlets, such as major dailies and network news still drive public opinion, but they have competition that didn't exist in their worst nightmares two decades ago. New dynamics include a variety of Internet and wireless communication services and products that shape the opinions of many segments of society. Their numbers grow every day. There are interactive websites and blogs. There are web pages addressing every imaginable topic. There are electronic magazines, newsletters and web commentaries. There are cyberspace gossip columns. And they are all even more unbridled than the mainstream media.

And they are all interconnected. News in the gossip and celebrity pages becomes news in the government and politics pages. And they have contributed to the resurrection of advocacy journalism, adversarial journalism and other forms of opinionated reporting that date to the American Revolution but have been more commonly associated in recent years with the British tabloids than with American media.

Most modern day journalists will tell you that the news media serves at least three basic functions in American politics.

First, they serve as a chronicler of history in the making. Much of what we know of the political history of our country, for instance, comes from the pages of newspapers. In more recent times, the footage of broadcast media has contributed to the historical record. The news media serves the nation by recording its history. It is not the only witness to history, but it is certainly one of the primary sources on which we as a nation depend.

That role has brought with it an incredibly important responsibility, one that has been diminished greatly by new forms of information dissemination via the Internet. We live in an era when raw material can be thrust into the public dialogue irrespective of its legitimacy or accuracy. The icon of this new era is Wikipedia, a modern-day encyclopedia of information to which anyone can contribute anything, regardless of whether it is true or false.

It is incumbent on Congressional staff to always be mindful of how history is recorded because they are making it.

Second, news media provide oversight. They consider themselves watchdogs. They are a check and balance outside the Constitution's governmental boundaries. How many times have you heard expressions such as, "Will it play in Peoria?" patented by Richard Nixon, or "Will it pass the smell test?" or "Can you say it with a straight face?" or "Is it credible?" or "Can we say that publicly?" The media provide a check on what you say, how you say it, and more importantly what you do and how you do it.

Media constantly define and redefine the term "appearance of impropriety," and often set a standard for ethical behavior that far exceeds legal or regulatory restrictions. The media can, for example, turn a time-honored procedure such as earmarks into a political liability. The media challenge behavior, question the application of laws and regulations, and heighten the awareness of otherwise unseen and unheard of issues that have the potential for significant impact on the way we govern and the way we live. They challenge statistics, question the interpretation of facts and second-guess conclusions. Granted, much of what the media do in the way of oversight originates from leads they get from government agencies and congressional committees. At their best, the media are the ombudsmen for the people who pay your salary. At their worst, they are agents of confusion, misinformation and obstruction. Yet no other mechanism in our system is so capable of putting issues and behavior under the white heat of public scrutiny.

Third, the media disseminate information with speed and efficiency. Some turn information into junk. Others translate it into the vernacular so that readers, viewers and listeners can understand much of what in politics and government affects their lives. Some use information to titillate and entertain, others use it to educate. But news media transmit information, lots of it, more of it than any other source available to you or your constituents.

It is impossible to deal effectively with the media without a basic understanding of their past and what motivates them in the 21st Century – and to a lesser degree, how the fundamental freedoms enshrined in the First Amendment are applied in this new era. Some of our Republic's first newspapers, and many since, were intensely partisan and ideological. They were advocates rather than impartial observers. Thomas Jefferson and Alexander Hamilton launched their own dueling publications, a characterization that may be of questionable taste, given Hamilton's fate at the hand of Aaron Burr. These publications became the instruments rather than the chroniclers of the budding new political parties in America. They advanced causes supported by their patrons, smeared their adversaries and otherwise fought for the hearts and minds of early Americans. Well into the 20th century, newspapers were known for their loyalty to one party or ideology over another.

Times have tempered some of the media's politically parochial instincts, but the history of journalism in the United States is anything but a study in truth, justice and the American way. It is a study in conflicting interests – commercial, professional, political and ideological – brought together to advance the agendas, some noble, some not, of owners, editors and writers.

The news media have always vacillated between subjectivity and what passes for objectivity, from news to entertainment, from highly partisan allegiances to non-alignment, from independence to conglomerate owner-ship and from cutthroat competition to absolute monopolies. These varied interests continue to drive journalism today, sometimes along conflicting lines.

Speed Skills

There are differences not just in the roles the media play or the interests that propel them, but also in the pace at which stories develop, the ques-tions of accountability raised by technological advances affecting tradi-tional and new media, and the ferocious competition for dominance as a source of information. Clark Kent-style journalism doesn't exist anymore, if it ever did.

Today the media may exercise enormous power but when all is said and done, they are businesses, scrambling for as big a share of the market as they can get, just like any other commercial enterprise. They experi-ence the same struggles between executive suites and the production line, similar to those in any other business.

In order to attract the attention of potential audiences in the modern world, they have blurred the line between news and entertainment –spawning what has been called "infotainment," an entirely new way of looking at the world, including political life.

Important information isn't always interesting or easy to understand. It takes time to explain a comprehensive healthcare plan, for instance. Most journalists don't have the talent to make a complex topic compel-ling. Even if they could, most audiences don't have the patience to absorb all the details and understand them. Our fast-paced society demands data in small, easy-to-digest doses that tickle us, that are intended to stimulate emotions more than encourage thought and reflection.

Audiences tune in where they can find easy answers, sarcasm or satire. Pioneering news entertainers such as Bill Maher, Don Imus, Stephen

Colbert, Rush Limbaugh, Bill O'Reilly, Lou Dobbs, Sean Hannity, Glenn Beck and Jack Cafferty exploit politics for fun, profit, ratings and a platform for their opinions.

Lobbying is no longer the only high-visibility second career available to Washington's out-of-work politicians and political operatives. The late Tim Russert was a former chief of staff to Senator Daniel Patrick Moynihan and counsel to New York Gov. Mario Cuomo before hosting NBC's Meet the Press; Chris Matthews was a one-time aide to President Jimmy Carter and House Speaker Tip O'Neill before hosting MSNBC's Hardball; George Stephanopoulos was an aide to House Speaker Tom Foley and later President Bill Clinton's communication director before hosting ABC's This Week; and former Congressmen Joe Scarborough, of MSNBC's Morning Joe, and John Kasich on FOX, were both Members of the House of Representatives. The list keeps growing.

Newspapers used to label opinion as editorials or commentary – terms that have been used by television and radio as well – and the opinions were almost always confined to specific pages. None bother much anymore. What used to be known as objective journalism has all but become a thing of the past. The manner in which journalists, producers and editors handle information that finds its way into print or onto the airwaves is shaped by a myriad of subjective factors such as personal prejudice, gender, age, religion or lack of it, politics, ideology and experience, career enhancement, peer pressure, ratings and a host of other factors.

Nonetheless, there are a good many journalists who strive for high journalistic standards and want to serve as unbiased observers of current events. Those of you who deal directly with the media will get to know them and appreciate the role they play. Those of you who don't will benefit from the efforts of those who do. But keep in mind that dealing with them takes serious study, professional finesse, sound judgment and a lot of caution.

The World of Blogs

Blogs – which is a contracted form of the phrase *web logs* – have become a primary source of news for many Americans and a source of leads for most media. Websites such as "The Drudge Report" and "Daily Kos" have exposed fault lines in the news operations of traditional media, revealing errors and in some cases calling into question the credibility of such luminaries as CBS anchor Dan Rather, whose career was destroyed when he was forced to apologize for unsubstantiated allegations involving President George W. Bush's military career.

Political blogs run the gamut from neoconservative to ultraliberal with output that ranges from urban myths to actual investigative reporting. Blogs have a strong appeal to partisans. They tend to attract audiences and commentary that share their point of view and are more forgiving of factual error than ideological apostasy. They represent an opportunity for far more personal interaction than the mainstream media, providing interactive forums where readers can comment, share opinions, ridicule political opponents, rally the troops and provide policy and other information aimed at specific political niches – all for a fraction of the cost of mainstream media productions.

While many blogs have become legitimate voices of political movements and parties, there are numerous sites that spew garbage – from vile white supremacist sites advocating hatred to ultra left sites that taunt and wish suffering on dying political opponents. Surf as carefully as a pet owner walking his best friend through the neighborhood dog park after dark.

According to the Pew Internet and American Life Project, nearly 40 percent of American adults used the Internet to get news about the 2008 political campaign. In fact, more people under the age of 36 get their news from the Internet than from newspapers. And the Internet continues to change politics – more than 10 percent of Americans have used a social networking site for political activity, and one in 10 Internet users has made an online campaign contribution. Since the election of Bill Clinton in 1992, the role of television, magazines and newspapers as primary sources of political news has declined, while the role of radio and the Internet has dramatically increased.

That doesn't mean a Member's communication director can ignore traditional media. It simply increases the range of opportunities – and challenges. So does a range of insider media that serves those working on the Hill but are accessed as well by other media, lobbyists and the Executive Branch. These include newspapers such as *Roll Call*, *The Hill* and *Politico*; online newsletters published by *Congressional Quarterly* and the

National Journal, including *Hotline* and *Congress Daily* and a host of other Hill-oriented outlets for information.

Demands of the Job

Today's communication staffs must possess the same media skills as their predecessors – creativity, salesmanship and the ability to render complex ideas in easy-to-understand prose. But they also must possess a range of high-tech skills such as the ability to quickly update websites, publish podcasts, make available video of the boss's Floor speech, publish a blog entry in a less formal and more conversational style than traditional press releases, arrange videoconferences and tele-townhalls that make it possible to reach remote audiences and produce e-newsletters. All this while continuing to build productive relationships with reporters, writing traditional press releases, arranging interviews, writing columns and op-ed pieces, drafting background papers, recording radio actualities (recorded radio quality messages sent out as a podcast or over the phone) and providing training to staff on when and how to deal with the media.

The ever-more abundant means of delivering a message complicate the process of delivering that message in a timely manner. Failure to get a Member's opinion on an important issue into the news quickly may mean missing the chance to have a voice in the debate or worse yet, allowing false information to go unchallenged long enough for it to become fact in the minds of many.

In a Fortune 500 office, it may take a week for a press release to pass through numerous levels of management – including marketing, legal and investor relations – unless of course, their product has been cited as a source of E. Coli. On the Hill, communication staffs often have only minutes to get a Member's perspective into a breaking news story or to respond to a charge that will be aired within the hour.

In addition to speed, accuracy is critical. In the good old days, there was time to call a reporter and clarify a comment. Even if it already had been published or broadcast, it could be corrected or rephrased or clarified. The same is not true of most websites. Once a story is published, no matter how rife with inaccuracies, it lives forever. An innocent mistake can be magnified or distorted beyond recognition and disseminated around the world in less time than it takes to say, "Congressman, we have a problem."

News has become a 24/7 process that doesn't take weekends off. Cable, then the Internet, forever changed the way Americans get information. Fox, CNN and MSNBC operate full-time news operations. Newspapers must continually be posting stories on their websites just to stay relevant. The Associated Press posts what used to be called bulletins, and then adds to them as information becomes available until the final report may be 10 times its original length. Seventy million-plus blogs have made potential reporters and commentators out of anyone with an Internet connection and a story to tell or an opinion to share. Television has followed suit by urging audiences to use the digital cameras in their cell phones to film news they come upon and share it with news staffs at affiliates or even the network.

You must build working professional relationships with reporters. Professional journalists are not likely, regardless of their personal ideology, to burn valuable relationships with a primary news source for "gotcha" politics. And, if they are, they are not professional, and you shouldn't bother establishing or maintaining a relationship with them. Learn from experience – yours as well as the experience of others.

Professional journalists face intense challenges. The pressure to scoop the competition creates the temptation to run with half the facts, abuse the anonymous source, and generalize to the point of misinterpretation. The symbiotic relationship that exists between a successful congressional communication staff and these journalists demands an understanding of the influences that govern the journalists' activities, from deadlines to editors or producers to the demographics of the audiences they serve to the standards and values that guide them as a group and as individuals. In essence, it is understanding what defines news to each one of them – and understanding that what is news to one isn't necessarily news to another.

A procedural dynamic that's driving a vote on an energy bill may be of interest to a writer for the *National Journal*, for example, but not to a correspondent for *NBC News*. An *NBC* correspondent, on the other hand, may be interested in the impact of welfare reform on a family in Iowa, while the *Journal* writer will not.

The fact that not every media outlet is interested in every story is complicated by the fact that all of them are interested in others – particularly the ones that involve controversy – and these tend to eat up space that from your point of view might be better devoted to the stories you'd like to tell. It's the way the world is. Don't waste time or energy being frustrated over it. Focus instead on absolutes that will benefit you in every situation:

Trust. The most important commodity a communication staff has is its credibility. It must not be undermined. Reporters must expect each member of the team to be a dependable source of information. Don't let a reporter learn from another source information that calls into question a position or a point of view you are putting forth – raise the question yourself and address it head on. Don't leave out facts, narrowly interpret them or stretch them beyond credulity. Don't say more than you need to say and make sure the facts and circumstances are absolutely clear in your mind before trying to impart them to someone else. Most importantly – never lie to a reporter.

Realize that trust is more than simply providing reliable information, explanations and observations. It manifests itself in returning calls, following up and providing good guidance. It manifests itself in candor and honesty as well. If you don't know the answer to a question, say so. If you know where the answer can be had, say that. And if you know the answer but can't reveal it, explain your situation.

Trust, obviously, is a two-way street. Reporters need to earn yours as urgently as you need to earn theirs. If you have even a hint of concern, probe deep enough to be sure.

Relevance. Communication staff must assure that whatever information provided is of value, that it is balanced, addressing both sides of an issue, and that it is of interest and importance to more than just the boss. You know what's important in your universe; know what's important in the reporter's.

Story Appeal. Not all, or even most, of press relations involves responding to news or reacting to events. Communications staff must devote time and talent to pitching story ideas, selling the relevance of information that by their very nature might not be particularly interesting. A story idea has to have appeal. It has to be compelling to a skeptical audience. This requires easy-to-understand background information. It requires humanizing the issues. You do that by bringing information and statistics to life, giving them a human face and form that dramatizes how the issue impacts the lives of the people for whom the journalist is writing or reporting.

The concept of welfare-to-work is a drab concept until you infuse it with life by telling the story of a formerly unemployed mother in Des Moines who is now working at a retail store, selling children's clothes. But it requires more than just an actor giving life to an issue of this sort. It also requires expert testimony from experts and analysts who can correlate that one success in Des Moines with thousands, perhaps millions, of others nationwide.

The challenge is to overcome the urge to proselytize, to preach, and to pack the story with partisanship. Keep personal opinions to a minimum and avoid criticism unless it's constructive and expressed in a positive way.

Journalists love a story that writes itself.

Unfortunately, it's sometimes hard to come up with one or with the time to develop it. Due to time constraints produced by day-to-day pressures and the demands of unexpected crises, coupled with the range of media to which responses must be addressed, capturing the essence of a *real lifestory* is one of the least honored absolutes in communication. You can help by identifying opportunities and passing them along to the communication staff.

A congressional district and surely an entire state can produce hundreds if not thousands of good human-interest stories, whether it involves someone helped by government, someone hurt by it, a business thriving because of it or a business impaled by it. If there is a compelling human element or a lesson that can be learned by others, or just something of drama or humor or sadness, there may well be media interest. It doesn't have to involve government, but it is government that ties the congressman or the Senator to the story, and, obviously, that is important. The halo effect of human-interest stories is immeasurable, whether they appear in a hometown newspaper, on network news or someplace in between. Just remember that when dealing with constituent interests and needs, you and the Congressman have a clear and critical legal and moral responsibility to protect the privacy of any constituent. Don't pursue a story idea without permission and don't apply pressure to get it.

There are distinctions between a story that is primarily local and one that has national potential. Local audiences are sensitive to social, geographic, cultural and commercial concerns – parochial peculiarities and idiosyncrasies are important, right down to word pronunciation and dialects. National audiences are less concerned about the correct pronunciation of Bexar County but share with local audiences a passion for stories that touch them on a personal level, that contain sympathetic characters grappling with challenges the audience is just as likely to face.

Chapter Nine Summary

- Communication is much more than the transfer of information.

- A fundamental principle of communication is to be circumspect.

- Relations with media have changed dramatically with the advent of new technology. New media have blurred the lines between news and entertainment and information and opinion.

- News media provide three basic functions in the political process: chronicler, overseer, and disseminator.

- The history of news media in America puts a lot of modern-day journalism in perspective.

- The world of blogs has changed the world of information gathering, verification and dissemination.

- Media relations demand many skills and work, all based on trust.

Any hope that the communication staff will have the time and resources to carry out even a fraction of their diverse missions requires that the communication director be intimately involved in strategic planning. By working backward from the goals identified in the planning phase, the communication director can identify where resources will be needed and come up with a game plan that will serve these needs. A strategic communication plan should address some or all of the following:

- The Member's priorities.

- National media relations.

- Regional/local media relations.

- Image and name recognition.

- An informed constituency.

- Crisis communications strategy.

- Message management.

The communication component of the overall strategic plan must recognize that everyone in the Member's office has a stake in successful communication and each must understand and fulfill his or her role in order for it to work. This is particularly true of the legislative staff. Communication personnel and those responsible for the office's legislative agenda must work in tandem if either hopes to be successful. You can't legislate without communication and you can't communicate without something to say. The vast majority of what is communicated is about legislation.

Elemental to the strategy is whether communication is done aggressively, timidly, safely or riskily or somewhere in between. Are you:

A. Avoiding pitfalls, playing it safe, being mundane, avoiding attention, reactive instead of proactive; or are you

B. Seizing issues, establishing a brand, being proactive and engaging controversy.

The timid approach is the least popular among most communications professionals. Today's political environment simply doesn't permit a politician to be a wallflower, nor does it enhance the fortunes of a press secretary to be one either. What matters, however, is the approach or style with which the Member is most comfortable.

The Member must be comfortable with the strategy and his or her role in carrying it out. A timid or studious politician cannot carry off an aggressive media strategy and no good communications professional would expect otherwise.

Another important criterion in building a strategy is gauging what kind of Member the Member wants to be. Is he or she primarily suited to fulfilling constituent needs with little interest in national issues or political agendas? Is the Member particularly dedicated to specific issues, such as trade or health care, rather than a generalist with broader interests? Is he or she a consensus builder or primarily a communicator, a messenger, one who defines issues rather than resolving them? There are shades of gray in all of these distinctions, but regardless of where a Member falls on this scale, it is important to tailor communications to the personality, character and proclivities of the boss.

It is equally important to assess resources and points of leverage that can be applied to the benefit of the Member: Committee assignments, for example, relationships with leadership and the Administration in power, staff, media accessibility, existing name recognition and branding, past exposure to media and communications, attitude, and demands on time and energy.

A key element of strategy development is rooted in your ability to create an image, an identity, a brand that distinguishes your Member from other Members and establishes him or her as a participant in the political process and not just an observer.

The most effective means of branding (a term that is overused and under-defined) a politician is through legislative action. Branding and name recognition can be built on the back of a legislative initiative if the Member is willing and able to devote the time and attention to it. The Member must champion an issue, develop a reputation for expertise in its various permutations and be engaged in the strategy and tactics necessary to move it forward. It requires building relationships with allies, including other Members of Congress, Executive branch advocates or experts and outside organizations such as trade associations, trade media and other interests that are considered leaders in the issue area. If, for example, the initiative involves cancer research, then a solid relationship should be built with the American Cancer Society, American Lung Association and

Do Members Have a "Brand?"

Members, Political Parties and even the Congress itself have a brand identity – whether it's intentional or not.

Keep in mind that a brand is not a marketing or campaign slogan (though a slogan might be adopted that highlights a brand). For an elected official, a "brand essence" is who that person really is. The brand conjures up certain characteristics such as attributes (committee, voting record, margin of victory), benefits to the voter (lower taxes, better health care), values (frugal, innovative, compassionate), culture (appealing to images different Americans have of their country), personality (optimistic, back slapping and cigar smoking), and what kind of voter (customer, in the business world) is likely to be attracted to that brand. The success of that brand is determined by whether people believe the elected official is what his or her brand claims they are, and whether they like what they believe the brand to be.

others, both in Washington D.C. and at home, who are involved in cancer research. Most issues and interests have a cadre of bylined reporters and information organizations that specialize in that subject or subjects closely related to it. For instance, major news organizations have health care reporters.

A legislative initiative has many moving parts, usually including a bill that serves as the primary mechanism for defining the issues, and defining the ultimate goal.

The introduction of a bill can be the catalyst for press releases, interviews, blogging, tele-townhalls and other forms of communication that address the problem and the need for the Member's solution. Through each stage of the process, similar proactive initiatives can be performed: committee hearings, committee votes, incorporation into other legislation, floor action, action in the other chamber, conferencing and ultimately signing into law by the President. There are many and varying opportunities through the process to engage in tactics that help brand the Member, giving him or her a positive identity.

Other activities and events, aside from legislative vehicles, are marketable as well and can serve as useful tools in shaping images and brand. This might include walking in a local cancer fundraising parade or highlighting an individual's plight with a speech for the *Congressional Record* – which is distributed to the people who are interested in the issue.

The best approaches to media are direct ones, a solid pitch made with an enticing story line, interesting and concise background information, a current event or occurrence that can serve as a backdrop for a story, and when possible, an element of exclusivity for the medium. A reporter who knows he or she will be getting the story before a competitor will be more attracted to your pitch. It should go without saying, however, that exclusivity, partial or whole, should not be promised if it cannot be delivered. The enticement of exclusivity puts the reporter's credibility on the line with his or her own editors and producers.

By the way, don't be afraid to "cold call" a reporter you have never met. Calling people they don't know is something most reporters do for a living, so they are not likely to be put out if you have an interesting pitch to make.

Staff also must recognize that what works on television may not work for newspapers, magazines and Internet. A good tool for electronic media, for example, are radio actualities – audio press releases that typically include a high-quality recording of a statement by the Member – distributed over the Internet to stations that may not have the budget for a news staff. A press conference may be a convenient way for Members of Congress to tell the media what they want them to know but scheduling one doesn't guarantee the media will attend – far from it. Press conferences should be employed sparingly and timed to accommodate deadlines and other news events. More often than not, media turnout will be disappointing. Props should be used to attract attention and clarify the message – charts, graphs, celebrities and other high-visibility supporters can distinguish what the Member has to say from what thousands of others have already said. It's called putting a face on the story.

Press events don't take place just in D.C. – if constituents back home don't know what the Member is doing, they're likely to perceive him or her as out of touch. Activities must be coordinated and synchronized with the state and district constituencies, and media.

If everything the boss does or thinks or says is presented the same way every time, the communication staff undermines its own ability to communicate. There's a time to shout and a time to whisper. There's a time for comment and a time for quiet. There's a time for emotion and a time for reason. There's a time for principle and a time for pragmatism.

No Member can afford to be the lightning rod for every issue that comes up in the Congress. In order to be effective, each Member must pick and choose which causes they'll make their own, which they'll support *sub rosa* and which they'll be willing to compromise on. Each Member also must decide how widely these choices should be publicized.

Calculating Risks

Communication strategy requires calculation, not only as it relates to getting the word out, but protecting sensitive information within. Everyone, regardless of whether they're part of the communication staff, should remember:

- Never put anything in writing you don't want to appear on the front page of the *New York Times*.

- Everything that is said or done should be the product of planning and should be said or done with a purpose or outcome in mind.

- Planning must take into consideration what vehicle or vehicles will be used to deliver the message – a webcast, for example, or a press release or participation in a network roundtable or an appearance on a late-night talk show or a combination of more than one of the avenues that are available. Not all avenues will be available at any given time, so alternative routes must be added to the list in descending order, thus enabling the greatest concentration of effort on the most advantageous, with the option of moving to the next tier if the top picks fall through or take less time than anticipated to attain.

- Planning also identifies who is authorized to speak publicly and under what circumstances – on the record, off the record, not for attribution, on background.

Those authorized to speak on the issue must be perpetually cautioned and eventually trained not to rush to the microphone with their mouths outrunning their brains, not to react in anger unless there's purpose behind the outburst, never to react instinctively; and to be prepared for any question, even if it must be answered with "I don't know."

Admitting ignorance is far preferable to demonstrating stupidity.

The integrity and credibility of the Member, of his office and of his or her communication staff depend on acquiring the facts and a willingness to share them, all of them. Provide your target audience with all sides of every issue. Put all the facts on the table and present them and interpret them in such a way that your audience can't help but reach the same conclusion you have. Some call that spin. There's nothing wrong with spin if it is practicing the art of persuasion and not perpetrating a fraud.

The effectiveness of what is said on behalf of the Member depends on the audience's ability to identify with the messenger and by extension, the message. It is not an ability the audience brings to the discussion. It is one that is produced by the medium and the message. If you are the messenger, you must be believable and able to make what you say important, interesting and persuasive. This maxim applies to news stories, feature stories, debates and any of the multitude of other communication vehicles used to ensure a message reaches its target audience in as many different ways as possible.

You Didn't Get This From Me, But...

It is prudent to make clear prior to speaking with the media as to the ground rules for the exchange. Here are the most common:

Off the Record: Nothing I say can be quoted or attributed to me or my office in any way.

Deep Background: Nothing I say can be attributed to me or my office or in any way that would lead to me.

Background: Nothing I say can be attributed to me by name, but can be sourced in a more general way.

On the record: Anything I say can be quoted and attributed to me by name and title.

Basic Rules for Talking to the Press

Here are some more basic rules that will serve you well in almost every situation:

- Don't say more than you have to say to make your point. Someone once said that the First Amendment gives every American the right to make a damn fool of themselves – but you don't have to exercise it. It has also been said that there is nothing wrong with having nothing to say – unless you say it.

- Stay on message. Don't be diverted. Don't digress.

- Limit the number of points you make.

- Reinforce what you say with selective research, expert testimony, background data, anecdotes, charts, graphs and other evidentiary material – but don't overdo it.

- Be serious, but not stuffy. Employ humor when possible, particularly the self-deprecating kind.

- Make whatever you say or do a call to action, whether the desired action is careful consideration or actual steps – inform, educate, stimulate, and ignite passions.

- Avoid clichés. They are called clichés because they are overused and are usually hackneyed expressions whose meaning is so broad as to be meaningless. The exception is when you can give a cliché a humorous twist, as Ronald Reagan did when he freshened up the time-honored canard that suggests prostitution is the world's oldest profession: "Politics is supposed to be the second oldest profession. I have come to realize that it bears a close resemblance to the first."

- Avoid acronyms and other communication shortcuts – they often divert your audience from what you have to say to the way you're saying it. Acronyms are lazy, presumptuous, often confusing and rude interruptions to the flow, particularly the ones that have been made up to brand a subject, project, initiative or a piece of legislation: *Help Employ Active Retirees Time (HEART) Act.*

Someone once said the most creative acronyms usually describe the worst programs. If you have to use acronyms, use them properly – no matter how universally understood you believe it to be, spell it out on first reference: *North Atlantic Treaty Organization (NATO)*.

- Whether writing or speaking, keep it simple. Use simple sentences. Use small words. Avoid adjectives, big words and cumbersome phrases.

- Understand and appreciate your audience. Who are you trying to communicate with? Speak to them in language with which they are familiar. If you are going to use your audience as a vehicle to communicate with another audience, give the audience that is serving as the intermediary the same respect you'd give to the one you're really aiming at.

- Understand and appreciate the individual for whom you are writing. Each Member of Congress has his or her own idiosyncrasies, styles, cadences and other peculiarities that give communications its personality and character.

- Be consistent. Get a stylebook – AP or *New York Times* – even if you're not on the communication staff. Master it. Then follow it whether speaking or writing on behalf of your boss. Be one person to all audiences.

- Be careful not to overplay your hand. You can beat an issue into irrelevance by giving it too much attention, exaggerating its implications, setting the rhetoric aflame or being overly righteous in your indignation. Keep it real.

- Always keep in mind that listening is among the most important aspects of communication. Listen carefully when asked questions. You will pick up clues about attitude, how interested the reporter is, and whether you are getting through.

- Read the book *On Writing Well* by William K. Zinsser.

Finally, if you are on the communications team, don't forget to communicate with your own office. It might sound obvious, but many a staff assistant has been embarrassed when a constituent on the phone was the first to tell them what his or her own boss said on the radio. Everyone on the staff needs to know what the Member's external message is and what constituents are likely to be hearing in the media. If you send out a press release, email it to those who work with you.

The Webs We Weave

While you're at it, do everything in your power to lobby for the best website in Congress. As Harvard's Michael Porter has observed in *Strategy and the Internet*: "The key question is not whether to deploy Internet technology – companies [*and governments*] have no choice if they want to stay competitive – but how to deploy it."

By and large, Congress does not deploy it effectively. Although websites are where most people turn for information about Members, most congressional websites are woefully inadequate. In their 2006 Gold Mouse Report, the non-partisan Congressional Management Foundation awarded A's to only 14 percent of all congressional websites. Nearly 60 percent got C's or worse. Here are some of Congressional Management Foundation's conclusions:

- Almost half of all Member websites do not clearly explain how or why constituents should contact the office regarding a problem with a federal agency.

- 32 percent do not have links to sponsored or co-sponsored legislation.

- Only 16 percent have clearly identified information on the Congress and the role of its Members.

- Only 26 percent tell visitors the best ways to communicate with the Member's office.

Many congressional websites are little more than online repositories for press releases, the Member's biography, some basic facts about the district and who to call for various congressional services. Offices historically have allocated little money to Internet communication. As a result, their websites tend to be little more than a personalized version of one of the dozen or so templates provided by House Information Resources or the Senate Sergeant-at-Arms office. They are a mere fraction of what they should be. In the vast realm of websites, they are equal to the lowest common denominator.

A study by the Congressional Institute, meanwhile, has revealed that constituents want useable information from which they can draw conclusions. They don't find it on most websites. Few websites contain transcripts of the Member's Floor speeches, and the vast majority of them do not include summaries of legislation or explanations of why a Member would vote for or against it. In *tsk-tsking* this sorry state of affairs, researchers pointed out that the absence of such obvious information suggests to visitors that Members are trying to obscure their voting records – that they've got something to hide.

Researchers pointed out to lawmakers that many of their sites do not have functioning search engines that can help visitors find information they're looking for: "Constituents go to a legislator's website to find a specific piece of information, and you need to make it easy for them to find it. If something is difficult to find they will assume it is not available."

There is no reason for an office not to have an online video of every floor speech the Member makes – they're easy and inexpensive to provide. Offices that rely on C-SPAN coverage to give the folks back home a glimpse of the boss in action are deluding themselves. The percentage of constituents watching C-SPAN when their Senator or Representative gives a two-minute speech is statistically insignificant.

Cable television offers on-demand programming so audiences can watch movies, children's shows and other offerings whenever they want. Congress should be just as attentive to the needs of constituents.

A website should also provide a blog that appears on the website and can also be subscribed to through access to an RSS (real simple syndication) news feed. Such blogs are less formal than press releases. They're more conversational and can be used to provide impressions gathered by a Member during a visit to soldiers at an overseas military base or the Member's thoughts on a major issue that has been receiving widespread attention in the media.

Each Member should have a general e-newsletter that goes out once or twice a month, and offers constituents the option of receiving only those containing information they're interested in such as the budget or defense or energy or the environment.

An e-newsletter list is an unfiltered means of communicating directly with constituents. Not only is delivery immediate, but also so is feedback. List server software tells you if and when your email was opened, and even whether it has been forwarded. And of course, constituents can instantly reply.

It is important for every email communication to include a way for the recipient to opt-out or be removed from the Member's emailing list. It doesn't pay to make a pest of yourself by sending material where it's not wanted – constituents will consider it spamming.

Getting names and addresses on your emailing list is somewhat more challenging. Every form of communication with constituents should contain an invitation to have names added to the Member's email list so they can be kept up to date on issues affecting them.

E-newsletters should not be massive rehashes of everything the Member has done, said or contemplated since the last time subscribers heard from your office. It should be a series of short teasers with links to items on the website that provide flesh and bone to whatever topics individual readers are interested in. For those who prefer to get such information in an audio format, a growing number of Congressional offices have produced podcasts of floor speeches and audio versions of articles written by Members.

The 2008 Obama presidential campaign successfully exploited two new forms of communication that are especially popular with young adults – social networking accounts and text messaging cell phones. You can be sure variations of this will quickly make their way into congressional offices.

Social networking sites such as Facebook and MySpace are online communities where people discover and share common interests. The Obama campaign combined this high-tech opportunity with the oldest form of political communication – word-of-mouth endorsement – to produce an invaluable campaign tool. The word of "friends" on Facebook carried more weight with some audiences than the same argument put forth by someone on radio or television. Though this approach is often referred to as "viral marketing," it's actually nothing more than online word-of-mouth messaging – whose impact is exponentially increased by technology.

Through social networking, President Barack Obama's campaign not only motivated hundreds of thousands of young people to vote, but raised millions of dollars through small online campaign contributions – all for a fraction of the cost of traditional marketing and fundraising.

The Obama campaign also developed text messaging as a means to communicate with targeted audience. The campaign realized that younger voters tend to be enthusiastic text-messengers, so it began "capturing" cell phone numbers over which campaign messages could be sent. A clever inducement was the announcement that those people who had signed up to receive text messages from the Obama campaign would be the first to know who his vice-presidential running mate would be. Though the 3 a.m. delivery of this message drew some criticism, the effort enabled supporters to accumulate hundreds of thousands of cell phone numbers that the campaign used to communicate everything from policy messages to information about upcoming campaign stops by the candidate.

Tele-townhalls are growing in popularity as well. These are nothing more than massive conference calls in which constituents participate from their homes. Organizers typically dial up random households in the district or state and invite constituents to take part and ask questions. Such events have proven to be an excellent alternative to traditional townhall meetings, which are more difficult to arrange and orchestrate. Most people, including Members of the Congress, are too busy to squeeze another meeting into their schedules. In addition, traditional townhall meetings have become popular targets for agitators whose sole intent is disruption and playing to the media.

The Science of Messaging

Not everyone is receptive to every message. That's because not all of us respond to stimuli in the same way. Research suggests that it is important to recognize how people process information in conversations and to recognize traits that can influence communication on a broader scale as well.

Upon the outset of World War II, Isabel Briggs Myers and her mother, Katharine Cook Briggs, set out to find practical applications for Carl Jung's theory of psychological types. Their efforts have been perpetuated by the Myers-Briggs Foundation, whose research continues to identify distinguishing characteristics but suggests that four types of communicators are among the most common. These are *Feelers*, *Sensors*, *Intuitors* and *Thinkers*.

None of these categories is necessarily absolute – individuals and groups may shift from one to another as easily as they experience a change in mood, so it's helpful to know the clues to look for if you are hoping for enthusiasm, compromise or cooperation.

- **The Feeler** uses language to express emotion. He or she is what's referred to as an empath, someone who wants to connect, who wants to make you feel comfortable. Listen for signals that indicate frustration. The *Feeler* needs to know that you recognize he or she is having difficulties, something along the lines of, "high gas prices are making it harder to afford groceries...." The Feeler also needs to be recognized and appreciated: "You're good in situations like this one."

- **The Sensor** thrives on deadlines and lives to get things done. A *Sensor* does everything – including communication – in spurts and can make "Good morning" feel like an intrusion. They respond most positively if they know you have a plan. Prepare ahead and communicate in easily digestible bites with Sensors. In the workplace, Sensors want to know that you can reduce their workload.

- **The Thinker** operates on logic. He or she loves organization and systems and likes to see projects through to the bitter end. They thrive on numbers and facts, are logical and realistic, and will reference projects that failed in order to deflate any plan that seems farfetched. *Thinkers* love problem solving. When you communicate, reassure them that you are grounded in reality and will get all the facts before coming up with a plan to deal with a problem.

- **The Intuitor** is conceptual, a long-range planner, a problem solver – but not necessarily interested in doing the work that's necessary to implement the solution. He or she would rather move on to the next problem. They're likely to have big ideas that are difficult to understand but are presented as if you ought to have no trouble whatsoever grasping what they've said. They seldom provide context or last names when discussing an idea or a situation and become impatient if you interrupt with a question. *Intuitors* would prefer you let them talk out their ideas before you begin asking questions. Questions to them are best received if they are phrased in a way that indicates you like the *Intuitor*'s ideas and simply need more information in order to get a clear picture.

Political leaders with the highly refined communication skills of Ronald Reagan, Bill Clinton and Newt Gingrich are able to embrace entire audiences – *Feelers, Sensors, Intuitors and Thinkers* alike.

Effective communicators think about the communication styles of their audience. A message intended for scientists would be skewed toward a Sensor/Thinker style while social workers would get a Sensor/Feeler message. The essence of the message should be consistent, but how it is delivered might be different for each audience.

For large audiences, emulate Clinton and Reagan and talk first to Sensors (who have the shorter attention spans) and then talk to Thinkers. This is particularly true for television where Sensor elements (who, what, when) combined with Feeler (empathy and sympathy) is best for interviews and 30-second sound bites.

In short, choose your speaking tactics for any given situation as carefully as you choose your words. Delivering a speech on the Floor of the House in an effort to persuade colleagues to vote in favor of a bill you co-sponsored isn't the same as delivering an emotional appeal on the Floor of the House directly to constituents by means of C-Span's cameras.

Chapter Ten Summary

- Strategic communication involves the entire office.

- If the Member isn't comfortable with the strategy the strategy won't work.

- A key element of strategic planning is the brand.

- The introduction of legislation is among the foundation tactics of communicating an idea.

- The types of media are many and each has distinctive needs and objectives.

- Communications strategy involves many calculations.

- There are basic rules for talking with the press. Among them is admitting ignorance is far preferable to demonstrating stupidity.

- Communication is an outside and an inside exercise. Communicating is also listening and understanding how your audience listens and perceives.

- Strategy should incorporate the new technologies and new venues for communicating ideas.

Public Opinion and Public Judgment

For more than two centuries, new Members of Congress have grappled with whether they were elected to make wise decisions based on their own good judgment or to vote the will of their constituents regardless of their own views. The surest approach is a blend of the two.

Just as the Founding Fathers balanced republican and democratic principles of government in the Constitution, so must the Congress balance the good of the nation against the parochial interests of each constituency or balance the judgment of the elected with the will of the electors. When those needs and opinions mesh, life on the Hill can be very sweet indeed. When they don't, the skills of individual Members and their staffs, and sometimes their courage, can be tested to the limit.

This struggle is seen best when looking at public opinion and public judgment. Public opinion is a snapshot in time – a look at what people are thinking at the moment they are polled. Public judgment reflects the deeply held values that shape the philosophical and moral principles of individuals over time.

Public opinion is subject to change – and can shift with surprising speed. President George H.W. Bush trailed Governor Michael Dukakis by 17 points the day after the Democratic National Convention in 1988 – he went on to win a fairly comfortable victory just two months later.

On the other hand, public judgment changes slowly, if at all. For example, for 60 years the Gallup Organization has asked Americans if they believed in God – and for 60 years nine out of 10 Americans have said they do.

Public opinion is when people compare the facts – as they know them and as they continue to gather them – against their core beliefs or judgment. The core beliefs do not change – at least not quickly and easily – but how an individual perceives facts in light of those beliefs may change in the time it takes to view a 30-second commercial.

The founders assumed that those who serve in the Congress would be better educated and more enlightened than their constituents. Armed with knowledge and information their constituents lack, they are expected to make reasoned decisions on behalf of those who were less informed.

Alexander Hamilton was among the first to recognize the distinction between this sort of *public judgment* and common, everyday, garden-variety *public opinion*. It is a theme that was elaborated on in 1991's *The Quickening of America: Rebuilding Our Nation, Remaking Our Lives* by Frances Moore Lappé and Paul Martin Du Bois. It contends that *public judgment* is possible only by listening to points of view other than your own and thinking through any clash of values.

"It comes from engaging respectfully and creatively with our differences," the authors write.

Over time, the challenge of balancing the two has increased as public opinion has become ever more readily accessible and strident. The nation's population has become urbanized, more technologically empowered and better educated. At the same time, a more sophisticated public has created the need forever more sophisticated methods of gauging how the electorate feels about issues.

Polls have become an invaluable tool. So much so that some observers contend that political positions that once were solid as oaks now are more like the willow that bends and sways gracefully in the breeze. Public opinion surveys, and the poll results they produce, date to the 1920s. But as recently as the mid-20th Century, the populations of Congressional districts were small enough for the average Member to figure out what his constituents were thinking.

When they were unable to do so, representatives knew where to go. Society was less complicated and less nuanced then. Community leaders were easier to identify. Interest groups were fewer in number and less complex. The purveyors of news and information were just a few broadcasters and the local newspaper editor. Personal relationships were simpler and so was the economy.

Members of Congress knew their constituents, who relied primarily on ingenuity, their neighbors and local government to resolve the issues that concerned them. A Member could learn much of what he or she needed to know merely by talking to local unions, church leaders, bankers, local service organizations such as the Rotary and Kiwanis clubs and Chambers of Commerce.

As recently as 1950, the American Association of Retired People (AARP), the Semiconductor Industry Association (SIA) and Greenpeace did not exist. Nor did thousands of other trade groups, social and political associations and global corporations employing thousands of lobbyists trying to steer the course of a multi-trillion dollar government that operates and manages hundreds of thousands of federal programs with millions of rules and regulations.

America had about 135 million residents in 1950 compared to over 300 million today.

In the 50 years in which the nation's population more than doubled, the number of seats in the House of Representatives has remained constant. Despite improvements in transportation and communication, the challenge to keep up with constituent interests and needs has become immense. District size, demographics, social and educational diversity, aging and a host of other factors have combined to make public opinion polls an essential source of information about the will of the electorate as well as national trends.

On Capitol Hill, polls are ubiquitous, yet multiple pollsters consistently provide differing results to the same question. If polling is a statistical science, how can this be?

Most professional pollsters freely admit that the primary danger associated with surveys is that their results are subject to misinterpretation, and what they reveal can be easily exaggerated, over-dramatized and over-applied. Polls produce a snapshot of attitudes at a given moment prompted by a given question addressing an issue that has been simply defined. They require scientific design, scientific analysis and an understanding of their limitations to be of any real value.

The challenge is to get the science right.

Margin of Error

Many people are familiar with the term *margin of error*, which is a measure of the survey's accuracy. Generally speaking, the more people you survey the more accurately the survey will reflect the entire group being sampled. It's like the elementary school experiment where you flipped a coin 100 times to demonstrate that the closer you got to 100, the closer the heads-to-tails ratio was to 50-50.

Unfortunately, arriving at an acceptable margin of error is the easy half of the science. Even more significant is what's known as the *survey sample*. In order for survey results to be accurate, this sample must reflect the pop-

143

ulation whose opinion is being sought. Say, for example, 60 percent of your sample consists of women and 40 percent men, but the ratio of the population you survey is 53 percent women and 47 percent men. The results are likely to be skewed because women will have been *oversampled*.

This is the cause of most variations in surveys asking essentially the same question. A survey will yield inaccurate results if it oversamples one of the political parties, ideologies, genders, generations or any other number of variables, including race.

Successful pollsters must ensure samples accurately reflect the population considered relevant to the poll. In an election campaign, for instance, the sample should consist exclusively of people who will be casting ballots. The challenge lies in figuring out who that's going to be. Pollsters must make educated guesses. Sometimes they guess wrong. Those casting ballots often represent variables that were not expected to be a factor or voters representing the variables that were considered significant may decide to stay home.

In the most highly contested presidential elections, 20 percent of all registered voters don't vote. In an off year, when congressional elections take place but there's not a presidential contest to be decided, fewer than 50 percent of registered voters may cast ballots. To address this problem, many pollsters insert a series of questions designed to identify *likely voters*. But even the best laid plans go astray, as they did in both 1998 and 2000, when pollsters who didn't bother to distinguish between *likely* and *unlikely voters* were more accurate than the ones who focused on so-called *likely voters*.

The Numbers Game

Such anomalies aren't always acts of nature. The polling process can be easily manipulated by intentionally oversampling a key demographic. A partisan surveyor or one on the payroll of politicians can make a candidate appear stronger than the opposition – creating an impression of political strength or momentum – simply by oversampling members of the candidate's party.

Equally disturbing is a practice known as *push-polling*, which isn't polling at all but an attempt to prostitute the process by asking a leading set of questions, intended not to measure voter opinion but to sway it. In his book *Playing to Win*, CBS news analyst Jeff Greenfield cites the infamous push-poll used by the 1950 campaign of George Smathers against then Florida Senator Claude Pepper. The question by the so-called pollster supporting Smathers was: "If you knew that Claude Pepper's brother is a practicing *homo sapien*, his sister is a known *thespian*, and that he openly *matriculated* when he was in college, would you still vote for him for Senate?"

Pepper lost that race by 60,000 votes, but was elected to the House in 1962 and served there for the next 26 years.

Today push-polls tend to be more sophisticated and more effectively disguised, but the objective is the same – to manipulate not only those who are polled but those who are targets of the polling, including unsuspecting media.

Push-polls aren't the only problem surveys that attract a great deal of undeserved attention. Add surveys on the Internet, for example. The results are nothing more than a reflection of attitudes shared by those people who frequent the website hosting the survey or who happened upon the questionnaire and took the time to answer it. The same can be said for Member polls conducted on their websites or in newsletters. Any similarity between those results and the opinions of the population as a whole is entirely coincidental.

Conducted and interpreted properly, opinion polls taken over time and reflecting the same sample provide an equilibrium that allows sophisticated policy makers to perceive temporary and permanent changes in the public's mind. In the wrong hands, however, polls can produce interesting headlines and generate a great deal of heat – but very little light.

Public opinion instruments measure progress in the journey to public judgment. It is a weather vane, a means of telling which direction opinion is headed, a gauge of attitudes toward a range of issues that occupy the Congress. This is particularly true when a survey reveals only part of the equation – and why it is important to keep in mind the fact that public opinion can appear to change without notice. It can be swayed by new information that exposes a conflict in values or by the day of the week when a survey is taken – those taken on a Friday night during football season, for example, always under-sample Republicans who are more likely than their Democratic counterparts to attend high school games.

Impact Takes Time

Change occurs all the time in Washington D.C. – that's one of the reasons the tax code takes up more than 10,000 pages and is amended every year. Complex change, however, is rare. Even when it does occur, it can take years to understand how it occurred or what long-range affect it will have.

- In the 1960s, major change produced new laws on voting rights, desegregation and Medicare.

- In the 1980s, the United States economic policy underwent a dramatic change from a semi-Keynesian economy to a supply-side Monetarist economy – where spending and inflation were replaced by tax reductions, tighter budgets and a money supply geared to lower inflation.

- In the late 1990s, the social welfare infrastructure of President Lyndon Johnson's Great Society underwent dramatic reform that redefined entitlement to government assistance and reversed disincentives to work and marriage – dramatically reducing welfare rolls across the country.

- The dawn of the new century produced change in the way seniors received prescription drug coverage – creating a massive new program based on free-market competition. The program went from cautious resistance and opposition to widespread acceptance and even popularity within a year of passage.

Regardless of whether we agree with these policy changes, they represent complex shifts in thinking that have significantly altered the way the country views fundamental issues. These changes required an appeal to deeply held values and judgments.

"People's opinions go through various stages as they gradually come to grips with an issue," Daniel Yankelovich told a Congressional audience in 1992.

Public opinion seems to fluctuate constantly, says Yankelovich, who is widely recognized as an architect of the modern polling process. New information, the timing of a news story or the timing of a public opinion survey or even the phrasing of the questions the survey asks can influence such fluctuations. Yet the results such surveys produce are valuable in forming short-term tactics. When it comes to formulating public policy, however, elected leaders should rely more heavily on public judgment.

The distinction, according to Yankelovich, is that public opinion tends to be momentary, while public judgment is long-term. Think of public judgment as a timeline on which public opinion appears as a series of snapshots measuring its evolution. Public judgment is strategic, while public opinion is a running commentary on whether it is succeeding.

When we discuss complex change in the Yankelovich model below, we are talking about fundamental change to the way society approaches problems and institutes solutions – so-called Big Issues, such as Social Security, Medicare reform, immigration, the role of the military in promoting democracy or fighting terrorism in other countries, changes in how we generate and use energy or free-trade versus protectionism.

In *Coming to Public Judgment*, Yankelovich defines a seven-step process that people go through in forming opinions on complex issues:

Awareness: "*This issue I keep hearing about is a problem.*"

Through hearsay, the media or public comments, individuals or groups become aware that change might be needed. They are aware, but not motivated.

Urgency: "*The problem must be solved soon.*"

The public recognizes that a problem not only exists, but that it must be dealt with. A new revelation – perhaps a news event or a personal life event – gives the problem a sense of urgency.

Reviewing alternatives: "*What solutions exist?*"

People assess what can be done to confront the challenge: Can they avoid the change? Are there options? Can someone else deal with it?

Wishful thinking: "*Maybe I can find a solution that doesn't require much change on my part.*"

People latch onto options they hope will resolve the problem. This is where resistance to change becomes visible: "They can cut government spending, and they probably ought to – but not by cutting programs that benefit me. Something's gotta give, but why should I have to pay for it? Maybe they can tax the rich or keep out the immigrants or control Hollywood…."

The chart below illustrates the evolutionary process Daniel Yankelovich says opinions go through as people come to grips with an issue – and does so from three different perspectives: personal, organizational and societal.

Objective:	Individual Lose weight.	Organizational Install computer system to manage inventory.	Societal Modernize electrical grid.
Stage 1: Awareness	You hear news that overweight people live shorter lives.	You hear a rumor that computer specialists have been meeting with the boss.	You hear news of blackouts on the other side of the country.
Stage 2: Urgency	Doctor informs you that extra weight is stressing heart: "You'll probably have a heart attack in the next 12 months."	Boss announces that a new system is to be installed and all staff will be required to take computer lessons.	Your hometown has a blackout that closes your business for hours and damages your inventory.
Stage 3: Looking for alternatives	You pick up a booklet at the supermarket checkout touting solutions that burn fat and do not require a reduction of food intake or bring pangs of hunger. You consider joining Weight Watchers.	You consider telling the boss that since your job is not related to inventory and you'll be retiring in five years anyway; it doesn't make sense for you to go through the training. You seriously consider an offer from a firm that does not use computers.	You think about buying a backup generator for your business and one for your home. You also suggest that local electric company officials install hydroelectric or wind generators independent of the grid.
Stage 4: Wishful Thinking	You remember overweight family members who lived to a ripe old age and assume that genetic history is on your side. You consider shifting to diet colas – that might help.	You think about having your neighbor's kid show you how to turn on a computer so you can avoid the classes, which will expose your inability to type. You even consider paying a co-worker to do your computer work.	You call your legislator to suggest taxing smokers since you don't smoke and to use the revenue to rebuild the grid. "Stop spending money on foreign aid," you tell your representative, "and we'll have plenty for an improved grid."

Objective:	Individual	Organizational	Societal
	Lose weight.	Install computer system to manage inventory.	Modernize electrical grid.
Stage 5: Pros and Cons	The birth of grandchild reinforces your desire to be around as the child grows up. But you fear that reducing the intake of favorite foods will cause irritability.	You recognize that quitting your job would jeopardize your retirement and health insurance. "Will computer skills enable you to be in regular contact with your grandson, who's almost 1000 miles away?" you wonder.	You realize that disruptions to his work for even a few hours is more expensive than your share of the costs associated with rebuilding the grid, which will give you a competitive advantage over businesses in less forward-thinking areas.
Stage 6: Intellectual Acceptance	You decide to lose weight and begin studying systems that may help.	You dig out an old manual typewriter and begin learning to type.	You attend a meeting, where you call on political leaders to rebuild the grid and increase user fees to offset the costs.
Stage 7: Institutionalization	You've succeeded in losing the excess pounds and maintaining your reduced weight for a couple of years through exercise and diet changes.	Not only do you handle inventory on a computer, but now you have a computer at home that you use to keep in touch with relatives and even do some shopping on-line.	You can't remember the last time the power was interrupted. And you didn't lose any customers when you increased prices to cover the additional costs.

149

Weighing pros and cons: *"If I have to change, which alternative best fits my values?"*

People begin to calculate trade-offs and confront conflicts in personal or societal values: "Yes, I want better schools, but no, I don't want to be required to personally tutor my child every night" or "No, I don't think we should bear the expense of inspecting every package, but I do think transportation must be made safer."

In every case, a conflict between at least two values must be resolved.

Consider, for example, flag-burning. When protestors abroad or at home burn a flag to show disgust or defiance over a U.S. policy, the majority of Americans are indignant. Activists in Congress move to outlaw such behavior, but when the value of patriotism is weighed against a value that's just as important – free speech – the majority reconsiders.

Members of the Congress and their staffs must be attentive to real, value conflicts and be able to frame them in such a way that they make a change in policy more valuable or more acceptable than existing policy.

Intellectual acceptance: *"I might not like the solution, but I can live with it."*

People have decided that change is the best course, even if, in their hearts, they still want to resist it. Public leaders are frequently undone at this juncture. They assume the decision of the affected individuals does not need reinforcement. Sometimes this is precisely when a Member and staff need to work overtime to keep acceptance firm.

Most truly contentious debates are over core values and therefore laden with emotion and ideology, defying logical resolution and pragmatic compromise. Even when the decibel level declines, care must be taken to determine whether the solution is durable enough to withstand changing perspectives or renewed opposition.

Institutionalized: *"Why revisit that issue when the new set-up works?"*

Institutionalization occurs when the acceptable solution is in place and becomes the status quo. Public judgment – which is far more stable than public opinion – has been attained. It is accepted both intellectually and emotionally. When true institutionalization exists, there is no need to consider change.

For purposes of clarity, the process described by Yankelovich has been presented here as a chronological progression, which it seldom is. New information or changes in circumstance often intrude, causing people to revert to earlier stages of thinking. A classic case occurred in 1988, when the federal government made a can't-miss leap in healthcare policy and fell flat on its face.

President Reagan and the Congress responded to concerns that catastrophic illnesses were bankrupting Americans on Medicare. Medicare covers the first 60 to 90 days of long-term care in a nursing home or comparable facility. Medicaid then picks up the slack – but only if most of the patient's life savings have been exhausted. The solution the Reagan Administration came up with was a premium-based catastrophic insurance plan that would cover 100 percent of expenses after the patient ponied up the $2,000 deductible – and the coverage would cost only $59 a year.

The Congress decided to be even more generous and lowered the annual deductible, while tacking on additional benefits. By the time Reagan signed the bill just before the 1988 election, the new law was thought to be hugely popular – after all, the Congress had created peace of mind for the elderly without increasing taxes. The problem was that few people understood how the package would be paid for.

They didn't realize the Congress had decided that lower-income seniors couldn't afford the premiums that originally were proposed, so it provided a complex formula that exempted those who couldn't come up with $59 a year and required higher-income seniors to pay as much as $800 per year to make up the difference. Adding insult to injury, the coverage duplicated what many retirees' union and federal pension plans provided, in effect, forcing them to pay for coverage they not only didn't need but also couldn't use.

Retribution was unprecedented. As more and more interest groups railed against what they perceived as a *seniors-only tax,* popular opinion shifted from strong support to strong opposition. A massive letter writing campaign, punctuated by House Ways and Means Committee Chairman Dan Rostenkowski being mobbed by his own constituents on national television, resulted in the act being repealed before it could actually go into effect.

Supposedly painless reform, lean and clean, had become downright mean. The Congress had relied on logic and math without taking into consideration the resistance inherent in change. Public opinion in favor of the new federal program had been undermined by failure to achieve *public judgment*.

Members and staff alike need to understand the limitations of public opinion and the impact of public judgment. Advocates of change must anticipate the resistance they will encounter and appreciate the conflicting values that are behind it. Opponents must expose the changes it will produce and reframe the debate to focus on values that are likely to be undermined. Reliable polling techniques can give both sides what they need to argue their point of view effectively.

Very little in the policymaking process had prepared millions of retirees to consider the tradeoffs in the catastrophic health insurance bill. Once they were informed that they had to pay the bill, their acceptance turned to rejection despite the fact that the change would have provided badly needed healthcare security. As a result, valuable ground was lost in the effort to deliver catastrophic coverage for seniors. The issue reverted to the earliest stages of Yankelovich's progression – where people could grasp the importance but weren't prepared to seriously consider alternatives. The prospect of security in the face of potentially onerous health care costs had been weighed against having to pay for that peace of mind – and those who would have benefited decided they'd rather live with the comparatively long odds against being bankrupted by a catastrophic medical bill than pay to be protected against it.

Proponents of the catastrophic health care bill were undone by their failure to perform due diligence. They did not anticipate opposition and failed to persuade, educate and consult with their constituents. But they did learn valuable lessons. When the Congress enacted prescription drug coverage 20 years later, Members spent enormous amounts of time explaining the new program to older constituents. In addition, the federal government launched a massive campaign to help people sort through any confusion. Opponents attacked various aspects of the program in an effort to derail it, but the education campaign won the day. By anticipating resistance, addressing it head on, measuring progress with public opinion surveys, and relentlessly educating the potential beneficiaries, Members turned the initial skepticism among older Americans into an 80 percent approval rate in less than one year, thus accomplishing a long promised change.

Chapter Eleven Summary

- The Founders created a complex governing tension in establishing the United States as both a republic and a democracy.

- Because congressional districts are so large and conflicting views on public policy so rampant, Members have come to rely on public opinion tools as one way to gauge public attitudes.

- Public opinion polls are a great tool but they are lacking when trying to ascertain more complex public judgment – the values based beliefs of the citizenry.

- Public opinion is subject to change – and can shift with surprising speed.

- Public judgment evolves much more slowly, when it shifts at all. Members who vote or act counter to public judgment will frequently find that a vote that looked reasonable the day it was cast will look unwise in coming months or years.

- Reading and using public opinion polls can be challenging for Members and staff. It is critical to understand the dynamics of sample size, margin of error and the nature of the survey sample.

- Because public judgment reflects core values held by the population, it both changes more slowly and at the same time is more reflective of the deepest attitudes of the populace.

- Public judgment on most significant attitudes is stable but it does move over time. When it does, it goes through a series of steps, at no specific timetable. It begins with an awareness of the need to examine an attitude. When awareness is motivated by urgency to act, it ignites a reexamination of the status quo.

- Once urgency to act has been acknowledged, the public looks for alternative solutions and is prone to focusing, initially, on those that appear to require the least amount of change.

- The public, with the help of good leadership, weighs the ramifications of the alternatives against their own core beliefs. There is usually a contest between two or more values in evaluating alternate avenues for solving the problem.

- Once the public decides which core value is most critical to protect, they come to an intellectual decision on how the problem should be resolved.

- Finally, the decision becomes ingrained or institutionalized in the public attitude and the problem no longer dominates the public debate.

Most of what we have discussed in preceding chapters has focused on the normal business of Congress: making corrections in the course of government, engaging in oversight of the Executive and the Judiciary, advocating and implementing change as mandated by the public in the last election or deemed warranted by political currents that will dictate the next election.

In recent elections prior to 2008 there have been no clear public mandates for change. Some may argue that the restoration of the Democratic majority in 2006 reflected such a mandate, but if it did, that mandate went unfulfilled. The 110th Congress failed to generate a major shift in policy or accomplishments of that portent.

The same held true for the Republican Congresses before it. They came in like a Hawaiian wave in 1994 and exited in a trickle 12 years later. Relatively rarely in American history does a Congress produce a major shift in the philosophies that drive congressional action or a major transformation in the country's social or economic life.

Major, transformational change (and the authors apologize now for the record-setting times the word "change" will be read in this chapter) takes time and an unusual synergy of energy, resources and need. There is usually a good deal of adjustment that must take place politically, socially and maybe culturally before change is achieved and accepted. Bringing about such change requires deep commitments from those who seek it.

The most dramatic and defining example of transformational change in America was the abolition of slavery.

Our founding fathers knew that abolition slavery could not be successfully written into the new Constitution. They deliberated and debated and declined. Those who favored abolition decided that that degree of change would take more time and conditioning, some thought as much as 12 years or more. In fact, it took almost 70 and a civil war.

There were a good many incremental steps such as the Missouri Compromise and the Compromise of 1850, which, in themselves, were transformational changes. When you look beyond the Civil War, through the ratification of the 13th, 14th, and 15th amendments to the Constitution, the trail of change continues to be highly illuminating and instructional, right up to the present day.

Our history offers other examples of what major change requires.

Creation of a national bank, its dissolution and creation again; westward expansion; women's suffrage; prohibition and its repeal; the McKinley tariffs; the Sherman Anti-Trust Act; the Civil Service System, the designation of public lands and parks; trade protectionism; Social Security; the Marshall Plan; welfare reforms; Medicare and Medicaid; space exploration. There are periods in our history when the times demanded change that would transform the way we live and the way we think. And most of the time that change took years, and sometimes decades.

Most Congresses are dominated by Members and staff who have their hands full meeting constituent demands, satisfying their committee assignments, and focusing on a few of their own legislative priorities. That is just the culture of Congress. Today there is so much strident, partisan and personalized conflict, not to mention classic political witch hunts, much of it exaggerated by the media's diversion of attention from the serious performers to the circus performers. There's little attention to critically needed long-term change.

Unfortunately, however, this is one of those periods in American history when transformational change is not only desirable, it is desperately needed. Energy independence and security, accessible and affordable health care, retirement security, domestic security, immigration, privacy, technology, public debt and taxation are just a few of the issues that are rapidly growing from problems into crises.

And, seldom have we had to wrestle with such an entangled array of threatening worldwide problems from terrorism to climate change, trade and hunger, globalization and economic development. Seldom has there been such a dire need for behavioral and attitudinal change in America, from social integration to civility in our political behavior, and seldom have the institutions of government been less prepared and less able to deliver it.

So how do Members of Congress and their staff rise to these challenges? How do they get beyond the weight of normal policy processes into a whole other realm of big new ideas, weighty and complex decision-making, and uncommon determination? Where do they get the resources, the time and the energy?

There is no manual that tells you how to do it, but there are some basic steps to transformational change that you can follow.

If confronted with one of those rare opportunities to be a leader of change the first priority is managing the process, adopting a sound strategic plan, creating a disciplined organization, and making best use of resources such as time and personnel.

Other chapters in this book address legislative and communications strategies, public judgments, and parliamentary procedure. Those chapters contain valuable charts for navigating the political waters. We will try to avoid repetition here, but there are some observations and practices, some discussed previously and some not, that need to be emphasized when addressing transformational change.

Let's divide this task into two components: (a) reaching consensus on what you want to accomplish, partially swiped from the Yankelovich research described in the previous chapter; (b) organizing and managing the process.

First, a framework is needed for what you want done.

Defining the Mission

What is it you seek to accomplish? Do you want to achieve energy independence in America through reliance on a private sector incentivized by government policy and enforced by government regulation? Do you want to create a retirement security system in America that emphasizes individual ownership and investment?

What is the mission? Where do you want to end up when the initiative has run its course?

Defining the Problem

In order to convince policy makers, the public and the media that drastic action is necessary to achieve, say, energy independence, you must define a problem that warrants a drastic action. You must define a problem that has widespread implications for large blocs of people. You must define a problem that cannot be solved with small, incremental adjustments in public policy. You must define a problem with a sense of urgency. You must define a problem stark enough that risk is warranted.

Defining the problem means beginning the process of overcoming natural public resistance to change.

All major change encounters resistance. It is a natural human reaction that has served our species pretty well. People resist change because it usually requires them to modify their expectations and deal with the unknown. The status quo is predictable. Change is less so and maybe not at all. Even if the current status is not ideal, something different may be worse.

A smoker *knows* the dangers of the habit, but puffs away until the coughing gets so bad it's hard to breathe or he/she has a heart attack or gets cancer. It is amazing how fast most habitual smokers find the strength to change after a heart attack or cancer diagnosis.

In public policy, warning signs of trouble are not as clear. A Federal program's failure may not be apparent or may be tolerated for years upon years, despite wasted funds and unserved constituents. Traditional welfare in America went unchanged for decades despite clear and flagrant failure to meet the needs of the needy. It took new leadership and new thinking to right the wrong. Resistance was natural and structural, and too often when resistance rises the advocates of change shrink in the face of it, only because they did not understand it and did not anticipate it.

Breaking down resistance requires patience. It takes time to convince people that the problem with which they are confronted is serious enough and broad enough in its effect that major change is required and that the risks of change are worth facing.

Identify The Affected

You must identify those segments of society who are affected by the problem and would, therefore, have the largest stake in bringing about a solution.

Energy, for example, affects almost all of us in different ways, but before you can fashion an acceptable solution, you must know who is affected and how. Some of us – such as lower income individuals and families, small businesses and transportation intensive industries – are hit harder by higher gasoline prices. Some are more affected by the residual affects of higher energy costs – families who face high heating and air conditioning bills – and industries, such as food, that use large amounts of energy to produce their products or get them to market. Some place higher priority on the electricity grid that brings energy to us. The impact must be clearly understood, so that varying alternatives can be considered and woven into a final outcome.

Developing Alternative Policy Solutions

The process of finding solutions means keeping an open mind to many alternatives. The more people invited to offer alternatives the less likely they are to engage in opposition early in the process. And the more alternatives you consider, the more likely you are to arrive at the best and right solution. Some suggestions can and are taken off the table at the outset. Again, in the case of energy, few are going to tolerate any solution with the inference of public takeover of energy companies or energy rationing. However, beyond the most radical solutions, most options should be reviewed.

Alternatives should be fully and widely aired, whether in media coverage, or in public hearings and discussions, such as town hall meetings, or through the activism of interested coalitions and organizations engaging in grassroots education and information programs.

Eventually, the public and the dynamics of political pressure will begin to point you in the right direction, toward a collection of alternatives that can be cobbled together into a workable, achievable solution. The process could take months. It could take years. Concluding it too early, moving too quickly to one solution, may spell disaster. A classic example is President George W. Bush's proposed reform of Social Security. His solutions were on the table before the public was convinced there was a serious enough problem to demand a solution, and his solution was the only one on the table, other than doing nothing. It was a no-win formula.

Finding the Solution

Finding a solution requires the careful analysis of the alternatives that have been aired and building a strategy around one or more of them.

There is no easy way to settle on a solution. It lies somewhere in between the mission you set out to accomplish at one end, and acceptance by the people affected at the other. The terrain in the middle includes building the successful coalitions needed to win. But enacting a law or laws to implement your goal is not the other end. Laws can be repealed. Policies can be reversed. The last step in the process is educating and convincing the public that what you are intent upon doing is the right course for them and the country. That is institutionalizing the outcome, making it as permanent as permanent can be.

There are a number of considerations in finding the right solution. Some of the more elemental are:

1. Making the case. All sides of your solution must be well thought out and highly defensible. Look at your solution, not from your perspective, but from that of the potential opposition. What elements need fortification? What elements need to be jettisoned? What elements speak for themselves? What elements are so complex, they cannot be easily explained? If you find it difficult to convince yourself that one part of the solution is workable, maybe it isn't.

2. Assess the elements of the solution in the context of achieving the mission. Which elements are essential? Which may be desirable, but not essential? What is negotiable? What isn't?

3. From which interest groups can you draw a majority coalition strong enough to win passage and enactment? What elements of the prospective solution bring which members of a prospective coalition? Are some potential members of the coalition more attractive than others? How important is bipartisanship? What do you give up to get it?

4. How will the media respond to each element of the prospective solution? As they say, are there dogs among your alternatives that just won't hunt?

Selling Your Solution

The second element we mentioned earlier is creating the organization and management infrastructure needed to achieve the change you want, winning acceptance of your solution by government and the public.

Some of the keys to success involve building out from the epicenter of the campaign:

- Building a team

- Developing a legislative strategy

- Communicating the message

Building the Team

Understanding the roles of key players is critical to success. Change is easier to lead in the private sector than in the public arena. In the private world, a clear hierarchy usually evolves, with a boss at the top and clear lines of authority and responsibilities underneath, making it easier to overcome resistance. Our Founders wanted no such concentration of power in our form of government. Public leaders, therefore, are required to follow a more complex course to success, and the roles they and their followers play are not always clear or well defined. But they should be as best as is possible.

There are four general roles and variations of the mix:

- In the business world the *Sponsor* is the individual or group with the power to bring about the change. The sponsor is the originator. In a democracy the *sponsor* (not to be confused with the legislative term) is the institution able to enact change – the President, Legislature and Judiciary. No one person in a democracy can accomplish political change by themselves – our Constitution designed it that way.

- An *advocate* recognizes that he or she does not have the personal or situational power to bring about the change and instead focuses efforts at influencing the process and working with other advocates to meet the objectives of the strategic plan.

- *Agents* often carry the main responsibility in shepherding the proposal to victory through the authority or empowerment afforded them. Staff will most often find themselves the agents of change promoted by their Member, committee or leadership. And this is where good staff work can actually change the country, perhaps the world, for the better.

- The final role is the beneficiary or the *target* of the change. Political change impacts citizens, federal agency employees or anyone whose behavior and expectations will be affected. Until the targets agree that the risks of change are preferable to the status quo, they have the power to resist. Unlike the private-sector worker who could be fired for too much resistance, the citizen has the power to fire the sponsor or advocate for disrupting their expectations. This reality makes leading change in the public world exceedingly complex and illustrates why most Members settle playing at the safer edges of policy.

The success of these actors of change requires commitment greater than an expression or feeling. It must become a life-altering reality. Transformational change is an endurance contest. Your obstacles include rejection, exhaustion, criticism, doubt, division, abandonment, and numerous other dynamics that evolve from natural and synthetically created resistance. It is commitment that must be hard and fast.

Affecting Public Judgment

As was discussed in the previous chapter, attention to convincing the public to embrace change is critical. It is usually assumed that if politicians advocate major transformational change that the public is already well enough aware of the problem for them to embark on such an endeavor. That is not necessarily true. While politicians usually don't champion policies unless there is public support behind them, the actual exercise of making change requires a high degree of public awareness and public acceptance, first in concept and then in practice.

The next ingredient is educating the public to the urgency of solving the problem.

The alternatives under consideration must be framed as both reasonable and necessary. The natural resistance to change will move the public mind to put off solutions with which they are not comfortable or feel may not be necessary.

Finally, the public must be convinced the arrived at solution is consistent with their values and is the best course for them – and that it demands and deserves their support.

Key to this process is defining the mission, defining the terms of the debate, and creating the language best suited to communicating the message.

Issues that make up the fabric of change must be framed and reframed by its proponents and not its opponents. If the opposition defines the issues, then defeat is likely. Those who resist change will make arguments for preservation of the status quo. No doubt half a century ago those who resisted school integration based their case on culture and tradition. But school integration was not simply about culture and tradition. It was about the equal opportunity and education, justice, fairness and progress. If you engage the issues on their terms, you lose. If you engage the issues on your terms, you stand a better chance of winning. Frame the issues from the outset and reframe them to meet the challenges of the opposition.

The Policy Strategy

Much of the strategic preparation for moving legislation through Congress and the Executive are addressed in other chapters. However, here are some observations appropriate to major change.

Designing A Process Specific To Your Mission

The policy process – the legislative strategy – must be developed to accommodate the change being proposed, like a well-tailored suit. That means the initiative should be bipartisan and bicameral, and done in cooperation with the Executive Branch. In other words, your potential supporters in both houses of Congress and the Executive Branch, must, along with the general public, be convinced of the need for change and its urgency before the legislative process is launched.

That, of course, is a tall order, and why conditioning the environment for change usually takes longer than the change itself.

The policy process should accommodate a sophisticated means of identifying policy options and vetting those options among four critical groups: (a) the general public, with emphasis on segments of the public that will be affected by the change being proposed; (b) legislators who will ultimately vote on the solution; (c) the interest groups that will have an impact on grassroots mobilization and media; and (d) the trade, Internet-based and mainstream media.

While stakeholders in the process, particularly committee and subcommittee chairs, must have ample opportunity to air options, express opinions and influence the decision-making, no stakeholder can be allowed to hijack the initiative and turn the team away from its mission.

Hijackers can also be found in the political organizations of both parties that are responsible for conducting and financing campaigns. National committees, congressional and senatorial committees, and tax-exempt political organizations all, for one reason or another, may decide that the best partisan advantage can be gained by exploiting, discrediting or reframing the elemental issues involved in change.

The Timeframe

A timeframe for action and a timeline of specific benchmarks in the legislative process should be established so that alarm bells go off and tactical adjustments are made when the process gets bogged down or threatened by opposition that is stronger than anticipated.

Decision-Makers and Decision-Making

The strategy should include a hierarchy for legislative and political decision-making, particularly as more and more individuals and organizations are empowered to influence the process.

Sometimes making a wrong decision is a better alternative than making no decision at all. Indecision leads to confusion and creates a power vacuum that in politics is usually filled quickly. The decision structure, however, must be accommodating enough to meet the needs of team leaders responsible for various phases of consideration, ranging from senior members and staff in the subcommittees and full committees, to the primary spokespersons and political leaders.

The Communications Strategy: Creating The Brand

Framing the issues is part of creating a brand for your initiative that makes your team members comfortable and motivated. The brand is an easily recognizable and positive personality that gives your audience confidence they know what you are talking about and what you want to accomplish, whether those people are your closest teammates and advisors, the press or the general public. It may sound a little too Madison Avenue to put branding among your top priorities, but the fact is the natural resistance to change must be offset by a naturally-feeling incentive to change that begins with a familiar and friendly face for the initiative.

The communications strategy has three principle audiences: (a) the media that will carry the message to the public; (b) the supporters who will mobilize national grassroots behind the implementation; and (c) public officials who must enact laws to implement the change.

Creating the Messages

Messages define the brand a little more specifically. They should be few in number and give context and meaning to your mission and your brand.

Message one could be that there is a problem and it is serious enough to demand immediate attention. Message two could be that there are good, constructive alternatives available and that a solution can be achieved if we all work together. The third message could be that the solution must be dictated by certain principles and values that are important to all of us.

Identifying the Messengers

It is important that the messages be delivered by skilled messengers and that the messengers are disciplined to stick to the essential messages without creating confusion or misunderstanding.

The messengers should be trained in media relations and experienced in addressing questions intended to confuse the messages or distort the purpose.

The messengers must be convincing and persuasive public speakers. They should be directed to proactive outreach programs designed to get messengers in situations where the messages can be delivered to the targeted audience most effectively. The messengers should speak to and represent the various interest groups you consider important to ultimate victory, maybe including both political parties, both houses of Congress, and key members of the coalition.

The Venues for Message Delivery

Selecting the right venues for message delivery can be important. Some media outlets will probably be more productive and accessible than others. Some public forums may be more receptive. Some organizations may be more helpful in message delivery than others. There will be some media, some environments, and some venues that you should avoid.

Electronic communications, as discussed in other chapters, offer team members a wide variety of venues from which to choose. There are unique aspects with each variety of media, from broadcast, to print, to cable, that require their own individual treatment.

It is important to remember that more often than not communications should be done with a rifle and not a shotgun. Pick your targets. Pick your ammunition. Pick your territory. Pick your timing.

Tools of the Trade

Make sure that your messages are backed up by solid research, well written and easy to understand briefing papers and talking points that intellectually and emotionally connect with the people you are trying to reach. In other words, we are not talking about an academic white paper for the American Political Science Association. The points you want to make must be clear. Your rebuttals of opposition arguments must be complete. Make sure your messengers and your supporters have what they need to do what you want them to do, whether that is a weekly update on activities, draft speeches, press releases, or graphics. Bring the best tools of the trade to the job.

When legislative proposals are drafted, they must be reinforced by both short and long summaries, talking points and briefs and background papers tailored to your messengers and your audiences.

Timing

Each strategic move should be carefully timed, not only to accommodate media outlets and their deadlines, but also predictable events that may overshadow what you are doing. Communications activities have to be intimately coordinated with the timing of legislative activities.

History offers excellent examples of Members of Congress, supported by good staff, who have been effective leaders of change. Some examples are more profound than others, but the examples are there to learn from: welfare reform (Rep. Clay Shaw, Jim Talent and Sen. Rick Santorum), the BRAC (Base Realignment and Closure) initiative by Rep. Dick Armey, creation of Medicare and Medicaid (President Johnson and Wilbur Mills) and most recently No Child Left Behind (President George W. Bush, Rep. John Boehner and Senator Edward Kennedy), the ultimate outcome of which is still undetermined. Leadership of change can begin and end in Congress.

Rep. Jack Kemp, the former Member from Buffalo, New York was a tireless advocate of creating economic growth and prosperity by lowering tax rates. His effort became known as supply-side economics. Ronald Reagan adopted Kemp's position and made it his own when he became President. Yet it was Kemp who gave the hundreds of interviews and speeches necessary to build public support for the most dramatic tax cuts in American history, launching over 20 years of mostly unbroken economic growth and prosperity.

Newt Gingrich woke up slumbering Republicans in the House who had grown accustomed to, and some suggested comfortable with, their inferiority after more than 40 years in the minority. His guerilla tactics on the House floor and confrontational use of issues and ideas in the Contract With America launched the 1994 Republican Revolution that radically changed the balance between the political parties. At times Gingrich annoyed establishment Republicans almost as much as he afflicted the Democratic majority, but there can be no doubt he breathed new life into Congressional Republicans and led them out of the political wilderness.

The late Wilbur Mills, a Democrat from Arkansas, was one of the most successful leaders of legislative change, even though he came up short in his personal behavior. He probably owed his success more to intuitive understanding of how the world works than to disciplined study. Mills was largely responsible for the legislative success of Medicare, Medicaid, Revenue Sharing, significant trade legislation, and President John F. Kennedy's major tax reforms lowering marginal income tax rates and capital gains tax rates.

Mills, once asked why he took two years to bring about adoption of a major change, responded that the first year was devoted to getting the public and his colleagues to recognize the problem (awareness) and the need to act (urgency). He, through a variety of public hearings and discussions, got those audiences to look at a range of options that might solve the urgent need for change. As they coalesced around his preferred solutions, after he had reframed their objections to various ideas, he'd introduce a proposal. Once it was ready for prime time, he would move it through his committee allowing non-fundamental amendments and alterations, and fending off others. Finally, he would take it to the Floor of the House where it was always adopted. Mills only lost one Floor battle in his career – the first bill he brought to the Floor after becoming Chairman of the House Ways and Means Committee – and that was the last time he brought a proposal to the Floor without going through the process he later adopted and followed for the rest of his long career.

Mills was one among many committee chairs, speakers, majority and minority leaders, or just committed individuals, in both houses who had a capacity for achieving change. While many exercised power in different ways, the most successful understood the limitations of power and the need to cajole, compromise, convince and sometimes confound in order

167

to overcome resistance and make people comfortable with his/her desired outcome. All of them understood that transformational change required the hands and minds of many – in more recent years, particularly good, competent, professional, and in no small measure, humble, staff.

Chapter Twelve Summary

- Leading transformational change takes time and an unusual combination of leadership, commitment, resources and an understanding and application of established fundamentals of change.

- Most Members and staff spend their time dealing with traditional congressional challenges, but certain times in history call for leadership of more important changes and we may be living in such a period.

- To be an effective leader of change Members and staff must do more than simply introduce legislation. They must build a team that develops a vision and define the ultimate solution.

- Members and staff seeking to bring about a major change in policy must objectively identify the targets or beneficiaries of the change.

- Other key players in the dynamic of change include the sponsor or leader, his or her agents and advocates.

- The process for implementing major change is well developed and practiced in the private sector but the Constitution makes public change harder.

- Understanding and defining roles is critical because no one in our divided form of government is an ultimate authority. In the private sector top leaders can demand compliance, but in a democracy more people must agree to change.

- Resistance is a natural reaction to all major change proposals. For that reason, creating public awareness of the problem is a critical task. There must be an urgency to change if there is any hope of overcoming resistance.

- Communications become the avenue through which resistance is confronted and objections reframed to conform to higher value attitudes.

- A communications strategy is much more than issuing one or even a multitude of news releases. An effective strategy has different stages of implementation. Initially it is to build awareness and urgency of the proposed change. Later it is to deal with resistance. Finally, the communication strategy must advocate the solution.

- Successful change requires the commitment of leaders. Yet, day-to-day pressures of Congressional offices undermine long-term commitment. Without sustained commitment and planning, major change is unlikely to succeed no matter how desirable the intended solution.

Playing By the Rules

Few professions are subject to as high an ethical standard or as much transparency as elected federal officials. They are under constant scrutiny. Their words and their actions are parsed and dissected by their constituents, the media and their rivals. The mere whiff of scandal can destroy a career, even if allegations later prove false. And what taints one official has a tendency to taint the rest as well.

When it comes to trust, the American public tends to rank Members of the Congress in close proximity, oddly enough, to journalists.

Members have always produced more than their share of scandalous behavior, from the earliest days of the nation.

The truth is, however, that the vast majority of Members of Congress have served with distinction and without the hint of impropriety. Perhaps the question should be: Is Congress a microcosm of the country morally and ethically?

It is the scandals that people remember, however, and it is the scandals that lead to such exasperations, as "All of them are corrupt." The slightest innuendo makes good and decent Members guilty until proven innocent in the eyes of the public. And all too often, even if they're exonerated, the fact that they're not guilty seldom gets reported, leaving a lingering perception of wrongdoing.

Public office today is a high-wire act performed before a live audience – without a net. One slip, one miscalculation can be fatal – and not just to the culprit, but his or her staff as well. It's why both the Senate and House have enacted and amended codes of ethics that govern the activities of Members, their families and their staffs.

You're likely to hear staff and even Members complain about the restrictions. Avoid the temptation to join in. It is Congress' constitutional obligation to *"determine the rules of its proceedings, punish its Members for disorderly behavior, and, with the concurrence of two thirds, expel a Member"* (Article I, Section 5).

Expulsion is typically reserved for Members who are convicted of crimes, but there's little precedence for other activities that might get you in hot water. The House couldn't even muster a two-thirds vote in favor of punishing South Carolina Rep. Preston Smith after Smith caned Massachusetts Sen. Charles Sumner so severely in 1856 that Sumner could not return to the Senate for several years. Beating another member of the Congress may be considered bad form in some corners of society, but in the contentious days leading to the Civil War, it apparently didn't meet the disorderly behavior standard – in the House of Representatives, anyway. Don't bet your career that it wouldn't be frowned on in this day and age, however. A good deal of other activity is.

In the years since Smith let actions speak louder than words, Congress has all too often adopted rules and procedures in reaction to scandal and the ensuing public outrage. But in its haste to meet public expectations, it often has issued rules that are confusing or absent of clear guidance for how they should be implemented. It often takes years of precedents to clarify their meaning and their application.

What is the logic that drives ethical standards in Congress?

It boils down to this: Not only are Members and their staffs expected to obey rules to the letter, they are expected to avoid even the *appearance* of misconduct. The operative word is *appearance*. Most professions demand *adherence* – few judge their membership on the basis of how their actions might appear to others.

Congress does.

The problem is that judgments as to what constitute *appearance* change daily.

The appearance standard is critical. It expands the range of those who make and prosecute accusations, from attorneys general, judges and juries to the press, Internet blogs, political opponents and interest groups that make their living questioning the behavior of public officials. Anyone with access to the media or the web can allege wrongdoing and drum an adversary out of office without the allegation ever being uttered in a courtroom. And the media can, and do, perform such exorcisms themselves without prompting or precedent.

Your career may depend on your ability to judge accurately how the rules of the institution tell you to behave, how federal statutes require you to behave and how critics will interpret your behavior. At the very least you've got to know enough to ask questions or seek advice when red flags are raised. Your knowledge of the rules will never be deep enough to guarantee safety in every situation. The rules are complex and confusing. They inevitably snare unsuspecting victims. And this always bears repeating: The rules are not the only determinant of right and wrong.

Responding to Allegations

When a Member or employee stands accused of abusing the rules of the House or the Senate or violating Federal statutes, the accusation must be confronted directly and immediately. The only universally acknowledged rule of thumb is that stalling, covering up and righteous indignation are losing tactics. Those who have been singled out must consider all options, but the overarching quandary can be reduced to this simple set of truths:

> **Passing the Smell Test**
>
> The mere appearance of impropriety can be as devastating to a political career as actual malfeasance. It's why staff members sometimes lose jobs and Members lose elections even when they haven't done anything wrong or violated any rules.
>
> Staffers refer to avoiding the appearance of impropriety as "passing the smell test" – an expression that refers to the way Moms historically have gauged whether leftovers have been in the refrigerator too long. Regardless of how fresh they looked they had to pass Mom's smell test.
>
> It's the same with the rules – even if activities are legal and allowed under the rules, the only reliable gauge of whether they're safe is to consider how the media, the public and political opponents will view them.

- The most basic principle of American jurisprudence is that we are all innocent until proven guilty.

- The surest reality of political life is that this basic principle doesn't apply. The unwritten but even more universal rule of political prudence holds that appearance of wrongdoing is as damaging as actual guilt.

The first step in assessing the situation is to seek counsel you can bank on – legal counsel from an expert in the rules and the law. Get media advice from someone with expertise and experience in crisis management and communication. But get opinions as well from family, friends, counselors and anyone else whose judgment you value and whose discretion you can count on. Get political advice from trusted advisors, particularly individuals who know and understand your district or state. Finally, get the benefit of experience by seeking out those who've been through a similar crisis – and do it quietly.

There are no clear-cut guidelines for what to do once all that advice has been gathered. The decision rests with whoever is under the microscope, their conscience, their political judgment, their integrity and the tenor of the times.

You just have to hope that political expediency does not dictate punishing the alleged offender before guilt or innocence has even been determined – an action referred to in Washington D.C. as "being thrown under the bus."

Major Pitfalls

The No. 1 cause of *accidental* ethics violations is well-meaning staff trying to save money or time. Getting it right is worth the extra time and expense it might take. An example might be a big donor offering to discount rent on a district office space or a Member failing to properly report having hitched a ride on a corporate jet so he or she could attend the funeral of a community leader in the home district and get back to Washington D.C. in time to vote on an important bill. Both of these actions might save tax dollars and enable the Member to successfully perform the duties of office, but both would violate the rules.

Rules and regulations surrounding political campaigns can also blow up in your face, particularly those pertaining to campaign finance.

For a variety of reasons, including media costs, the size of districts and early primaries, campaigns now require sophisticated operations. They are expensive. On average, Representatives must raise $1 million for each two-year election cycle if they hope to remain in office. That's what a campaign costs. And that's just your common, run-of-the-mill campaign. A heavily contested, hard-fought campaign is likely to eat up even more cash.

The law requires a separation between campaigns and the duties of elected office that is as inviolable as the one that supposedly exists between church and state. Members may not use the resources of their elected office for campaign purposes. They may not design or conduct fundraising appeals on official time or use official equipment. They can't mail campaign solicitations from Congressional offices or use government postage. They absolutely can't ask for donations when lobbyists or others visit their offices.

These rules are, as they should be, absolute.

All these prohibitions apply to staff as well.

Recent modifications do, however, permit a Member to designate one staff member as liaison between the campaign and the elected office, but only for specified purposes such as coordinating the Member's schedule. Like all other staff members, however, the liaison is prohibited from performing any campaign duties on government time or using government resources to do them.

Keeping arm's length between campaigns and the elected office is vital to the integrity of the Congress, but it does contribute to inefficiency and confusion. After all, in certain respects there is no distinction between serving constituents and running for re-election. The lines are sometimes very grey and narrow. Inconvenient or difficult as the rules sometimes might seem, it is foolish to skirt their edges and risk breaking one of them.

Each chamber's Ethics Committee governs the official actions and activities of its Members just as the Federal Election Commission, which enforces a variety of complex laws governing campaigns, regulates the actions and activities of candidates for federal office. The ability to keep track and make sense of the labyrinth that candidates, elected officials and their staffs must negotiate each day is why attorneys who specialize in election law are paid so much money.

175

The Role of the Media

The role of the media in the prosecution of ethics rules has to be recognized and weighed carefully by those who must live by them.

The are three basic roles the media might play:

- The media serve as a straightforward purveyor of information regarding allegations of misconduct or a behavior that is simply suspect, without attempting to sway public opinion one way or the other, generate outrage or pass judgment.

- The media can serve as accuser, prosecutor, judge and jury in situations where a public figure has put him or herself in a compromising position by engaging in behavior that invites criticism. The behavior may be an apparent violation of the rules – or it may be an activity that is not covered by the rules but the media decided it ought to be – or it can be neither, simply an excuse for the media to come down on an individual it dislikes.

- The media can play the role of echo chamber for someone else's attempt to bring down a politician, beating the drums loudly and often enough that the accuser is able to orchestrate public demand for punitive action. That someone else might be an aggressive prosecutor who leaks damaging information, or any number of interest groups that make their living denigrating public officials, political parties or party organizations.

The media perform these roles sometimes responsibly and sometimes not. The choices they face are not fun, and those on the receiving end of the judgments they make will invariably credit them to prejudicial reporting, political bias or just plain cynicism.

You make your own judgments based on what facts you have and not what emotions you feel. And you, like the rest of us, will draw conclusions about whether the press performs well, not so well or despicably in these circumstances.

We think there are a few general truths regarding media treatment of "scandal."

First, it is clear that media judgment and rules of engagement have changed dramatically since the Administration of President Franklin

Roosevelt when neither his infirmities nor his alleged liaisons were reported. The press protected Presidents in those days, as it did with the personal life of John Kennedy, whose use of painkillers and his alleged liaisons were not reported.

There was a different standard in place before Vietnam, Watergate, before the range of subjects and circumstances considered off limits began to shrink until today when it's impossible to think of a topic that's unlikely to be scrutinized.

It is safe to say that there are no general standards governing the activities of those individuals or enterprises that consider themselves media these days. Media cover or fail to cover what they will and each will justify its decisions to suit the circumstances – if it bothers to provide any justification at all. In 2008, for example, the mainstream media reported on an affair involving Senator John McCain– an allegation that was later debunked – but did not report an affair involving Senator John Edwards that it was aware of for a year before he admitted to it publicly.

Whether the subject is earmarks, relationships with lobbyists, personal behavior, the behavior of children and relatives, drinking or dalliances, some media go to great lengths to score points in the game of political "gotcha," making up new rules and drafting new standards of behavior to suit the situation.

Other media are less reckless and more circumspect in assessing how far to go before putting someone's reputation on the chopping block.

Irresponsible reporting isn't new. All of the Founding Fathers felt the sting of the pen – from Washington being accused of senility to Andrew Jackson's belief that published attacks on his wife led to her untimely death.

Today, however, the instantaneous and near-ubiquitous nature of information reported by competing and ever changing outlets, makes it more critical than ever for media to handle accusations responsibly – and more tempting than ever to do just the opposite.

The Ins and Outs of the Ethics Rules

Take the time to learn the rules and never act without certainty – if you don't know whether the action might be a violation, check it out with the House Committee on Standards of Official Conduct or the Senate Select

Committee on Ethics. Both committees offer advice by phone and provide staff attorneys with whom you can confidentially discuss ethics questions. Take advantage of the one that serves the chamber in which you work.

Ethical behavior cannot be legislated. Character cannot be fabricated. Scoundrels will break the rules. What follows isn't written with them in mind. This is written to help prevent good and decent public servants from making innocent and dumb mistakes. It is not written as legal advice, nor is it an excuse to avoid reading the rules or asking questions.

Unless specifically stated, these rules apply to both Members and staff.

Gifts

The rules prohibit staff and Members from accepting anything of value from a lobbyist or an entity that employs one. This is an important point. The manager of a plant in your district, for example, cannot take you to lunch if the company he or she works for employs a lobbyist.

If you are not sure whether a *venti latte* is going to get you in trouble, ask or pay for it yourself.

The same applies to tickets to sporting events and fancy pens – a former chief of staff was actually indicted for fraud against the House of Representatives after taking tickets to a Wiggles concert for his toddlers from a Jack Abramoff associate.

"Just say no" is a good rule of thumb even in situations that don't involve drugs.

A seemingly harmless violation can land you in hot water.

You can accept a gift or meal with a value up to $50 as long as it's from someone who is not a lobbyist or a foreign representative. You can even accept two of them but not at the same time – and no more than two in a given year since there is an annual limit of $100. That means that if a non-lobbyist wants to conduct a series of luncheon meetings and each meal is valued at $25, you can go four times during the year. If you attend more sessions than that, you'll need to pay your own way.

You also may receive gifts from relatives, even if the relative is a lobbyist, but he or she has to be a relative before the gift is given. It used to be that a potential groom only needed the permission of a bride's father to give his love an engagement ring. Not anymore – at least not if he's a lobbyist and she works for Congress. The Ethics Committee must grant written permission for any gift from a lobbyist, even one you're going to marry. (No word on whether the committee will offer marriage counseling in the future.)

There are no limits on gifts from federal, state and local governments, including sporting events at public universities. Informational materials such as books and DVDs, home-state products of "nominal" value and commemorative items such as inscribed plaques are also permitted.

It is always a violation, however, to ask or solicit a gift.

Remember, there's no such thing as a harmless violation.

Attending Events

You may go to a reception that offers food and refreshments of nominal value – milk and cookies, for example – but not if the food constitutes part of a meal.

You may attend an event where you are invited by the sponsor, but not if a lobbyist or someone other than the sponsor buys the ticket, and only if the event is deemed to be *widely attended* – which is an extremely important consideration. A *widely attended* event must have at least 25 non-Hill guests or participants and must either be open to the public or to individuals representing a range of characteristics and must be relevant to your official duties.

Sounds pretty vague, doesn't it?

Plan on spending a good deal of time conferring with the Ethics Committee to confirm that events you'd like to attend qualify.

If an event does qualify, you are permitted to accept transportation and a meal as long as the same meal is offered to everyone else who's there.

You may not accept a gift bag or souvenir.

You may attend a charity event if you are invited by the charity. A lobbyist cannot buy you a ticket to the Federated Cancer Fighter's ball, for example.

Your spouse or dependent child may join you at such an event, but you must pay for a ticket for any other guest including a sibling, parent or date.

If it is a campaign event, however, all bets are off.

A lobbyist can buy a table for $25,000 at a fund-raising banquet and provide tickets for you and your date and no one will raise an eyebrow. Eat and drink and be merry. You're off the hook.

Confusing?

We don't make the rules we just explain them.

Privately Sponsored Travel

Travel for which someone else foots the bill may be permitted under very strict circumstances. A trip sponsor must complete a multi-page certification form. The staff member who will be making the trip must then submit this form, along with a separate request for permission, to the Ethics Committee. Staff members also must have advance authorization from their boss.

At the conclusion of the trip, the traveler must file a disclosure form with details on exactly how much was spent on transportation, lodging and food. These disclosure reports become public record.

A U.S. college or university may sponsor trips up to four days domestically or seven days internationally, as can any group or other body that does not employ a lobbyist or foreign representative or agent. An organization that does employ a lobbyist can sponsor a one-day trip as long as the lobbyist is not involved in planning and does not travel with the participant on any leg of the event.

If all of these qualifications are met, the Member or staffer may accept coach or business class accommodations and meals that are reasonably priced – as defined by the Ethics Committee on a case-by-case basis – and served to everyone else making the trip.

The exceptions to these travel rules include official overseas travel by CODELs (Congressional delegations) or trips sponsored by state or local governments, travel paid for by foreign governments and campaign travel, as long as the campaign committee reports the trip to the FEC as a campaign expense.

Campaign travel may not be on official time.

Campaign Work

Staff members may perform campaign work – paid or voluntary – on their own time but not on the Congressional clock and only of their own volition. It is a felony for an office to compel an employee to perform campaign duties.

Campaign activities are prohibited in any Congressional office – including district offices. Solicitation and acceptance of campaign contributions also are prohibited. If a contribution is inadvertently sent to the Congressional office, it must be forwarded at the campaign's expense within seven days.

You may not make a campaign contribution to your boss – even if you want to and even if you contributed before you were employed on the Hill. With the exception of travel, an employee may not expend personal funds to cover a campaign expense even if the expense would be reimbursed. And if you aren't reimbursed the full amount of campaign travel, the difference will be considered an illegal campaign contribution.

Constituent Casework

On behalf of a constituent, you are permitted to inquire of federal agencies about the status of inquiries or applications. You also may request full and prompt consideration.

You may NOT, however, ask an agency to make an exception to the law or the agency's regulations. You cannot threaten or make any promise to an agency official. You may not conduct communication with any official with decision-making authority in a legal or administrative proceeding. You may not contact an agency on a matter where you or your boss has a personal financial interest. Nor may a Member or staff show preferential treatment to a supporter, contributor or friends in a casework matter. By the same token, however, they are not required to recuse themselves from providing such assistance to supporters, contributors or friends.

What is demanded of them is simply that they treat everyone equally.

Offices are severely limited in the types of recommendations they can make for civil service positions – study the rules carefully before making any recommendations.

Official Events

An office may not use outside resources to conduct official business. This means a Member may not jointly sponsor any kind of event with a private group or anyone else, for that matter. And you are not allowed to accept cash or in-kind support for an official event or meeting.

Allowances for the expenditure of campaign money in support of official events are limited – food and beverage costs, for example, room rental, printed materials and travel expenses for guest speakers. Nor can campaign funds be used to advertise an official event. Check with the Ethics Committee before using campaign funds for anything other than obvious campaign expenses.

The rules also limit how a Member's name can be used in conjunction with a private event. A Member can be listed as an honorary co-host, for example, but only if the invitation clearly identifies the sponsor of the event. Use of official letterhead or the official seal by an outside group is, however, prohibited. As is the use of official resources, including the office's press-release capability, its website or franking privileges to promote an event sponsored by a private enterprise, no matter how local or how emotionally compelling the cause may be. A Member may send a "Dear Colleague" letter about a private group's event after the group has issued an invitation to those same colleagues but only if the event is taking place in a House or Senate room.

Outside Employment and Financial Disclosure

Staff members may work or volunteer for an outside group or other entity – including charities and non-profits – but such activities are subject to strict guidelines. They cannot conflict with official duties. They cannot involve House or Senate resources and no work on their behalf may be performed in Congressional offices or while on the Congressional clock. In addition, any staffer taking part in such activities must have his or her boss's approval to do so.

If you are considered senior staff – earning in the neighborhood of two-thirds the pay of a Member – the caveats increase in number. How much you can earn moonlighting is limited to 15 percent of the Member's salary. Campaign pay is considered outside income and can be accepted for work done in your spare time – but there are strictly enforced limits.

Senior staff also are prohibited from working in or having an on-going affiliation with any profession that bears a fiduciary responsibility – this includes the law, real estate, insurance and financial planning. An outside firm cannot use your name and you cannot be a paid officer or board member of any such organization.

In addition, you are required to have advance written approval from the Ethics Committee before accepting any paid teaching position. There are strict limitations on outside royalty income, as well. No Member or senior staff may receive an honorarium – non-senior staff can but not for anything related to their official duties or if the source of the honorarium has interests before the Congress that the employee might in any way influence.

In other words, a non-senior staff member may be allowed to write a book on butterfly collecting – but only after the issue has been thoroughly vetted.

If you are a Member or senior level staffer, you must file an annual financial disclosure report. Senior-level employees must also file a disclosure within 30 days of joining a staff and 30 days after leaving one. The report lists income, assets, liabilities, property and security transactions, certain types of gifts, travel expenses, outside positions and employment agreements. Financial information regarding spouses and children also must be disclosed.

In offices where no one earns enough to qualify as senior staff, the Member designates a staffer to file such a report. Usually it is the chief of staff, but it can be anybody who was on staff as of December 31 of the preceding year.

The Justice Department is authorized to take action on willfully erroneous information, so have your report reviewed by Ethics Committee staff prior to submitting it to make sure you got everything right.

There are fines for late filings.

There are also a number of post-employment restrictions for *senior-level* employees (those who earn 67 percent of a Member's salary), but considerably more for those who earn *very senior* staff salaries(75 percent of what the boss makes). Those leaving very senior staff positions in the House are prohibited from trying to influence formal activities in their former office for a full year. If they are committee staff, they are prohibited from lobbying the committee or its Members for a year, and leadership staff may not lobby leadership of either party in the House for a like period of time. Very senior Senate employees can't lobby anyone in the Senate – Members or staff – for a year as well.

Very senior staff in both chambers must disclose in writing any negotiation with a prospective employer within three days and recuse themselves from any issue where there might be a conflict of interest with a prospective employer.

Conflict of Interest

Common sense is all it takes to keep you from violating the host of conflict of interest rules. First and foremost among them is the prohibition against using your official position or any confidential information for personal gain. Any violation of the confidential information clause is the Legislative equivalent of insider trading.

A Member is prohibited from hiring family members in his or her congressional office and cannot in their official capacity do any special favors for family members.

And That's Not All

This is but a snapshot of the ethics rules that will guide your activities and those of your bosses in the Congress – and an idea of how serious and all encompassing they are. The manuals in which they are contained run to several hundred pages, and the Ethics Committees regularly add updates and guidance. Mastering them all will take time. But even when you're confident you know the rules, it's a good idea to confer with the umpire before setting foot on the playing field.

This is serious business. The penalties for making a mistake can be harsh. The whole experience can make you second-guess the attraction of public service. We hope not. We hope instead that by being aware of the rules and making a commitment to ethical behavior, that you might become the type of high-quality public servant that helps Congress restore its damaged reputation.

Chapter Thirteen Summary

- Few professions are subject to as high an ethical standard or as much transparency as elected federal officials.

- The mere whiff of scandal can destroy a career, even if allegations later prove false. And what taints one official has a tendency to taint the rest as well.

- The truth is that the vast majority of Members of Congress have served with distinction and without the hint of impropriety.

- The Senate and House have codes of ethics that govern the activities of Members, their families and their staffs.

- Not only are Members and their staffs expected to obey rules to the letter, they are expected to avoid even the *appearance* of misconduct.

- The most basic principle of American jurisprudence is that we are all innocent until proven guilty. The surest reality of political life is that this basic principle doesn't apply.

- The No. 1 cause of *accidental* ethics violations is well-meaning staff trying to save money or time.

- The law requires a separation between campaigns and the duties of elected office that is as inviolable as the one that supposedly exists between church and state.

- The role of the media in the prosecution of ethics rules has to be recognized and weighed carefully by those who must live by them. The are three basic roles the media might play: a straightforward purveyor of information; accuser, prosecutor, judge and jury; or an echo chamber for someone else's attempt to bring down a politician. The media performs these roles sometimes responsibly and sometimes not.

- Take the time to learn the rules and never act without certainty – if you don't know whether an action might be a violation, check it out with the House Committee on Standards of Official Conduct or the Senate Select Committee on Ethics. Both committees offer advice by phone and provide staff attorneys with whom you can confidentially discuss ethics questions.

- Ethical behavior cannot be legislated. Character cannot be fabricated. Scoundrels will break the rules. This chapter is written to help prevent good and decent public servants from making innocent and dumb mistakes.

- The penalties for making a mistake can be harsh. We hope that by being aware of the rules and making a commitment to ethical behavior, that you might become the type of high-quality public servant that helps Congress restore its damaged reputation.

There are few terms in politics more derogatory than ... (Dare we say it aloud?) ... *special interests*. Special interests have probably played a role in every incident of influence peddling ever recorded. Even the words themselves – *special* and *interests* – sound undemocratic.

Who are these evil interests?

And what makes them so special?

In point of fact, special interests are not evil – nor even undemocratic. Quite the contrary. We all have special interests, and they are being represented on our behalf in the halls of Congress. If you own a car or a refrigerator, travel on an airline, watch television, go to church, get sick, eat, fish, hunt, invest in a mutual fund or have a hard time breathing, you are a special interest, and there are associations and organizations campaigning on your behalf at both the state and the national level.

Few people realize, for instance, that AARP, one of the largest associations representing the interests of seniors, tops Fortune magazine's list of the most influential special interest in Washington D.C.

Boy Scouts of America is a special interest. So are barbers, bakers, basketball players, bird lovers, beauticians, bingo players, buglers, bureaucrats, bricklayers, bar owners, caterers, churchgoers, circus performers, car dealers, cartoonists, cab drivers, cooks, can manufacturers, cable operators, chaplains – and that doesn't even get us through the C's. They are all represented in Washington and they all employ lobbyists. The fact is that a $3 trillion government, with thousands of programs and millions of rules and regulations, affects just about everyone. At one time or another, we all need relief or assistance from the federal government or one of more than 87,000 state and local government agencies with over 513,000 elected officials all trying to be helpful, including counties, regional transportation authorities, cities, towns, townships, sanitary districts, school districts, water districts and the list goes on.

Generally speaking, *special interests* do not refer to concerns so much as to the groups representing them – in fact, the phrase typically is shorthand for *special interest groups*. They're also called *advocacy*, *lobbying* and even *pressure* groups. Their primary reason for being is to influence political decisions and public policy.

Special interest groups are a necessary component in a pluralist democratic republic. They provide lawmakers and executive agencies with valuable information that can help shape legislation. They also provide information on the political, economic, social and environmental impact that legislation or policies are likely to have. And they provide a barometer for how activities in the Congress are likely to affect the next election. And for each special interest advocating one position, there are other special interests advocating the opposite or another opinion.

There are four kinds of special interest groups:

Corporate: Thousands of companies and corporations of all varieties maintain a presence in Washington, whether in the form of a Washington office with full-time employees or through a contractual relationship with one or more law firms, lobby firms or trade associations. Private companies ranging from global conglomerates like General Electric to upstarts like Notification Technologies Inc. find a presence in Washington necessary to protect their interests or advance public policies that enhance their business opportunities and, in the process, make life better for their stockholders, their customers and their employees. Most present their case before the legislative and executive branches, regulatory agencies and quasi-governmental agencies.

While print and broadcast journalists often rail against special interests, the companies for which they work – *The Washington Post*, the *Wall Street Journal*, the *Chicago Tribune*, ABC, NBC, CBS, CNN and Fox – are represented by Washington lobbyists and trade associations advocating on their behalf over everything from content piracy to taxes, postal rates to protection of sources, and any issues that can have an impact on their ability to produce a product and make a profit.

Associations and Organizations: These fall into two categories: Some, such as the National Manufacturers Association, the Chamber of Commerce, the American Medical Association, the National Federation of Independent Businesses, and the Newspaper Publisher's Association, represent professions, occupations, industries, individual companies and even labor unions. Others, such as Common Cause, Citizens for a Responsive Politics, the American Heart Association and the National Rifle Association represent causes or issues and are self-perpetuating movements that rely on the loyalty and commitment of individual donors to fund their efforts. Theirs are among the literally thousands of lobbying efforts aimed at the same people and the same governmental agencies that corporations try to influence.

Associations represent the shared interests of their members – individuals and organizations that contribute financially to them, whether their contributions are in the form of union dues, annual membership fees or ad hoc contributions.

In most cases, associations do not exist for the sole purpose of lobbying. For many, lobbying isn't even their primary function. The Food Marketing Institute, for example, may lobby at the federal, state and local levels, but its primary concerns are food packaging and food safety research, membership education programs, public opinion research and hosting conventions and conferences where members can exchange information.

Associations such as the National Federation of Independent Businesses and the National Association of Realtors provide a means for local Mom and Pop stores and one-person contractors to band together and have a voice equal to or greater than big corporations.

Some *special interests* attempt to wrap themselves in the cloak of altruism by contending that they're actually *public interest* groups. It's a slick branding strategy aimed at convincing outsiders that their objectives are more honorable – and by extension that the objectives of anyone who disagrees or has a commercial interest in the same issues are not. The motives of an organization whose mission is campaign finance reform, for example, are no purer than those of the Association of Can Manufacturers; they both advocate their own interests. People who run both organizations respond to the demands of those who pay their salaries.

The so-called *public interest groups* do not like to be called special interests. They prefer to think of their interests as somehow different. But they lobby the Congress and the Executive Branch as aggressively as any other special interest. They are particularly effective at influencing public opinion through the media. They have media access that few others do.

Single-Issue Organizations: These are similar to not-for-profits in terms of variables such as membership, financial support and tax status. They distinguish themselves by representing just one issue or set of related issues. While a labor union may have positions on a range of topics, including trade, minimum wage, health care and workplace conditions, the single-issue organization focuses all its energy on one, like abortion or gun

189

ownership, a specific form of tax-reform or saving the whales. Single-issue organizations are less permanent. When their issue has been resolved to the satisfaction of the organization's backers, they often disband, or sometimes gravitate to another similar issue. One example of this phenomenon is the March of Dimes, which has been so successful in helping to wipe out polio – its original purpose – that it has been able to shift focus to preventing premature birth, birth defects and conducting maternal education programs promoting good health practices, care for unborn children and their pregnant mothers, and prevention of infant mortality.

The reality is that few single-issue organizations ever disband. The issues that motivate them seldom get resolved to anyone's complete satisfaction.

Many organizations and associations have full-time employees representing their interests in the state capitals and Washington D.C., and even some foreign countries, but they also hire additional professional advocates or lobbyists to represent them. These professional advocates might be associated with law firms, with public affairs firms that specialize in both government and public relations, with large and small lobbying firms – or simply independent contractors.

Lobbying Companies, Multiple Advocacy or Consultant Organizations: There are about 1700 firms in Washington D.C. that lobby on behalf of their clients. These advocates are hired for a variety of reasons: The firm may have a particular expertise or an area of specialty – many firms employ former Members of Congress and committee staff with unique knowledge about pertinent issues and programs – or the client may find that hiring the lobbying firm is less expensive and faster to get started on its behalf than creating an in-house staff.

Some professional advocates have long-term contracts. In other cases, relationships are brief and involve a single, clearly defined task. If, for example, hedge-fund operators find their livelihood suddenly threatened by negative publicity that threatens punitive action in Congress, they may need the help of outside pros to improve their image and fight legislation that could have a negative impact on their livelihood.

Coalitions: Corporations, associations, foundations and single-interest lobbies will occasionally form coalitions to advocate an issue or action that is in their common interest. Coalitions are usually temporarily financed and structured to meet a specific mission or common goal. Normally a coalition will hire independent staff and solicit what might be referred to as *dues* even though contributions are actually based on what each member can afford or is willing to devote to the effort. An executive director who answers to a board of directors or board of advisors, usually made up of the biggest contributors, generally manages them. Coalitions sometimes operate out of the office of a consultant, lobbying firm, public relations firm or law firm that is hired to handle the campaign.

Governments: The world of special interests also is populated by state governments, public and private colleges and universities, regional governing authorities, cities, counties, townships and associations of governors and attorneys general and other bodies of elected officials or units of government. Governments also employ lobbyists and hire outside public affairs specialists. In addition, there are foreign governments represented in Washington– most of which also depend on paid lobbyists to represent their interests.

By most estimates, there are from 15,000 to 20,000 lobbyists in Washington, D.C., supported by staffs that take the advocacy community to 40,000 employees. There are more than 2,000 corporations, more than 8,000 non-profit and trade associations and thousands of government or quasi-governmental agencies with Washington representation.

All of these special interests realize that direct pressure may not be and often is not enough to solve their problems. If nothing else there is strength in numbers and power in public opinion. That's why many, particularly when in trouble, will invest so much time, energy and money in indirect advocacy – grassroots/grasstops mobilization, research and public relations. All three forms of advocacy have evolved in recent years into highly sophisticated means of influencing public opinion and public policy.

An effective grassroots operation can educate thousands of people in a very short time and motivate them to write or email their Representatives and Senators, write letters to the editor of the local newspaper, participate in radio call-in shows, show up at townhall meetings and engage in other activities designed to influence the actions of their elected representatives and staffs.

The term *grasstops* describes campaigns that aim to educate and motivate public officials, opinion leaders and prominent local citizens. The

> **Reasons Governments Lobby**
>
> - **Financial:** Governments often seek federal grants to support services and infrastructure.
>
> - **Corporate:** A government might participate in a corporate lobbying effort that affects the community's largest employer.
>
> - **Not-for-profit:** It might be associated with a not-for-profit such as one working to increase federal aid for homeless programs.
>
> - **Single-issue:** It might be involved in an effort to modify water-purity standards.
>
> - **Coalition:** It might be part of an effort involving businesses and governmental bodies hoping to persuade the Congress to allocate funds for a comprehensive transportation program.

goal is for these individuals to call and put pressure on Congress to take a particular action, and begin word-of-mouth advocacy that gets those in their circle of influence involved in the campaign.

Intensive public relations campaigns can include paid and unpaid advertising, the creation of websites, and pitches to journalists to encourage coverage of pertinent issues and development of a positive brand for an individual, an organization or an issue. In support of these initiatives, opinion polling and survey research provide data and themes for their messages.

An individual needing help with a problem usually can get it from an elected official. But the efforts of individuals rarely change laws or keep laws from being enacted. That takes many individuals working together. It takes a clearly defined strategy and a coordinated lobbying effort. No elected official has the time or the staff or the mental capacity to learn, retain and understand all that influences the lives of constituents, let alone all that influences the country as a whole.

The Founding Fathers may not have envisioned the level of sophistication that advocacy efforts have attained, but they codified the practice in the First Amendment of the Bill of Rights, which guarantees the right to petition government for redress of grievances. The Founders didn't go into a lot of detail about how such redress could be sought, but they made it clear that it was a right they wanted protected.

In the days before the volume became unmanageable, citizens were encouraged to actually submit written petitions directly to the Congress, where the House set aside time to address them. One of the first petition drives was led by Benjamin Franklin and advocated the abolition of slavery.

Like every avenue to influence, the role of special interests is subject to abuse. Special interests have been tainted by scandal since the founding of the nation.

Take the dispute between Alexander Hamilton and James Madison that led to the formation of the Federalist and Republican parties. The Continental Congress was so poor throughout the Revolutionary War that it paid General George Washington's Continental Army with bonds, which were essentially IOUs. Believing the government would never redeem the bonds, most soldiers sold them to speculators at a fraction of their face value. These speculators held onto the bonds until 1787, when they began lobbying the new federal government for payment in full. Hamilton favored paying the face value to whoever held the bonds but Madison objected. Virginia had gone into debt redeeming bonds that had been paid out to soldiers from that state. Veterans deserved to be repaid, he argued, and should receive half the value of any bonds that were redeemed. Hamilton won out when, at a private dinner arranged by Thomas Jefferson, Madison dropped his demands in exchange for a commitment on the part of the federal government to pay off Virginia's debt and build the new Capitol on the Potomac River.

It was lobbying on behalf of multiple interests that resolved the issue and led to the location of Washington D.C.

The first efforts to regulate lobbying at the federal level didn't occur until 1876 when a resolution approved by the House required lobbyists to register with the Clerk of the House.

The excesses of monopolists and the economic and societal impact of the industrial revolution led to exposés by muckrakers in the last decades of the 19th Century – and those, in turn, led to a number of reforms with teeth and new regulatory agencies to give them bite. With each new scandal in the interim – from Teapot Dome to Abscam to Jack Abramoff – have come calls for greater regulation.

In response to the Jack Abramoff scandal, in which several Members and staff were implicated in alleged influence peddling, Congress placed new restrictions on the activities of lobbyists. These dramatically increased disclosure requirements and the paper work they must maintain and file, imposed harsh criminal sentences and fines for violations of the rules, and imposed new restrictions on Members and staff in their interaction with lobbyists.

The Congress considered but rejected provisions that would have restricted Members' ability to solicit political contributions from lobbyists.

What was enacted is a confusing set of restrictions that, on the one hand, prohibits a lobbyist from buying a Member lunch so they can discuss the merits of a legislative issue, but allows him to buy that same Member the same lunch if he brings up to a $2300 campaign contribution with him.

Advice for Staff

A Congressional staff member should take full advantage of the expertise and resources special interests have to offer – but do so with a clear understanding of the petitioner's intent and motivation and the restrictions surrounding your interaction. Here are some simple rules to help guide you:

- Know who is financing, managing and controlling any special interest you encounter, particularly coalitions with noble-sounding monikers. A lobbyist may be paid by a corporation that is a wholly owned subsidiary of a larger one or a holding company that hopes to conceal its interest in the issue at hand. By the same token, a coalition calling itself the Energy Efficiency Organization may seem like an all-American enterprise if you neglect to take into consideration the fact that energy isn't a purely American concern – and that a coalition could have foreign interests. Know with whom you are doing business.

- Find out if the special interest or coalition is providing only its side of the issue or is willing to acknowledge opposing viewpoints and identify organizations that are advocating on behalf of the opposition.

- Don't reach a conclusion without examining all sides of an issue. If you hear from one side, make it a point to listen to the other side as well.

- Follow up; ask questions, demand answers and additional information or verification of the information that has been presented.

- Maintain an arm's-length relationship with special interests and coalitions – and make sure your activities are always within the Rules of the House or Senate and comply with federal statutes. But don't resist developing professional relationships with lobbyists through periodic or frequent contact. The system is, after all, still based on mutual trust and respect.

- Don't be afraid to use trusted representatives of special interests as an information resource when dealing with issues in which they have an expertise.

- Never make a commitment without a clear understanding of precisely what it is you're committing to. Lobbyists look at their meetings with you – whether in person, by email or by phone – as an

194

action-producing mechanism. They want something to come of the contact. There's nothing wrong with taking action, but make sure you are comfortable taking the action you're being pressed to take.

- Be sure, as well, to understand the special interest's relationship to your interests – your district or your boss's committee assignments.

- Before you sit down with representatives of a special interest, understand not only the issues they're interested in, but also their relevance to your sphere of influence. Going into a meeting cold is disrespectful and unproductive. If you don't have time to prepare, let the meeting participants know so they can bring you up to speed, at least from their perspective.

Friendly Persuasion

Imagine that it's your first week on the job. Your boss took his oath of office yesterday and you're still trying to figure out which restroom you should be using. Out of the blue, the receptionist tells you a college buddy you haven't seen in years has stopped by to welcome you to D.C.

You invite him in and after briefing one another on what's been going on in your lives since the last time you shared a pitcher of beer, he tells you he's a lobbyist for XYZ Corporation.

More out of politeness than interest, you ask what sort of issues he focuses on.

"Net neutrality," he replies.

"Never heard of it," you say with a laugh.

"It's pretty significant," he says and manages not to sound critical of your ignorance.

With little prodding, he does what a good lobbyist SHOULD NOT DO, he provides you with a one-sided subjective explanation claiming that existing regulations severely limit the Internet's usefulness, threaten to produce unfortunate precedents that will severely limit the nation's competitive telecommunications edge, severely limit investment, deny providers the ability to offer services that distinguish them from one another and give other communication providers an unfair competitive advantage.

Sounds downright un-American.

Exactly the kind of issue your boss is interested in.

You're about to commit your office's support for a bill when you stop yourself. Instead, you promise to look into the issue.

Wise decision.

When you do look into net neutrality, you'll discover it is among the most contentious issues facing the Congress. To paraphrase Churchill's description of Russia, it is a riddle, wrapped in a mystery inside an enigma. Those opposing any change in the rules include content providers. They argue that allowing DSL (digital subscriber line) providers to charge for access would be tantamount to providing them with near-monopolistic authority over the Internet. By duplicating the content of providers and making it available free to their customers while charging the providers for delivering it, DSLs would be in a position to drive the competition out of the market, opponents say. And in the process, other opponents such as software manufacturers add that charges for DSL access would discourage innovation and development.

As one lawmaker said in sidestepping the controversy: "A lot of us believe that we don't have a problem, and we're not going to overly regulate a product that might stifle the entrepreneurship and the progress we want to make in the future."

What lesson do we learn from all this?

Do your homework, welcome advice but make your own judgment.

Chapter Fourteen Summary

- We all have special interests, and they are being represented on our behalf in the halls of Congress.

- The Founding Fathers may not have envisioned the level of sophistication that advocacy efforts have attained, but they codified the practice in the First Amendment of the Bill of Rights, which guarantees the right to petition government for redress of grievances.

- The fact is that a $3 trillion government, with thousands of programs and millions of rules and regulations, affects just about everyone. At one time or another, we all need relief or assistance from the federal government.

- Special interest groups are a necessary component in a pluralist democratic republic.

- There are four kinds of special interest groups: corporate, associations and organizations, single-issue organizations, and lobbying companies and consultants.

- Corporations, associations, foundations and single-interest lobbies will occasionally form coalitions to advocate an issue or action that is in their common interest. Coalitions are usually temporarily financed and structured to meet a specific mission or common goal.

- State governments, public and private colleges and universities, local governments and foreign governments, also populate the world of special interests.

- An effective grassroots operation can educate thousands of people in a very short time and motivate them to act.

- Intensive public relations campaigns can include paid and unpaid advertising, the creation of websites, and pitches to journalists to encourage coverage of pertinent issues and development of a positive brand for an individual, an organization or an issue.

- The first efforts to regulate lobbying at the federal level didn't occur until 1876. With each new scandal in the interim – from Teapot Dome to Abscam to Jack Abramoff – have come calls for greater regulation.

- Staff should know who is financing, managing and controlling any special interest they encounter, particularly coalitions with noble-sounding monikers.

- Do your homework, welcome advice but make your own judgment.

To summarize some of the key messages from previous chapters and conclude this introduction to the Congress, we have drafted the following memo to illustrate strategic planning and the role you might play in it. The memo is from a legislative director to his boss, a congressman who has been asked by the President and the leader of his party in Congress, to assume the leadership role in developing and winning congressional passage of a major reform of the Social Security System. While the memo does not delve into the specifics of strategic planning for a project of this dimension, it does address the key elements, all of which have been touched on in one way or another in previous chapters.

MEMORANDUM

TO: Congressman James E. Cricket

FROM: Wright A. Law, Legislative Director

RE: SOCIAL SECURITY REFORM: Spearheading Or Beheading?

I am reminded of Oliver Hardy's line in the old Laurel & Hardy films: "Here's another fine mess you've gotten us into." But in this case, it was the President, in the presence of our House Leader, who convinced you to assume the leadership of a task force to reform the mess the Social Security System is in. And this is beyond anything Oliver Hardy ever imagined.

What follows is a preliminary overview of how the goal might be accomplished. I hope you will forgive me if it seems from time to time to overstate the obvious, but for the sake of clarity and for those who will eventually be recruited to this process, the obvious may be worth restating.

During my initial conversations with you and our chief of staff, we addressed the massive volume of personal and professional resources that will be required. We paid special attention to the commitment you must make and the risks involved in dedicating the lion's share of your energy and attention to this endeavor at the expense of all other priorities. As we observed, the risks are substantial, particularly if the President or the leadership is tempted by unforeseen events to reduce support, leaving you without badly needed leverage and resources until you can regain their commitment. You concluded that the need to enact a solution to the Social Security problem outweighs the risks involved.

You then asked me to produce an analysis of the challenge and a blueprint for meeting it. This blueprint contains steps we, the senior staff in our office, think necessary to produce a viable strategy, launch a campaign and implement change on a scale seldom seen in Washington or the nation.

In a separate document, we will detail the crisis Social Security faces and the impact that crisis will have on every American citizen. For the moment, we will focus on developing a strategy to guide us through the gathering storm.

The 9 Key Elements of Strategic Thinking

The first element is getting some help. You need to begin immediately creating a task force or executive committee or leadership team – or whatever designation you give it – that will work closely with you through every step of this process, from the mission statement to enactment. A project of this nature has little if any potential for success if it is viewed as partisan. Therefore, long before the effort is even rumored around town, it is critical to recruit a colleague from across the aisle that is as committed to the task as you are. From this two-Member nucleus, you will build outward to form your task force.

We recommend that this task force be made up of 15 or more members:

- Six or more Members of Congress (equal numbers from the House and Senate) reflecting the interests of the committees of jurisdiction, the leadership and the two parties. These colleagues will eventually become the core of the movement that will define for the American public the urgency of the situation, build support for legislation and implement the legislative strategy.

- The four representatives of the Executive Branch with expertise and jurisdiction over Social Security and direct access to the President. This would include a representative of the Commissioner of the Social Security Administration, the Secretary of the Treasury, the Secretary of Labor and the Secretary of Health and Human Services, all of whom are trustees of the Social Security Trust Fund.

- Four representatives of the private sector with expertise in retirement security issues, experience in problem solving on a national scale and national outreach capability – access to a substantial constituency, the public and the press. These individuals must represent the diverse interests that have a vested interest in the Social Security System, and more broadly in the nation's retirement security. Those interests may include Wall Street, a corporate executive, a leader of organized labor and a leader from the senior community.

- Two representatives of the public or private sector with expertise and experience in public relations and public opinion research. This is a group whose role will be invaluable in the development of what may be a massive public education initiative, constant media relations, grassroots organization, and the monitoring of public opinion as various policy options and alternatives are explored.

The second element is defining the mission and the major objectives you seek to accomplish. The mission must be clearly enunciated, in a manner the public, the Administration and the Congressional Leadership, as well as those who will do the heavy lifting, can embrace. It must be a clear and succinct statement of what you want to accomplish. The process can survive reservations and flat out opposition, but we cannot afford widespread public disagreements over what we see as our basic mission and whether it is even desirable or necessary to pursue. The mission must have broad approval.

Once the mission has been adopted, specific objectives flowing from that mission should be identified. Will it be an objective, for example, to preserve the fundamentals of the Social Security system, as we know it? Will it be an objective to achieve reform within a specific timeframe? The two or three objectives, extensions of the mission statement, must be seen as credible and achievable.

The third element requires us to define the problem, which is both critical and complex, in language that is clear and concrete. In a separate document we will offer a brief history of Social Security reform, the various economic scenarios demonstrating the severity of the problem and other problems inherent in reform. For the moment, let's focus on the fact that there are a number of political realities to consider:

- There is no political imperative to reach a long-term outcome because the crisis has not yet arrived, the public has not been educated or energized.

- The entire political process and system of governance is resistant to solving long-term problems – anything with an anticipated crisis point more than six months in the future.

- The problem of Social Security insolvency impacts each generation differently, with the likely outcome of pitting one generation against another.

- There are no silver bullets.

- Social Security and issues related to it are highly exploitable. They can be framed in ways that trigger emotions and ignite opposition.

- The issue's complexities make consensus difficult.

The fourth element is very much related to the third. It entails identifying the various segments of society who are affected by the Social Security System – natural enemies as well as potential friends – and the potential impact changes in the status quo would have on them.

Who stands to feel the effects of a systemic overhaul? Everyone in America, obviously. But that doesn't answer the question. There are influential interest groups, such as AARP, that would have a powerful stake in any action that might be taken.But there are so many others, ranging from labor unions to multi-national corporations – and most important of all, those citizens who will be eligible for Social Security benefits over the next two decades, younger generations who may be asked to pay for those benefits and those concerned about the financial security of their parents or grandparents.

By identifying vested interests we are identifying all the pieces of the puzzle before setting out to assemble them: spreading those pieces out on the table so we can see where each piece fits, what contribution it will make to the big picture. It may enable us to see a problem or solution not otherwise visible. It may even enable us to transform an adversary into an ally as options are considered, discarded or accepted.

For some of these constituencies, the potential change is personal. Others will be more objective. Some reactions will be emotional and others will be analytical. It is essential that we recognize distinct perspectives.

The fifth element involves fashioning a policy process capable of accommodating change. Clearly, the normal legislative, procedural and political processes will not produce the desired result. Serious innovation will be required to force action within a strict timetable.There are three major characteristics of this effort that make it extraordinary:

- It must be bicameral, involving both houses of Congress concurrently.

- It is must be bipartisan, involving both political parties working together.

- It must involve two branches of government – the executive and the legislative – working concurrently on the same problem.

Normally, one house of Congress will wait for the other to act, or they will act separately but seldom together. By the same token, the two parties in the two chambers will normally not work together on one solution. In addition, it is normal for the Congress to act legislatively by passing a bill and for the Administration to react by signing or vetoing it.

We propose homogenizing the process and the personalities. This way, no one party to the process can stray too far from the center without bringing the entire enterprise down.

This may, for example, require abbreviated committee consideration in both chambers of the Congress. There are at least six House and Senate committees and twice that number of subcommittees with some element of jurisdiction over the Social Security program – for each of them to act independently on a major reform would take years. This effort may require heavy involvement by committee chairmen willing to fast track their procedures and by Leadership of both parties committed to producing results.

The sixth element is bipartisan cooperation that makes the initiative impervious to attack from either party's hierarchy, even if it cannot be protected from ideological attack from their base constituencies. Obviously, freedom of speech cannot be denied, but an attempt can be made to reach out to partisan leaders – the Republican and Democratic national committees and their Congressional counterparts– to endorse the process if not the outcome, buying time for the task force to do its work.

Bipartisan leadership is essential in the creation and funding of the core group. If this endeavor is founded and funded by statute, it is much more likely to succeed. That cannot be accomplished without the commitment of each party's leadership.

This is not an original idea – the last major reform of Social Security, the Greenspan Commission of 1981-1983, followed this model and produced a package of reforms that received expedited Congressional action.

The seventh element is a communications and public relations strategy that accomplishes four goals:

- Builds awareness and urgency for reforming the current Social Security program and defines the consequences of failure.

- Integrates the mainstream media in the process by keeping them fully informed from the outset and providing news leads that demonstrate the need for change, emphasizing the openness of the process and the caliber of the people leading the change. This is critical to building momentum.

- Provides for the mobilization of active grassroots support throughout the process, so that legislative proposals, when introduced, have support.

- Creates a brand – a name and image for a nationwide campaign, just like a new model car. One that persuades everyone with a vested interest in the existing system that it is in their best interest to support the changes that are being proposed. Creating this kind of packaging also emboldens the leaders of change, giving them a cause they can explain and sell.

It may sound Madison Ave. to say so, but the reality is that while we are not creating and selling a product, we are marketing a bold concept to a new generation – we are unveiling "New and Improved Retirement Security!" And to succeed, the reform we want the American public to buy into needs to be encapsulated in a brand that's as comfortable and familiar as their favorite laundry detergent or breakfast cereal.

The eighth element is creating a timetable for action. Such a timetable has to take into consideration the influence of electoral cycles, subsidiary activities such as normal budget and appropriation processes that will have an impact on consideration and solutions, and the lengthy process of building support among allies and countering opposing arguments. As discussed earlier, we are attempting to bring together a bicameral, bipartisan legislative-executive strategy of unique proportion. Making it work will require discipline and timing.

The timetable is made more complex by the fact that each step is dependent upon successful completion of the previous steps. Creating a draft solution, for instance, cannot be done until after the public and the Congress accept the urgency to change. So the time required accomplishing some steps might be impossible to predict since others must be completed before they can begin.

The ninth element is budgeting. This project will require a substantial financial commitment, much of it federal funds that will need to be made available through the appropriations process.

From a financial and ethical perspective, not to mention the credibility of the effort, Congress should give statutory authorization to this task force by making it an official commission. Legislation to that effect should be drafted immediately and put on a fast track for consideration as soon as the members of the task force are ready to be announced.

As your leadership team considers the budget, it should provide for very strict and transparent accounting procedures and wherever possible the assignment of projects, particularly in research, that can be accomplished by existing public agencies and staff. Every effort must be made to avoid duplicating what already has been done – it is critical, for instance, that funds not be wasted by repeating research that has produced data that's already sitting on a shelf somewhere waiting to be put to good use.

There's a good chance that sources outside government will be eager to become involved and even offer to foot the bill for some aspects of the overall effort, but as you know, we cannot co-mingle public and private money in a process that is authorized and funded by the Congress. This makes staffing a doubly important consideration.

Clearly, this reform initiative cannot be achieved without substantial staffing and support. It should be our objective to staff the new Commission with highly trained professionals, drawing on congressional staff from committee and Members' personal staff. However, it would seem prudent as well to bring in experts, who could take leaves of absence from corporations, foundations and interest groups, to supplant the expertise on the Hill.

Those Members of the Congress who are part of the initial task force must select a member of their staff who can represent their views, speak on their behalf and in some cases, make decisions in their absence as we move forward. We cannot afford to be delayed in this process because a member of the core group is distracted for days or weeks by other priorities. Staff representatives will act as *agents* whose main responsibility will be shepherding the proposal to victory through the authority or empowerment afforded them. Members should choose these agents with the following criteria in mind:

- Willingness to work within the hierarchical structure you recommend and the team members adopt.

- Dedication to this reform initiative, with substantial time and resources also dedicated for this purpose.

- The experience, expertise and senior status necessary to move the process forward.

Additional staff will be necessary to carry out the mission, but it is critical that the senior staff structure described above be put in place as soon as possible.

A Bad Precedent

The following is a brief look at the most recent attempt at major policy change of the magnitude we are contemplating and some of the lessons learned.

The Clinton health care plan of 1993 is the most recent effort on the scale of the one we are about to undertake. The fact that President Clinton took office only a year before the plan was proposed suggests how Wilbur Mills would have rated its chances for success. As you'll recall, Mills was Chairman of the House Ways and Means Committee when he observed that it takes two years to get major legislation passed – the first to create a nationwide sense of urgency and the second to persuade colleagues in the Congress to adopt the solution being proposed.

We may need to tack on at least a year at the front end to accommodate research and development. We might as well accept the fact that this is going to require lot of attention for a very long while.

The Clinton health care debacle provides us with a number of other valuable lessons as well:

- At the time, Clinton appointed a health care task force, America was emerging from a recession and polls indicated that 42 percent of the nation favored an overhaul of the system. By the time the Clinton health care plan was unveiled, the nation was on its way to economic recovery and the demand for an overhaul had dropped into the teens.

Lesson: Timing is everything. Public relations efforts must build to a crescendo at the point when the plan we are developing goes to the Congress for a vote.

- The Clinton task force conducted its activities behind closed doors, which aroused suspicions and led to embarrassing litigation.

  Lesson: Maintain transparency. Let the media in. Let the public in, as well. The topic is so complex and potentially stultifying that the efforts of the task force are unlikely to draw sustained attention – and any attention they do attract should be easy to turn to our advantage.

- The task force presented a thousand-page, highly detailed bill to the Congress before it even succeeded in selling it to those who would have to get it through the committee process.

  Lesson: Break an effort of this magnitude into a package of digestible principles. Encourage bipartisan participation in the process. Invite Members, as well as those who will be affected, to take ownership. Charge them with the task of crafting and fine-tuning the various elements in the package. Give them an opportunity to buy into the solutions that are being proposed.

- The Clinton effort suffered from internecine and partisan attacks that had little to do with the plan but a great deal to do with the way the Clintons were conducting their efforts.

  Lesson: Share the responsibility and share the credit. From the outset, involve leadership from both parties and both chambers of the Congress and invite participation by independents, libertarians and every other stripe. Invite participation as well by government experts who oversee the Social Security system, as well as other agencies that interact with it or have even a remote interest in how it functions.

- Whether deservedly or not, the Clinton task force was perceived as Beltway insiders and intellectuals telling the rest of America what to do. This perception was aggravated by advertising, such as the famous *Harry and Louise* ads, paid for by health care industry insiders who might not have been happy with the status quo but were unconvinced that changes to it would be in the best interest of their shareholders.

  Lesson: Emphasize the roots of those named to the task force.

And don't limit the development process to research done for or by the task force. Invite everyone in America to participate, involve everyone in the process – especially those with deep pockets, a vested interest and access to organizations capable of producing campaigns that could sink the plan before it even leaves the dock. The task force must represent all interested constituencies.

The Challenge

No matter how pure our motives might be, a sizable portion of the public is going to be suspicious of any effort to reform the Social Security system if that effort is perceived to originate in Washington, D.C. Allegations of politics as usual and every other contemptuous intent that cynics can come up with will smother the initiative. Social Security reform must be seen as a campaign by the people to confront a national crisis head-on.

An addendum will be provided separately that will provide a detailed definition of the problem. The executive summary, if there were one, would highlight these realities:

- The Social Security Trust Fund will not be able to meet the needs of Social Security recipients – your banker would say the system will be bankrupt – in the year 2042. It is not actuarially sound and cannot be sustained any longer.

- Right now, excess Social Security revenues supplement other federal spending. In a year or two, the opposite will be true – other federal revenues will increasingly be needed to pay Social Security benefits. This will necessitate serious reductions in all other federal spending – creating a complex domino effect that has received little public attention.

- The population and economic demographics that bring actuaries to the conclusion that the system will be bankrupt in 2042 paint a dangerous picture – too many retirees supported by too few workers compounded by the reality of a huge Baby Boom population that will live far longer than previous generations.

- The payroll tax – the mechanism for financing current and projected Social Security benefits – is inadequate. Even if the tax were dramatically increased – which would be politically and economically untenable – the system could not be adequately financed.

- The current system of employer-based retirement programs is threatening to crumble under the weight of retiring Baby Boomers and its weakened state will exacerbate the Social Security system's problems.

- The retirement insecurity problem is not national, but global. While some nations such as Sweden and Chile have solved problems unique to them, most others face the same crisis as the United States. In sociological terms, the developed nations – particularly those in Europe – are aging faster than their less-developed neighbors.

- And the impending shortage of retirement benefits isn't even the most pressing concern – far more immediate are the needs of the Medicare program, which will go bankrupt within the next decade. Fixing Social Security is, as Churchill said, only the end of the beginning.

Social Security is one of the biggest problems facing this nation. It is the confluence of good intentions and unintended consequences, political timidity and political expediency.

There will be many obstacles to overcome in scaling this mountain. The biggest will be convincing the American people how high the peak actually is, that it must be climbed and conquering it will require them to overcome fear and doubt, shoulder some measure of sacrifice, and in the process, become activists and not just observers.

Adapting to Change

One of the certainties facing anyone contemplating change is resistance. The growing body of research on innovation and change suggests:

- Resistance to change is natural. We all like to think we favor change, but usually balk when confronted with its realities, especially when we realize at the outset that it's unlikely to meet our expectations.

- Resistance must be dealt with overtly, up front, without surprises.

- Resistance must be framed as a condition that defies the higher purpose and higher values reflected in the reform effort. In other words, maintaining the status quo must be seen as less desirable than the risks of change.

- Resistance is unlikely to prevail if the leaders of change remain resolute. If the chain of unity among the leaders is broken, so too will be the will of the people to follow.

One of the most serious studies on how Americans go about adopting change is described in the book *Coming to Public Judgment: Making Democracy Work in a Complex World* by Daniel Yankelovich. He defines the process of overcoming resistance with these descriptive terms:

- Awareness
- Urgency
- Alternatives
- Getting Beyond Simple Solutions
- Weighing the Pros and Cons
- Intellectual Acceptance
- Institutionalization

Previous attempts at Social Security reform have ignored the public's need to understand and accept the *why* before being presented with the *what* and the *how*. Opinion polls have told would-be reformers that the American people understand that Social Security is in financial trouble. What the reformers didn't take into account was that these same polls revealed the public had widely varying opinions on the severity of the problem, its cause, its urgency and the need to fix it. Nor did the polls reveal what levels of reform the public would tolerate.

We need to start at the beginning. We need to establish a common understanding of the need for reform and the level of reform that will be necessary. And we need to instill a sense of urgency that does not exist. Once the public accepts the severity and the urgency of the problem – and only then – will we be able to open their eyes to alternatives.

There are ample alternatives out there: higher taxes, fewer benefits, greater private-sector involvement, extending the retirement age, limiting some benefits or eliminating them altogether to some higher income recipients.

Such alternatives need to be aired so we can move beyond rhetoric and breakdown the resistance to change that occurs when people realize that no remedy will be painless. The public must know that retirement security in the 21st Century will require changes in the behavior and thinking of all of us. If they don't reach that realization after looking over the alternatives, they will be attracted by pie-in-the-sky promises made by those polarizing cynics who use crises of this nature for personal gain. They'll resort to wishful thinking rather than productive solutions or, perhaps more dangerously, they'll simply go into denial.

Once all the unworkable alternatives are swept from the table and only the serious contenders remain, we must encourage Americans to weigh the potential solutions from the perspective of their own values and circumstances. For example, the elderly may be asked to weigh a benefit cut that they do not believe they can sustain. The young may be asked to assume a heavier tax burden that they do not feel they deserve. Corporations may be asked to manage programs that detract from their global competitiveness. Each participant in the system has a perspective that must be considered.

If we are successful, the public will coalesce around a solution that does the least amount of harm and has the highest probability of success. It is this process that observers like Yankelovich refer to as *intellectual acceptance*, which leads to the successful enactment of a law dealing with the problem followed by the institutionalization of the solution.

The term *change* is tossed about in political campaigns like balloons at a convention. But as history shows, in our system of diffused national power, real change is never easy. It demands consensus building. It requires perseverance. And it always necessitates great leadership.

Let me know if you would like me to continue working on this project or go back to getting that highway in our district named for your recently deceased predecessor.

This hypothetical memorandum provides a glimpse into the complexity of challenges you're likely to help grapple with during your stay on Capitol Hill. Keep in mind the enormity of the impact that even seemingly innocuous contributions can have. Take pride in everything you do, no matter how insignificant it might appear to be.

Remember that you are a citizen of Capitol Hill, a small city with just two employers – the House and the Senate – which coexist and cooperate to conduct the nation's business. The 40,000 or so combined staff members working for Congress represent a cross-section of America. They come from every state, every race, every religion and every socio-economic background. They're mostly young people – ambitious, patriotic, intelligent, driven. They hold political views every bit as diverse as their bosses', but there is a common bond that generally fosters mutual respect and a kind of pride that comes with public service. Regardless of what opinion polls may say about attitudes toward the Congress, you'll rarely see a Hill employee bashful about saying where he or she works.

Working on Capitol Hill is one of those rare experiences that will never be forgotten and will make each employee better at whatever else they decide to do.

INTRODUCTION

Learn the rules and understand the precedents and procedures of the House. The congressman who knows how the House operates will soon be recognized for his parliamentary skills - and his prestige will rise among his colleagues, no matter what his party.

House Speaker John W. McCormack (1962-1971) of Massachusetts,
giving advice to new House Members

I. HOUSE IS CALLED TO ORDER BY THE SPEAKER

Time of Meeting:

The daily hour of meeting is set by a House Resolution adopted on the first day of each session. On January 4, 2007, the House adopted H. Res. 10, which established the following meeting times until May 14, 2007:

2:00 p.m. on Monday;

12:00 p.m. on Tuesday; and,

10:00 a.m. on all other days of the week.

Beginning May 14, 2007 until the end of the first session:

Noon on Monday;

10:00 a.m. on Tuesday, Wednesday and Thursday; and

9:00 a.m. on all other days of the week.

The hour of meeting can be changed by order of the House at any time, usually by unanimous consent after consultation between both party leaderships.

A Member's office is notified of any time changes by a Whip call. If in doubt, a Member's Office should check with the Republican Cloakroom at 225-7350 or the Democratic Cloakroom at 225-7330.

Three-Day Adjournment Limit:

Article I, section 5 of the U.S. Constitution prevents either House from adjourning for more than three days (not including Sundays) unless the other House concurs. Such adjournment authority for more than three days is accomplished through the adoption by both Houses of a concurrent resolution, which does not require the signature of the President.

In the case of an emergency in which the House may be under immediate danger, the Speaker may declare an emergency recess under clause 12 of Rule I. If during a recess or adjournment of not more than three days the Speaker is notified by the Sergeant-at-Arms of an imminent danger to the place of reconvening, the Speaker may postpone the time for reconvening the House. The Speaker may also reconvene the House under those circumstances before the time previously appointed to declare the House in recess again. These circumstances require the Speaker to notify Members accordingly. At the outset of the 110th Congress, the House agreed to H. Con. Res. 1, which permits the Speaker and the Majority Leader of the Senate to assemble at a place outside the District of Columbia whenever, in their opinion, the public interest shall warrant it (the Senate has yet to take action on H. Con. Res. 1).

Furthermore, at the beginning of the 109th Congress, the House adopted a rule to deal with the consequences of a terrorist attack or other catastrophe that incapacitates a large number of Members. This rule (clause 5(c) of rule XX) allows the House to act if a roll call vote is required following a catastrophe and a quorum cannot be achieved. Quorum is the majority of the whole number of the House and is calculated from those Members who are chose, sworn and living. Thus, if all Members of the House are alive, quorum is the majority of 435, or 218 Members. Incapacitated Members, though unable to vote, are nonetheless counted for purposes of quorum. If more than a majority of the House is incapacitated, the House would be unable to take a roll call vote because of a lack of quorum. The rule change allows for the House to conduct business with less than a majority of a fully constituted House – but only in times of catastrophe and subject to a number of procedural protections. This smaller number is called the provisional quorum. Operating with a provisional quorum lasts only until enough Members are revived for a regular quorum. Any legislation considered with a provisional quorum would be subject to the bicameral and presentment to the President requirements, and any votes adopted could be ratified or repudiated at a later time by a fully constituted House.

Legislative Schedule:

The scheduling of legislation for House Floor action is the prerogative of the majority leadership. However, the following table is useful in determining the time it takes to prepare legislation for Floor consideration:

Tuesday Committee orders a bill reported; views requested
Wednesday Day #1 for filing views.
Thursday Day #2 for filing views.
Friday Committee files report. (May be Day #1 of report availability if report is filed the day before.)
Monday Day #1 that report is available to the House.
Tuesday Day #2 that report is available to the House.
Wednesday Day #3 that report is available to the House. Floor consideration is possible.
Thursday Rules Committee meets to grant rule.
Friday Rule and bill may be considered on House Floor.

Usually on the last legislative day of the week, a representative of the minority leadership seeks unanimous consent to speak out of order for one-minute to address the House for the purpose of asking the Majority Leader about the legislative program for the upcoming week. Following the announcement, the Whip Offices will send Members "Whip Notices" for the next week listing the specific bills to be considered including how each bill will receive Floor consideration (for example, suspension of the rules, a rule from the Rules Committee, unanimous consent, etc.). Each office also receives copies of the legislation scheduled for Floor consideration (if available) in a "Whip Packet," which is delivered by the House Page Service. Offices will receive publications from the Republican Conference or the Democratic Caucus with

215

summaries of the upcoming legislation. Finally, if the bill is to be considered under a rule from the Rules Committee, information about the amendment process, debate time, etc is available on the Rules Committee website at www. house.gov/rules.

Even though the Majority Leadership announces a program for the coming week, it is possible for the program to change. Therefore, it is to a Member's benefit to follow any updates. The Republican Cloakroom provides recorded information for the week's program at 225-2020 and 225-7430 for the Floor program for that specific day. The Democratic Cloakroom provides recorded information for the week's program at 225-1600 and 225-7400 for the Floor program for that specific day.

In addition to the announced schedule of major bills, legislative matters may be called up for consideration by "unanimous consent." In keeping with the Speaker's announced policy, unanimous consent requests of that type must be cleared by the majority and minority leaderships as well as the bipartisan leadership of the committee(s) of jurisdiction.

Following clearance, these matters may come up with little notice except to the Members managing the request (i.e., the Chairman and Ranking Minority Member of the committee(s) of jurisdiction). If Members have a specific interest in something that might come up by unanimous consent, they should contact the appropriate committee and leadership representatives as early as possible. A Member might also ask the Floor staff to be on the lookout for the matter of interest.

In addition to the normal order of business as presented here, there are several "special legislative days." Bills may be brought up under "suspension of the rules" on Mondays, Tuesdays, and Wednesdays of each week, although this process is separate and apart from the calendar system. There is no "suspension calendar." Suspension of the rules will be discussed in detail later in Section VIII of this manual. Private Bills may be considered on the 1st and 3rd Tuesdays of each month.

Powers of the Speaker:

The Speaker traditionally opens the session each day, but may designate a "Speaker pro tempore," who is a Member of the majority party, to serve in this capacity for up to three legislative days. The Speaker or Speaker pro tempore may preside through one-minute speeches and other House business (such as debate on special rules) until the House resolves itself into the Committee of the Whole House on the State of the Union, at which time the Speaker appoints a majority Member to preside as the Chairman of the Committee of the Whole. The Speaker or Speaker pro tempore returns to the Chair when the Committee of the Whole rises to come back into the Whole House

NOTE: House Rule I details the numerous duties of the Speaker, many of which directly affect Members. It is also important to understand the Speaker's power of recognition under clause 2 of Rule XVII. In most cases, it is the Chair's prerogative to recognize a Member. The power of recognition cannot be appealed.

<u>Morning Hour:</u>
By agreement of both the majority and minority leadership, the House has instituted a "Morning Hour" period for special order speeches on Monday and Tuesday of each week. On those days prior to May 16 of each session, the House may convene ninety minutes earlier than normal for Morning Hour special order speeches.

On those Tuesdays after May 16 of each session, the House may convene 60 minutes earlier than normal for Morning Hour.

Morning Hour special order speeches are equally divided and rotated between majority and minority party Members. Members designated by the leaders may speak for up to five minutes on any subject of their choice (except for the Majority and Minority Leaders and Minority Whip, who may speak for longer blocks of time). If a Member wishes to participate, he or she must sign up for the time in their respective Cloakroom.

II. PRAYER IS OFFERED BY THE CHAPLAIN

The House Chaplain is the Reverend Daniel Coughlin. Guest Chaplains are permitted in the Chamber and each Member may consider inviting a clergyman from his or her district to offer the daily prayer. Members should contact Father Coughlin for further information at 225-2509.

III. APPROVAL OF THE JOURNAL

Article I, section 5 of the U.S. Constitution requires that the House keep a Journal of its proceedings, which is a summary of the day's actions. The Speaker is responsible for examining and approving the Journal of the previous day. The Speaker announces approval to the House immediately after the prayer is offered by the Chaplain. Following the announcement of approval by the Speaker, any Member may demand a vote on the question of the Speaker's approval. However, the Speaker has the authority to postpone a vote on agreeing to the Speaker's approval of the Journal until a later time on the same legislative day.

NOTE: The Journal is not the *Congressional Record*.

IV. VOTING BY ELECTRONIC DEVICE

When the Speaker or the Chair announces that the yeas and nays are ordered and a recorded vote is ordered or announces that a quorum is not present and the yeas and nays are automatic, the vote is taken by electronic device. A Member casts a vote by electronic device by inserting a voting card into the nearest voting station and pressing the appropriate button: "yea," "nay" or "present." It is advised that Members go to another voting station and reinsert their voting card until the light comes on and verifies the vote cast at the first station. Members should also visually check the voting board to make sure that the light next to their name reflects their intended vote.

Members that do not have their voting card should go to the table in the Well and obtain an appropriate voting card from the boxes placed there (green card for yea, red card for nay, orange card for present). The Member should sign the card and give it to the Tally Clerk who will be standing on the first level of the rostrum. The Clerk will then register the vote into the computer, but the Member should visually check the board to make sure the vote is recorded correctly.

Members deciding to change their vote may do so by reinserting their card into a voting station and pressing the appropriate button during the first ten minutes of a fifteen-minute vote, or at any time during a five-minute vote. However, during the last five minutes of a fifteen-minute vote, a change in a Member's vote can only be made by going to the Well, taking a card from the table, signing it, and handing it to the Tally Clerk on the rostrum. The Clerk then registers the change and a statement will appear in the *Congressional Record* indicating that the Member changed his or her vote. Members using this procedure to change their vote should be sure to check the board to see that it reflects the change. Also, Members may change their vote during a five-minute vote by machine and no statement about the change will appear in the *Congressional Record* unless it comes after the voting stations are closed and before the result of the vote is announced.

NOTE: Once the record vote ends (by the Chair announcing the result), and the motion to reconsider is laid on the table, the vote is final — no further voting or changing is permitted. However, if a Member has missed the vote they may submit a statement declaring how they would have voted had they been present. Such an explanatory statement containing the Member's original signature will be inserted in the *Congressional Record* at the point immediately after the vote. A suggested script for such an explanatory statement on missed or mistaken votes may be obtained from the Floor staff. It is important to remember that this statement does not affect whether or how the Member is recorded on the vote.

Clause 2 of Rule III specifically prohibits Members from allowing another person to cast their vote and from casting the vote of another Member. This unethical action was banned at the beginning of the 97th Congress.

The allotted time for a quorum call or recorded vote under the rules of the House is not less than fifteen minutes (clause 2 of Rule XX). It is the prerogative of the Speaker or presiding officer to allow additional time beyond the fifteen minutes. Often one will hear Members calling "regular order" when an electronic vote extends beyond fifteen minutes under the mistaken impression that recorded votes are limited to fifteen minutes — they are not limited. The regular order is to allow more time on recorded votes if the Chair desires. In the 110th Congress, clause 2 of Rule XX was amended to prohibit a vote from being held open for the sole purpose of reversing the outcome of the vote. Under the new rule it is Chair's responsibility to differentiate between activity toward the establishment of an outcome on the one hand, and activity that might have as its purpose the reversal of an already-established outcome, on the other.

It has been the custom of the House since the 104th Congress to attempt to "limit" these fifteen-minute votes to seventeen minutes. The Chair should allow all Members who are on the Floor before the final announcement to be recorded, but is not obliged to hold the vote open to accommodate requests through the Cloakrooms for Members "on their way" to the House Floor.

V. PLEDGE OF ALLEGIANCE TO THE FLAG

After approval of the Journal, the Speaker recognizes a designated Member to lead the House in the Pledge of Allegiance to the American flag. The

Member designated alternates between the majority and minority party on a daily basis. The Member is usually informed in advance if he or she is the designated Member.

I pledge Allegiance to the flag of the
United States of America and to the
Republic for which it stands, one nation
Under God, indivisible, with Liberty and
Justice for all.

VI. ONE-MINUTE SPEECHES

These short speeches (300 words) may be made by Members before legislative business each day. If the speech given at the beginning of the day is longer than 300 words or includes extraneous materials, it will appear in the Extension of Remarks section of the *Congressional Record*. Any Member may seek recognition to give a speech on a subject of his or her choice not exceeding one minute in duration. One-minute speeches are often coordinated by the majority and minority leaderships to focus on particular topics, but the speeches are not limited to such topics. Participants in these coordinated efforts usually receive priority seating and recognition.

The one-minute speech period is granted at the discretion of the Speaker, as are the number of such speeches. Some days one-minute speeches may be limited to ten or fifteen speeches per side. On other days, they may be unlimited. On occasion, this period is postponed until the end of the day if the business of the House is heavy and time is short. In this case, a Member may address the House for one minute at the end of legislative business for the day.

To give a one-minute speech, a Member should go to the front row of seats on their party's side of the Floor and sit down. The Speaker will recognize Members in turn, alternating between the majority and minority sides. At the appropriate point, the member should stand to seek recognition and address the Chair by saying: "Mr. Speaker, I ask unanimous consent to address the House for one minute and to revise and extend my remarks."

The Speaker will respond by saying: "Without objection, so ordered." The

Member may then proceed to the podium in the Well to give the speech. The Chair will tell the Member when the one minute has expired at which time the Member may finish the sentence, but no more.

NOTE: Members are strongly encouraged to read House Rule XVII, Decorum and Debate (especially clause 1), as well as section XVII of the Jefferson's Manual, Order and Debate. See also Conduct During Debate under Part XI of this manual, "General Debate in the Committee of the Whole."

It is not proper at any time for a Member to refer to the television audience. Rule XVII states that a Member must always address the Chair and only the Chair.

Furthermore, clause 7 of Rule XVII states specifically that Members may not introduce or otherwise make reference to people in the Visitors or Press Gallery.

It is acceptable to refer to actions taken by the Senate. A new House rule adopted at the beginning of the 109th Congress allows for references on the House Floor to the Senate or its Members. However, these remarks must be limited to the question under debate and may not include personalities. (See clause 1 of Rule XVII).

Not only is it inappropriate to address the President of the United States directly (Members must always address the Chair), but it is also improper to refer to the President in a personally offensive manner.

NOTE: A Member does not actually have to deliver a one-minute speech. He or she can simply ask unanimous consent that it be placed in the *Congressional Record* and yield back his or her time. The speech will be inserted at that point, but it will appear in different type to indicate that it was not delivered in person. Also, if extraneous materials are inserted with a one-minute speech, the entire speech will appear at the end of the *Congressional Record* just prior to special order speeches.

VII. UNANIMOUS CONSENT REQUESTS

The House does much of its non-controversial work by "unanimous consent" procedure, whereby a Member stands up and asks that something be done by or permitted by unanimous consent and no other Member objects to the request. These requests may involve debate time (similar to the language of a special rule) in order to consider a measure or conference report, or waive points of order against a measure. Before the Chair will recognize a Member for a unanimous consent request, it must be cleared by both the majority and minority leadership and relevant committee leadership.

In most cases, the Chair, hearing no objection, replies: "Without objection, so ordered."

If a Member is unfamiliar with the request or its motives, the best way to find out what is behind the request is to "reserve the right to object." This gives the Member the Floor and the opportunity to inquire about the request.

If the discussion during the "reservation of the right to object" proceeds for too long, any Member can demand "the regular order," which means that the Member reserving the right to object should stop talking and either object or withdraw the reservation. The Member reserving the right to object may yield to another Member on the subject of the objection.

VIII. SUSPENSION OF THE RULES

Under clause 1 of Rule XV, it is in order on Monday, Tuesday, and Wednesday of each week, and during the last six days of a session, for the Speaker to entertain motions to suspend the rules and pass legislation.

Bills brought up under suspension of the rules are spoken of as "suspensions" in Floor terminology. There is no suspension calendar. The purpose of considering bills under suspension is to dispose of non-controversial measures expeditiously. Consideration of legislation under suspension of the rules on other days of the week is possible by unanimous consent or a special rule.

A motion to suspend the rules requires a vote of two-thirds of the Members present and voting. No amendments are in order unless submitted with the bill by its manager as part of the motion to suspend the rules.

Debate on a bill brought up under suspension of the rules is limited to forty minutes, twenty minutes controlled by a Member who supports the bill and twenty minutes controlled by a Member in opposition, a division that does not always follow party lines. It is typical for the chairman of the committee of jurisdiction to manage the time. For control of the opposition time, priority is given to a minority Member of the committee that has jurisdiction over the bill. Often the twenty minutes "in opposition" is controlled by the Ranking Minority Member of the committee or subcommittee who may not be opposed to the measure because no one rises in opposition. However, he or she may be challenged for control of the opposition time by another Member who qualifies as being opposed to the measure.

The majority leadership usually schedules several bills under suspension of the rules on the same day and the Chair often exercises its authority under clause 8 of Rule XX to announce beforehand that recorded votes on passage of each suspension, if ordered, will be postponed until the debate is concluded on all such suspensions (or up to two legislative days).

At the conclusion of debate, the postponed votes may be "clustered" and put before the House. If several votes have been ordered and the Chair has announced that the time for voting will be reduced, the first vote in the series will consume not less than fifteen minutes and all subsequent record votes will take not less than five minutes each. It is important for Members to be mindful of when a five-minute vote is expected, so that it will not be missed.

In the event of a series of two or more votes in which any votes after the first one will be reduced to not less than five minutes, the Member will be summoned to the Floor by two bells followed by five bells.

IX. SPECIAL RULES FOR MAJOR BILLS

Each major piece of legislation, except privileged matters (such as appropriations bills, budget resolutions and conference reports) not in violation of any rule of the House, normally needs a "special rule" to be adopted before the measure can be considered. A special rule, also known as an "order of business resolution," is a House resolution that sets the terms for debate and amendment. A special rule is highly important because it controls what the House can and cannot do regarding the bill itself. Special rules are reported to the House by the Rules Committee, acting as an arm of the majority leadership. They require adoption by the full House by a simple majority vote in order to go into effect. Bills considered under suspension of the rules or on other special procedural days do not require a special rule in order to be considered on the House Floor.

Special rules should not be confused with the established procedures of the House. Generally speaking, special rules provide exceptions to, or departures from, the established procedures of the House. Those procedures are found in the Constitution of the United States, applicable provisions of Jefferson's Manual, rules of the House adopted on the opening day of each Congress, provisions of law and resolutions having the force of rules of the House, and established precedents by Speakers and other presiding officers of the House and Committee of the Whole.

Among the various types of special rules considered in the House, the most common are:

Open rules, which permit general debate for a certain period of time (one, two or three hours or more depending on the importance of the legislation and the legislative schedule) and allow any Member to offer an amendment that complies with the established procedures of the House under the five-minute rule.

Modified open rules, which permit general debate and allow any Member to offer a germane amendment under the five-minute rule subject only to a requirement that the amendment(s) be pre-printed in the *Congressional Record*. Modified open rules may also allow for any germane to be offered without pre-printing in the *Congressional Record*, but the rule may place an overall time cap on consideration of the bill for amendment.

Structured rules, which permit general debate for a certain period of time, but limit the amendments that may be offered to only those designated in the special rule or the Rules Committee report to accompany the special rule, or preclude amendments to a particular portion of a bill, even though the rest of the bill may be completely open to amendment.

Closed rules, which permit debate for a certain period of time, but do not allow amendments to be offered to the bill.

NOTE: To encourage Members to pre-print their amendments in the *Congressional Record* in advance of their consideration, the Rules Committee routinely includes a provision in open rules allowing the Chair to give priority in recognition to such Members. This common provision encouraging pre-printing should not be confused with the more restrictive provision in modified open rules requiring the pre-printing of amendments.

One of the most important features of a special rule is what it designates as the base text for purposes of amendment. This often may be the text of the committee reported amendment in the nature of a substitute, an amendment in the nature of a substitute as modified by another amendment or a completely new text printed in the *Congressional Record*, or in the report of the Committee on Rules accompanying the rule, or consisting of the text of another introduced bill, or consisting of the text of a Committee Print of the

Committee on Rules.

When a special rule waives points of order, it means that some standing rule or other established procedure of the House (such as germaneness or a provision of the Congressional Budget Act) is being set aside to permit the bill to be called up for consideration, or to permit certain amendments to be offered to the bill in question. Without such waivers, a point of order would lie against consideration of the bill or amendment and any Member could make that point of order, thereby preventing consideration of the bill or amendment.

Before a special rule is considered by the House, it is the subject of a hearing by the Rules Committee during which Members testify as to the type of rule and amendments they support. Members are usually notified by the Committee, in the form of a "Dear Colleague" letter and a Floor announcement by the Rules Committee Chairman, in advance of a meeting if a rule structuring the amendment process is anticipated. After a hearing is held, the Rules Committee will consider a motion to grant a special rule, and will then vote to report the rule to the House. The rule and accompanying report are usually filed on the same day.

A special rule may not be considered on the same day it is reported, except by a two-thirds vote of the House (unless it is within the last three days of the session). This prohibition (clause 6(a) of Rule XIII) is sometimes waived by the adoption of another special rule reported by the Rules Committee.

The process for considering a rule in the House is as follows:

- The rule is called up for consideration in the House by a majority Member (manager) of the Rules Committee.

- One hour of debate is permitted and the majority manager customarily yields one half of the time to the minority manager for the purposes of debate only.

- Amendments to special rules are very rare. Special rules can be altered by unanimous consent or the manager may offer an amendment. It is also possible but unlikely that the majority manager will yield for the purpose of amendment, or that the previous question will be defeated (see subsection E).

- The previous question is moved and put to the House by the Chair for a vote.

225

- Once the previous question is ordered, the House then votes on the rule. Upon adoption of the rule, the House may proceed to consideration of the legislation.

The previous question is a motion made in order under clause 1 of Rule XIX and is the major parliamentary device in the House used for closing debate and preventing further amendment. The effect of adopting the previous question is to bring the resolution to an immediate, final vote. The motion is most often made at the conclusion of debate on a rule, motion or legislation considered in the House prior to final passage. A Member might think about ordering the previous question in terms of answering the question: Is the House ready to vote on the rule, bill or amendment before it?

NOTE: The previous question is not in order under a motion to suspend the rules.

In order to amend a special rule (other than by using those procedures previously mentioned), the House must vote against ordering the previous question. If the previous question is defeated, the Speaker then recognizes the Member who led the opposition to the previous question (usually a Member of the minority party) to control an additional hour of debate during which a germane amendment may be offered to the rule. The Member controlling the Floor then moves the previous question on the amendment and the rule. If the previous question is ordered, the next vote occurs on the opposition's amendment followed by a vote on the rule as amended.

Adoption of the rule occurs after the previous question is agreed to. When the previous question is not a subject of controversy, it is simply disposed of "without objection." Next, the question of adopting the rule is put to the House, and the rule is either adopted or defeated. The underlying bill is not prejudiced for future consideration if the rule providing for its consideration is defeated. The Rules Committee can report another rule providing for consideration of that initial underlying bill.

X. RESOLVING INTO THE COMMITTEE OF THE WHOLE

The Committee of the Whole is a parliamentary device, derived from the practice of the English House of Commons, used to expedite the work of the House during the debate and amendment process. It involves several less formal arrangements to conduct business, including a lesser number of Members required for a quorum (100 as compared to 218 in the full House). It

226

also has a different procedure required to obtain a recorded vote (twenty-five Members standing in support as compared to the requirement of one-fifth of those present standing or a lack of a quorum in the full House). Certain motions allowed in the House are prohibited in the Committee of the Whole, such as motions for the previous question, to adjourn, to reconsider a vote, or to refer or recommit.

The Speaker does not preside in the Committee of the Whole, but appoints a Member of the majority party to preside with the full authority to keep order, rule on questions, recognize Members, and order votes. The Member designated to preside is addressed as "Mr. Chairman" or in the case of a female Member as "Madam Chairman." On entering the House Chamber and facing the Chair, an easy way to determine whether the House is in the Committee of the Whole or in the full House is to note the position of the Mace to the left of the Chair. If it is in the lower position, the House is in the Committee of the Whole.

XI. GENERAL DEBATE IN THE COMMITTEE OF THE WHOLE

There are two ways for the House to be resolved into the Committee of the Whole. Normally the House is resolved into the Committee of the Whole when pursuant to a special rule, the Speaker declares the House resolved into the Committee of the Whole, in which case the resolving action is automatic and no vote is put to the Members. The second less common way is when the manager of the bill moves that the House resolve itself into the Committee of the Whole (by authority of the standing rules in the case of a privileged matter such as an appropriations bill), in which case the motion is put to the Members.

Once the House has resolved into the Committee of the Whole to consider a particular measure, the parliamentary conduct of the Committee is dictated by the special rule previously adopted (refer to this manual's Section IX, "Special Rules For Major Bills") as well as general House Rules.

The "first reading" of the bill is normally dispensed with by the specific provisions of the special rule governing the bill. The Clerk reads the title and then the Chairman recognizes a majority and minority party member to manage the debate. This is usually the chairman and ranking member of the committee or subcommittee with jurisdiction over the pending bill.

One half of the general debate time is customarily allotted by the special rule to the minority and that time is usually managed by the Ranking Minority Member of the committee or subcommittee.

Speaking During General Debate:

The time for general debate is controlled by the majority and minority Floor managers of a bill and a Member should ask the majority or minority manager at the committee table for time to speak. Normally, Members of the committee with jurisdiction over the bill speak first, and those not on the committee speak later. The first speech is given by the majority and the order of speakers then informally rotates back and forth across the aisle.

If Members need additional time to speak, they must ask the Floor manager to yield more time. It is not in order to ask unanimous consent for additional time during general debate because the time is "controlled." A Member may instead wish to speak briefly about the bill and insert a much longer statement into the *Congressional Record* to cover all the points the Member wants to make. (NOTE: Different typeface will appear in the *Congressional Record* to distinguish unspoken words.)

How a Member obtains time to speak:

The Floor manager will yield time to a Member and the Chairman of the Committee of the Whole will recognize him/her for the allotted time. Once at a microphone, a Member's remarks may be prefaced by saying, "Mr. Chairman (or Madam Chairman), I ask unanimous consent to revise and extend my remarks." Then he or she may proceed to speak for the time yielded. The Floor manager may yield extra time to Members to complete their statements if requested and the time is available.

If a Member would like to ask a question of another Member who is speaking or make a comment, he or she should address the Chair and say, "Mr. Chairman (or Madam Chairman), will the gentleman (or gentlewoman from (STATE) yield to me?" If the Member wishes to yield, he or she may do so at his or her discretion and must remain standing while the other Member speaks. The Member who has yielded may at any time "reclaim" his or her time and then the other Member must stop speaking and allow him or her to continue. A Member to whom time has been yielded can yield time to another Member as long as he or she remains standing, unless he or she is the Member controlling the debate time.

Conduct During Debate:

Words Taken Down: A Member should avoid impugning the motives of another Member, the Senate or a Member of the Senate, the Vice President or the President, as well as using offensive language or uttering words that are otherwise deemed unparliamentary. These actions violate the Rules of the House and are subject to a point of order. A point of order may be made by a Member "demanding that the gentleman's (or gentlewoman's) words be taken down." If this happens in the Committee of the Whole, the Committee of the Whole rises and the Speaker must return to the Chair and rule on the propriety of the words used. In the case of remarks regarding the Senate and the President, the Chair may take the initiative and admonish Members for unparliamentary references.

Often the offending Member obtains unanimous consent to withdraw the inappropriate words or the demand is withdrawn before the Speaker rules and then the Member proceeds in order. However, if the Member's words are ruled out of order, they may be stricken from the *Congressional Record* by motion or unanimous consent, and the Member will not be allowed to speak again on that day, except by motion or unanimous consent (clause 4 of Rule XVII).

Relevancy: A Member may get carried away in debate and stray from the subject under discussion. If so, he or she may be subject to a point of order that their remarks are not relevant to the debate (clause 1(b) of Rule XVII).

Speaking Out of Order: If a Member has to make an important announcement to the House that is not relevant to the debate, the Member may ask unanimous consent to "speak out of order" for a period of time (usually one minute). If granted, the Member may then speak on the desired subject for the allotted time.

Addressing the Chair: A Member must be standing while speaking. If not, the Member may be subject to a point of order because of unparliamentary posture (clause 1(a) of Rule XVII).

Walking in the Well: Members should avoid walking between the Chair and any Member who is addressing the House. In addition, Members should not walk through the Well of the House when Members are speaking (clause 5 of Rule XVII).

Dress Code: Members should dress appropriately, which traditionally means male Members should wear a coat and tie and female Members should wear business attire. Members should not wear overcoats or hats on the Floor while the House is in session. Eating, drinking, and smoking are not permitted. The use of personal electronic equipment, including cellular telephones and personal computers, is also prohibited on the Floor of the House (clause 5 of Rule XVII).

Forms of Address: Members should not address their colleagues by their first name on the House Floor. They should be addressed as the gentleman or gentlewoman from (State).

NOTE: All of the same cautions and prohibitions mentioned above with respect to conduct during debate in the Committee of the Whole also apply to conduct during debate in the House.

Quorum and Vote in the Committee of the Whole:
A quorum in the Committee of the Whole consists of 100 Members. However, during general debate the Chairman has the discretion to refuse to entertain a point of order that a quorum is not present. If the Chair does permit a quorum call at this point and orders the call by electronic device, Members will be summoned by three bells to the House Floor to record their presence.

The Chairman must entertain a point of no quorum during consideration of a measure under the five-minute rule (the regular amendment process) if a quorum has not yet been established in the Committee of the Whole on the bill on that day. However, if a quorum has been established in Committee, the Chairman may not later entertain a point of no quorum during consideration under the five-minute rule unless and until the question is put on a pending amendment or motion. Whenever such a question is put before the Committee, any Member may rise and say: "On that question I request a recorded vote, and pending that, I make a point of order that a quorum is not present."

If less than 100 Members are present, the Chair will direct that Members record their presence by electronic device. The Chair at his or her discretion may order either a "live" or "notice" quorum call. For a live quorum call, Members must respond by recording their presence. A Member's absence will be noted in the *Congressional Record*. In the case of a "live" quorum call where a five-minute vote on an amendment is expected following the quorum call, Members are summoned by three bells followed by five bells.

Alternatively, in the absence of a quorum, the Chair may order a "notice" quorum call and vacate the quorum call at any time when 100 Members appear. The Committee then continues its business, and no indication of who responded to the call will appear in the *Congressional Record*. In the case of a "notice" quorum call, Members are summoned by one long bell followed by three short bells. In current practice, notice quorum calls are very rare.

XII. AMENDMENTS UNDER THE FIVE-MINUTE RULE

After all of the general debate has concluded, either by all time having been consumed or both sides yielding back the balance of their unused time, the Chairman of the Committee of the Whole will direct the Reading Clerk to read the bill for amendment. This is the so-called "second reading" of the bill. Under the standing Rules of the House, a bill is read for amendment by section (or by paragraph in the case of an appropriations bill), although a special rule may provide that it be read by title for amendment, or that it be considered as read and open for amendment at any point. A special rule may also specify the order in which amendments must be offered.

The special rule frequently provides for each section (or paragraph or title) to be considered as read. In that case, the Reading Clerk only designates each section as it is reached.

Offering an Amendment:
If a Member wants to offer an amendment, he or she must be on the Floor when the Clerk reads to the point at which the amendment is in order. At that point, the Member asks for recognition to offer the amendment. If a Member misses the opportunity to offer the amendment at the proper time, he or she may not be able to offer the amendment at all unless unanimous consent is granted to return to the appropriate place in the bill or the Member is able to redraft it to amend a subsequent section of the bill that has not yet been read for amendment. In general, Members should be sure that their amendments comply with the rules of the House.

Amendments must be "germane" to the bill and to the section to which it is offered. (See clause 7 of Rule XVI for an explanation of germaneness.) Failure to comply with this Rule means that the amendment may be ruled out of order if a point of order is made against it. Amendments should be reviewed by a Parliamentarian well in advance of the debate to ensure its germaneness and compliance with House rules.

Amendments should be shared with the appropriate Members of the committee of jurisdiction unless the element of surprise is desired. Review by the committee of jurisdiction, which may recommend alternative language to make an amendment more acceptable, will enhance the prospects for passage.

Members should also provide sufficient copies of their amendment (a minimum of ten) to the Reading Clerk on the rostrum. The Member may either take the copies to the Clerk in advance or may send the amendment to the desk as the Member offers it from the Floor.

Members should make sure the Floor and cloakroom staffs have information about their amendments so they can communicate them to the membership by posting them at the leadership desk on the Floor and in the cloakroom, and by informing Members over their pagers if record vote(s) are ordered.

Time Limits Under the Five-Minute Rule:

Under the normal process of debate during consideration of amendments, the author of an amendment is recognized for five minutes, followed by recognition of a Member who wishes to speak in opposition for five minutes. Other Members may speak for five minutes by standing to seek recognition and saying, "Mr. Chairman, I move to strike the last word."

This pro forma amendment is simply a device to get time without having to offer an actual amendment. Once a Member is finished speaking on a pro forma amendment, it is considered to have been automatically withdrawn and no vote is required on it.

When speaking under the five-minute rule, a Member may be able to obtain additional time by asking unanimous consent to proceed for the additional time desired. If an objection is heard, the Member may not proceed with additional debate time. Unlike general debate, time under the five-minute rule is not allocated to any specific Member, unless specifically provided for in a special rule. Additional time can be obtained by unanimous consent or by asking other Members who have not consumed all of their five minutes to yield time. When all Members who wish to be heard on an amendment are finished, the Chair puts the question to a vote.

In addition to time limitations that may be imposed by special rules governing consideration of bills, clause 8 of Rule XVIII outlines the manner in which the time for debate may be limited — either for tactical advantage or because all parties agree that enough debate has occurred. Such limits are proposed by a Member, usually the manager of the bill, asking unanimous consent that all time on an amendment and all amendments thereto be limited to a specified amount of time. A Member may ask that all debate on an amendment (or section) and all amendments thereto end at a certain time. These requests may be granted "without objection" or, if an objection is heard, they may be offered as a motion and be subject to a vote.

Protecting an Amendment:
It is advisable for Members to have their amendments printed in the *Congressional Record* (where they will be numbered accordingly) before their consideration. There are occasions in which a special rule governing a bill will require amendments to be printed in the *Congressional Record* prior to their consideration. Normally, however, such special rules, if open, will provide preferential treatment for pre-printed amendments. There is a special box for such amendments on the lower tier of the rostrum. If the Member submits an amendment for printing, it must be signed in the upper right-hand corner. Facsimile copies are not acceptable. Once printed in the *Congressional Record*, the Member is assured five minutes to speak on the amendment under an open rule, as will one opponent, even if a time limit is imposed by the Committee of the Whole. However, this protection will not apply if the special rule governing the bill adopted by the House includes a time limitation or the rule does not include the Member's amendment in the list of amendments that are to be made in order. The time for consideration of amendments may be limited overall by a rule, or the rule may specify time limits for each amendment made in order.

How to Get a Vote on an Amendment:
Once all debate has concluded on an amendment, the Chair will state, "The question occurs on the amendment offered by the Gentleman (or Gentlewoman) from (State). All those in favor will say aye. Those opposed will say no." Then the Chair will announce the outcome of the voice vote. Typically, if any Member is dissatisfied with the outcome of the voice vote, he or she may demand a recorded vote on the amendment.

NOTE: Rarely will a Member demand a "division" vote before requesting a recorded vote. Under this little-used procedure, the Chair will first ask those in favor to rise, then those opposed. The Chair will count the Members and announce the total. If the Member is still unsatisfied with the outcome, a record vote may be requested.

In order to obtain a record vote, twenty-five Members must rise to be counted by the Chair. As noted earlier, a point of no quorum can be made pending the request for record vote in order to get more Members to the Floor to support the request. If so, the Member should say: "Mr. Chairman (or Madam Chairman), I request a record vote and, pending that, I make a point of order that a quorum is not present." If a sufficient number of Members stand, the point of no quorum should be withdrawn and the request for a record vote restated.

XIII. CONCLUSION OF A BILL'S CONSIDERATION

Committee of the Whole Rises:
Usually a special rule will provide that, automatically following the disposition of all amendments, the Committee of the Whole rises and reports the bill back to the House with the recommendation that the bill, as amended, does pass. If the rule does not include this provision, the majority manager of the bill will be recognized to make such a motion. The Committee of the Whole then rises and the Speaker or a Speaker pro tempore resumes the Chair.

Separate Votes on Amendments Adopted in the Committee of the Whole:
The Chair, now the Speaker, asks the House: "Is a separate vote demanded on any amendment adopted in the Committee of the Whole?" Separate votes may be demanded only on amendments adopted by the Committee. Amendments that were defeated may not be voted on again. If there is no request for any separate votes, the amendments adopted are put before the House en bloc and adopted without objection. On the other hand, if an amendment has been adopted by a narrow margin or a voice vote in the Committee of the Whole, at this point, the opponents may try to reverse the outcome by demanding a separate vote on it in the House.

Previous Question:
Under a special rule, the ordering of the previous question is typically automatic to ensure that the measure makes it to final passage; therefore, no vote on the previous question is allowed. In the absence of such a provision (such as on appropriations bills considered without a special rule), the Speaker will move that the previous question be ordered "without objection." If an objection is heard, the motion for the previous question must be voted on.

Engrossment and Third Reading of the Bill:
This is a routine motion that orders the Clerk to prepare the measure for transmission to the Senate and read its title (the "third reading").

Motion to Recommit:

After the engrossment and third reading of a bill or joint resolution (but not simple resolutions, concurrent resolutions and conference reports), a Member opposed to the measure is given preference in recognition to offer a motion to recommit the measure, with or without instructions, to committee that originally reported the measure. This motion is traditionally the right of the minority and gives them one last chance to return the measure to committee or have its version voted on. The Rules Committee may not report a special rule on a bill or joint resolution that denies a motion to recommit with instructions if offered by the Minority Leader or a designee.

If the motion to recommit is without instructions, the adoption of the motion has the practical impact of killing the bill without a final vote on its passage. The motion is not debatable if it does not include instructions.

If the motion to recommit is with instructions, and is adopted, the bill is then returned to the originating committee. Usually the instructions are for the committee to "report the bill back to the House forthwith with the following amendment...." The text of the amendment is then read in full. The motion to recommit with instructions is debatable for ten minutes, equally divided, but not controlled, which means neither side may yield or reserve time, between the proponent and the opponent, although the time may be extended to one hour at the request of the majority Floor manager.

If the motion is adopted, the bill is recommitted with such "forthwith" instructions. The bill is immediately reported back to the House on the spot with the amendment, the amendment is voted on, and the House proceeds to final passage of the bill.

In order of priority, the Minority Leader and then minority party Members on the committee handling the bill, by seniority, have the right to offer the motion. This does not preclude Members of the majority party from offering the motion to recommit. They "qualify" to offer the motion if they state that they oppose the bill. The Member who qualifies and offers the motion usually votes against final passage of the bill if the motion to recommit fails.

It is worth noting that a motion to recommit need not instruct that an amendment be adopted. The motion may also direct that further hearings be held, or that an investigation be conducted and that a report of that investigation be made to the House, so long as the instruction is germane to the bill as amended and is in compliance with all other House rules. However, in the case of such general instructions, the committee cannot be required to report the bill back to the House, although it is certainly not precluded from doing so.

XIV. FINAL PASSAGE OF A BILL

In bringing a measure to a final passage vote, the Speaker is required under House rules to first put the question to a voice vote by stating, "As many as are in favor (as the question may be), say `Aye.' As many as are opposed, say 'No.'" The Speaker then makes the "call" on which side prevails. The only remedy available to any Member that disagrees with the Speaker's announcement on the voice vote is to demand a division or recorded vote.

Obtaining a Recorded Vote in the House:
Because the Constitution requires a quorum to be present to do business, whenever a quorum (218 Members) is not present, a recorded vote can be obtained by addressing the Chair and declaring: "Mr. Speaker, I object to the vote on the grounds that a quorum is not present and I make a point of order that a quorum is not present."

An alternate means of obtaining a recorded vote when a quorum is not present is to request the "yeas and nays," which requires that one-fifth of those Members present stand up to order the vote. This could be as many as 87 if all 435 Members are present, or as few as one if less than five Members are on the Floor. Once the Chair determines that one-fifth of those present support the demand for the yeas and nays, the vote is ordered.

A Member can obtain a recorded vote when a quorum (218 Members or more) is present by addressing the Chair and declaring: "Mr. Speaker, on that I demand a recorded vote." A "recorded vote" under these circumstances requires only one-fifth of a quorum (44 Members) to stand and support the request.

General Leave:
It is customary after consideration of a bill for the majority Floor manager to ask unanimous consent that all Members have five legislative days in which to revise and extend their remarks and to include extraneous material on the subject of the bill just passed. Once this request is granted, Members may insert remarks on the bill without having to ask permission personally. The remarks should be labeled "General Leave." If the material is submitted rather than actually spoken on the Floor, it will appear in different type in the *Congressional Record*.

Revising and Extending Remarks:

Once a Member has requested to see his or her remarks before they are printed in the *Congressional Record*, especially those made during debate when other Members are involved, certain rules of courtesy should be followed. As soon as the Official Reporter gives the transcript to the Member, it should be corrected for grammatical errors and immediately returned so that other Members may do the same.

The substance of a Member's remarks should not be changed — only grammatical corrections are allowed to be made. If elaboration is desired with tables or other "extraneous material," and permission has not been granted under general leave, specific permission must be obtained in the House and not in the Committee of the Whole. It will take approximately one hour between the time a speech is given and the time the transcribed remarks will be available on the Floor.

Motion to Reconsider:

The motion to reconsider is available to any Member who votes on the prevailing side of a question and who wishes to move reconsideration on the same or succeeding legislative day. This often occurs when Members (usually minority Members) determine there is a need to slow down the legislative process. After final passage, it is the common practice in the House for the Speaker to declare, "Without objection, the motion to reconsider is laid upon the table." If no objection is raised, this has the parliamentary effect of ending any possibility that another vote on the bill can take place.

Postponement of Votes:

The Speaker has the discretion to postpone votes for up to two legislative days on a number of questions, including final passage of bills. Other questions that can be postponed by the Speaker include adoption of resolutions, motions to instruct, agreements to conference reports, previous question votes on any of the above matters, suspensions, motions to reconsider (and motions to table reconsideration), and agreements to amendments reported from the Committee of the Whole. The Chairman of the Committee of the Whole has the authority to postpone and cluster votes on amendments.

Clustering of Votes:

The Speaker may reduce the voting time to five minutes for electronic voting on certain questions after a fifteen-minute record vote has been taken. Votes can only be clustered by the Chair when there has not been intervening business between the votes in question.

Vote Pairs and Missed Votes:

The practice of announcing "general pairs" or the "pairing" of votes was eliminated in the 106th Congress. While "general pairs" are no longer announced, "live pairs" are still permitted. A "live pair" is an informal agreement between one Member present and voting and another on the opposite side of the question who is absent. By agreement, the voting member withdraws his or her vote and records his or her self as "present." If the present Member wishes to announce the "pair," they must do so prior to the announcement of the final vote total.

If a Member misses a vote, they may have their position on the missed vote made part of the public record by inserting a brief statement in the *Congressional Record* at the proper point indicating how the Member would have voted. Such statements appear in the *Congressional Record* under the heading "Personal Explanation." For more information about this practice, contact the Floor staff.

Conflicts of Interest:

Each Member must be present in the Hall of the House during its sessions "unless excused or necessarily prevented" and "shall vote on each question put, unless he or she has a direct personal or pecuniary interest in the event of such question." It has been ruled that only the Member can decide whether such a conflict exists and not even the Speaker will question his or her judgment, nor can any other Member challenge his or her vote on such grounds. Members should let their consciences be their guide. If Members believe they have such a conflict, they can vote "present" on the record vote and include an explanation in the *Congressional Record*.

XV. CONFERENCE REPORTS

In order for a bill to be presented to the President for signature, it must pass both the House and Senate in the exact same form. The device used for reaching agreement between the two Houses is often, but not always, a conference committee. Sometimes differences between the two bodies are resolved by amendment — e.g., the House will agree to the bill as passed by the Senate with an amendment and the Senate will subsequently concur with that amendment.

A bill may be sent to conference by special rule or unanimous consent. If objection is heard, the bill may be sent to conference by motion or suspension. A motion to request or agree to a conference with the Senate is in order if offered by direction of the primary committee and of all reporting committees of initial referral. If such a motion has not been authorized by the committee, a special rule may be required to go to conference. The 109th rules of the House include a change that gives committees the option to adopt a rule directing the chairman of the committee to offer a privileged motion to go to conference at any time the chairman deems it appropriate during a Congress.

Following the motion to go to conference, but prior to the appointment of conferees, the Speaker will recognize a minority Member, with preference given to the minority Floor manager (if recognition is sought) to offer a motion to instruct House conferees. The motion is debatable for one hour, divided between the majority and the minority managers. If both support the motion, however, a third Member may demand time in opposition. All three Members are then recognized for one-third of the time. The motion to instruct conferees is not amendable unless the previous question is defeated. The instructions are not binding and they may not propose to do what the conferees could not otherwise do under the Rules of the House (e.g. exceed the scope of the conference). Additional opportunities to instruct occur when a conference report is recommitted or after twenty calendar days and ten legislative days if the conference has failed to report. A Member who wishes to offer a motion to instruct conferees after twenty-and-ten days must notify the House one day in advance of offering the motion.

Conferees are named by the Speaker and usually include Members of the committee(s) of jurisdiction and principal proponents of the legislation's major provisions.

When a conference agreement is reached, it comes back to the House in the form of a "conference report" that the House must consider and approve. Unless waived, the rules of the House require that a conference report be filed at least three calendar days (excluding Saturdays, Sundays, and legal holidays) before it can be called up for consideration. The rules also require that a majority of the conferees sign the conference report. After that time, it becomes privileged and can be called up at any time. If the conference report violates a rule of the House, it may be subject to a point of order that would prevent its consideration.

Debate on a conference report is limited to one hour, the time divided between the majority and the minority, unless the majority party manager and the minority party manager both support the conference report. In that case, one-third of the debate time will be given to an opponent of the conference report who makes such a demand.

Before adoption of the conference report, a motion may be in order to recommit the conference report to the committee on conference, either with instructions (that must be within the authority of the conferees and comply with the rules of the House) or without instructions, although separate debate time is not allowed on either motion. Such a motion is only in order if the Senate has not yet acted on the conference report, thereby discharging its conferees, and the instructions in the motion to recommit are not binding because the House cannot bind Senate conferees. A Member qualifies to offer the motion if he or she opposes the conference report and states that fact.

If the House is first to act and the motion to recommit is adopted, the conference must meet again and a new conference report must be filed prior to consideration of the measure again. The rule requiring a three-day layover of conference reports still applies unless waived by special rule.

Following debate on the conference report and in the absence of a motion to recommit or upon the defeat of such a motion, a vote then occurs on adoption of the conference report, which may not be amended on the Floor.

When dealing with appropriations conference reports, there may be times when conferees cannot reach agreement on all the amendments in disagreement. Also, there may be times when conferees must report provisions outside the conference report. For example, conferees may not exceed the scope of the conference or include legislative or unauthorized provisions in an appropriations bill. In those cases, the conferees will present a conference report to the House and Senate that includes all amendments on which agreement has been reached but excludes the amendments that remain in real or technical disagreement. The conference report is considered first and, assuming adoption of the conference report, the amendments in disagreement are then considered and disposed of individually.

XVI. DISCHARGE PETITIONS

After a bill has been introduced and referred to committee for 30 legislative days or more, any Member may file a motion with the Clerk of the House to discharge the committee from further consideration of the bill. A Member may also file a motion to discharge the Rules Committee from consideration of a special rule after the rule has been pending before the Rules Committee for at least seven legislative days and the bill has been reported by a standing committee or has been referred to a standing committee for thirty legislative days.

Discharge petitions may cover only a single introduced measure, not multiple bills. A motion to discharge must only provide for the consideration of similar subject matter. In other words, a discharge motion cannot waive the germaneness rule.

If a Member is successful in convincing a majority of the total membership of the House (218 Members) to sign a discharge petition, the petition becomes eligible for consideration on the second or fourth Monday of the month after a seven legislative day layover (except during the last six days of any session when the layover is waived). The discharge motion is debatable for twenty minutes, equally divided between the proponents and an opponent. If the motion to discharge a bill is adopted, it is in order to move that the House immediately consider the bill itself. If the motion to discharge a rule is adopted, the House turns immediately to consideration of the rule.

NOTE: Signatures on a discharge petition must be made available to the public by the Clerk and are made available on the Internet. The names of new signatories are printed in the *Congressional Record* on the last legislative day of each week.

XVII. END OF LEGISLATIVE BUSINESS FOR THE DAY

After completion of the scheduled legislative business, it is customary at the end of the day for the House to consider miscellaneous unanimous consent requests that were not made earlier in the day, including personal requests of individual Members.

Personal Requests:
Such requests can only be made by the Member benefiting from the request. These include to:

- Make a correction in the *Congressional Record*;
- Have a Member's name removed as a cosponsor of a bill or resolution (this request may also be made by the original sponsor of the measure);

241

- Include extraneous material exceeding two pages in the *Congressional Record*, which must be accompanied by a cost estimate from Government Printing Office.

Official Leave:

Members are allowed to be absent and excused on grounds of necessity which can include a death in the family, illness or official business. A request for a leave of absence should be made through the Cloakroom and signed by the appropriate party leader. Such requests are laid before the House each evening and made a part of the *Congressional Record*.

Extension of Remarks:

Members may insert comments in the section of the *Congressional Record* entitled "Extension of Remarks" by submitting to the Cloakroom such remarks with the Member's original signature. It is no longer necessary to obtain "permission" to include extensions in the *Congressional Record*. All material submitted must bear an original Member's signature in the upper right-hand corner of the front page — facsimiles are not permitted — and the Member's typed name to be sure of identification. Members must be sure clerks will title the extension themselves.

If the extraneous material to be inserted will exceed two pages of the *Congressional Record*, it must be submitted to the Government Printing Office in advance for a cost estimate. When the estimate is received, the Member must ask leave of the House in person that it be printed, notwithstanding the cost. At the beginning or the end of the day, the Member must ask unanimous consent to extend his or her remarks in the *Congressional Record* and to include therein extraneous material notwithstanding the fact that it exceeds two pages. As part of the unanimous consent request, the Member also should include a cost estimate by the GPO. (As of May 2004, it is estimated that each page of the *Congressional Record* costs $290.00.)

Extensions should be delivered to the Cloakroom, handed to the *Congressional Record* clerks who sit at the bottom tier of the rostrum during session, or delivered to the Office of the Official Reports of Debates in Room HT-60 of the Capitol by 5 p.m. or fifteen minutes after the House adjourns, whichever is later.

Special Orders:

Members may request special orders through their Cloakroom in five-minute increments up to sixty minutes in length. Special order speeches are given after legislative business is completed for the day. They may be on any topic, and may either be given orally or submitted in writing (as with extensions of remarks). Members are recognized first for five-minute special orders, alternating between the majority and minority. At the conclusion of five-minute special orders, the Chair will recognize Members who wish to speak for longer periods of time, also alternating between the majority and minority. Special orders cannot be requested more than one week in advance and cannot be entertained after midnight. Any questions concerning special orders should be directed to the Cloakrooms.

Adjournment:
A motion to adjourn closes the business of the day.

XVIII. EARMARK RULES

At the beginning of the 110th Congress the House adopted new rules concerning the consideration of Member directed projects or "earmarks," specifically clause 9 of Rule XXI and clause 17 of Rule XXIII (the Code of Official Conduct). These rules followed efforts in the 109th Congress to provide greater transparency in the earmarking process.

The rules are intended to prohibit the consideration of legislation that does not identify individual earmarks and the Members who sponsored them. The rules also require the distribution of the information in a way that makes it readily available before the legislation is considered, and certification by earmark sponsors that neither they nor their spouses have a financial interest in the earmark.

Point of Order:
Clause 9 of Rule XXI requires the chairman of the committee of initial referral to either disclose all earmarks contained in a bill, joint resolution, or conference report, or certify that the bill, joint resolution, or conference report contain no earmarks, and provide that information either in the accompanying report or printed in the *Congressional Record*. If the chairman of the committee of initial referral does not fulfill either of these requirements prior to the consideration of the measure, a point of order would lay against the consideration of the measure. This requirement also applies to unreported measures (in which case the information must be printed in the *Congressional Record*).

Clause 9(b) of Rule XXI prohibits the Rules Committee from waiving those disclosure requirements. If the Rules Committee reports a rule waiving clause

9 of Rule XXI, it would then be in order to raise a point of order against consideration of the rule. Disposition of the point of order raised against the rule would be determined by the Chair putting the question of consideration after twenty minutes of debate on the point of order equally divided and controlled by the Member initiating the point of order and a member opposed. At the conclusion of debate on the point of order the Chair will put the question as follows: "Not withstanding the assertion of the gentleman/lady from (STATE), that House Resolution XXX violates clause 9(b) of Rule XXI, shall the House now consider House Resolution XXX?"

Members should also be aware that clause 9(a)(3) of Rule XXI applies the point of order to the initial amendment made in order under a special rule from the Rules Committee if that amendment is authored by a Member of the committee of initial referral. Clause 9(a)(3) requires the sponsor of the amendment to comply with the same disclosure requirements by having a statement printed in the *Congressional Record* either disclosing earmarks contained in their amendment or certifying that there are no earmarks in their amendment.

Several Members raised concerns with the enforceability of these rules, particularly as they apply to conference reports. Specifically, Members were concerned that there was no way to debate the point of order if a Member questioned the accuracy or completeness of the list contained in the statement of managers. This problem arises because the current practice of the Rules Committee is to waive all points of order except clause 9 and 10 of Rule XXI, meaning that the point of order against a conference report is never armed.

In response to this concern, the House adopted H. Res. 491, which creates some enforceability for this provision against conference reports. This special order provides a point of order against a conference report to accompany a regular general appropriations bill (debatable as a question of consideration) for the failure to include a list of "air dropped" earmarks in the joint statement of managers. Unlike the current rule, this point of order does not have a congnizability standard, allowing Members to question the accuracy or completeness of the list.

Clause 17 of Rule XXIII (the Code of Official Conduct) imposes a disclosure requirement on a Member who requests a congressional earmark, a limited tax benefit, or a limited tariff benefit in any bill or joint resolution or in any conference report on a bill or joint resolution. The committee of primary jurisdiction over the bill shall determine, using the definitions of "earmark," "limited tax benefit," and "limited tariff benefit" provided in clauses 9(d), (e), and (f) of Rule XXI, whether any particular spending provision constitutes an earmark or a request for an earmark.

A Member can raise the point of order at the point the manager calls up the conference report by saying: "M. Speaker, I raise a point of order under section 1 of H. Res. 491 against the conference report for the failure to include a [complete/accurate] list of congressional earmarks."

If the rule providing for consideration of the conference report waives all points of order, the point of order automatically moves to the rule. The form of that point of order is: "M. Speaker, I raise a point of order against H. Res. ____ under section 2 of H. Res. 491 because the resolution contains a waiver of all points of order against the conference report and its consideration."

The point of order would then be debated as if raised under clause 9(b) of Rule XXI.

Earmark Certification:
A Member who requests an earmark or other provision must provide a written statement to the chairman and ranking member of the committee of jurisdiction of the bill, resolution, or report that contains the following information:

- The name of the Member;
- In the case of an earmark, the name and address of the intended recipient or if there is no intended recipient, the location of the activity;
- In the case of a limited tax or tariff benefit, the name of the beneficiary;
- The purpose of the earmark or limited tax or tariff benefit; and
- A certification that both the Member and the Member's spouse have no "financial interest" in the earmark or limited tax or tariff benefit.

Clause 17(a)(5) of Rule XXIII (the Code of Official Conduct), requires a Member who requests an earmark to certify that the Member and his or her spouse have "no financial interest in such congressional earmark." In the great majority of cases, Members should readily be able to determine whether they have a financial interest in an earmark by simply determining whether or not

245

it would be reasonable to conclude that the provisions would have a direct and foreseeable effect on the pecuniary interests of the Member or the Member's spouse. However; Members are strongly encouraged to consult the Standards Committee for guidance with any fact specific questions they have.

Adjournment to a Day Certain - Adjournment under a motion or resolution that fixes the next time of meeting. Under the Constitution, both Houses must agree to a concurrent resolution for either House to adjourn for more than three days. A session of Congress is not ended by adjournment to a day certain.

Adjournment Sine Die - Adjournment without definitely fixing a day for reconvening; literally "adjournment without a day." Usually used to connote the final adjournment of a session of Congress. A session can continue until noon, January 3, of the following year, when, under the 20th Amendment to the Constitution, it automatically terminates.

Amendments (Types of) - A proposal of a Member of Congress to alter the text of a bill or another amendment. An amendment usually is voted on in the same manner as a bill.

> **Amendment in the Nature of a Substitute** - An amendment that seeks to replace the entire text of an underlying bill. The adoption of such an amendment precludes any further amendment to that bill under the regular process (Also, see Substitute Amendment).

> **Pro Forma Amendment** - A motion whereby a Member secures five minutes to speak on an amendment under debate in the Committee of the Whole. The Member gains recognition from the Chair by moving to "strike the last word." The motion requires no vote, does not change the amendment under debate, and is deemed automatically withdrawn at the expiration of the five minutes of debate.

> **Substitute Amendment** - An amendment that replaces the entire text of a pending amendment.

Bills Introduced - In both the House and Senate, any number of Members may join in introducing a single bill or resolution. The first Member listed is the sponsor of the bill, and all Members' names following the sponsor's are the bill's cosponsors. When introduced, a bill is referred to the committee or committees that have jurisdiction over the subject with which the bill is concerned. Under the standing rules of the House and Senate, bills are referred by the Speaker in the House and by the presiding officer in the Senate. In practice, the House and Senate parliamentarians act for these officials and refer the bills.

Budget Authority - Authority provided by law to incur into financial obligations that normally result in the outlay of funds. The main forms of budget authority are appropriations, borrowing authority, contract authority, and entitlement authority.

Budget Outlay - Payments made (generally through the issuance of checks or disbursement of cash) to liquidate obligations. Outlays during a fiscal year may be for payment of obligations incurred in prior years or in the same year.

Budget Resolution - A concurrent resolution which outlines in broad parameters the levels of spending and revenues for the next fiscal year. The concurrent resolution, which is not signed by the President, contains allocations of spending authority for House and Senate committees which serve as constraints on their consideration of legislation. The Appropriations Committee gets an allocation for discretionary spending.

Calendar - An agenda or list of business awaiting possible action by the House or Senate. The House has four calendars (the Discharge Calendar, the House Calendar, the Private Calendar and the Union Calendar).

Chaplain of the House or Senate - He or she opens the legislative session with a formal prayer, a custom since the First Congress. The Chaplain provides pastoral counseling to Members, their families and staff. Guest Chaplains of various denominations regularly offer the prayer.

Chief Administrative Officer (CAO) - He or she is responsible for certain administrative and financial activities that support the operations of the House, including the finance office, Members' accounts, information resources, human resources, office systems management, furniture, office supplies, postal operations, food services, and various media services.

Clerk of the House - As the chief legislative officer, he or she directs administrative activities that support the legislative process including keeping the Journal, recording all votes, certifying bill passage and processing all legislation.

Committee - A panel of Members elected or appointed to perform some service or function for its parent body. Congress has three types of committees: standing, special or select, joint. Committees conduct investigations, make studies, issue reports and recommendations, and, in the case of standing committees, review and prepare measures on their assigned subjects for action by their respective houses. Most committees divide their work among several subcommittees or, in some cases, task forces, but only the full committee may submit reports or measures to its house or to Congress. With rare exceptions, the majority party in a house holds a majority of the seats on its committees, and their chairmen are also from that party.

Committee Allocation - The distribution, pursuant to section 302 of the Congressional Budget Act, of new budget authority and outlays to House and Senate committees. The allocation, which may not exceed the relevant amounts in the budget resolution, usually is made in the joint explanatory statement that accompanies the conference report on the budget resolution.

Committee of the Whole - A committee composed of all House Members created to expedite the consideration of bills, other measures and amendments on the Floor of the House. In the Committee of the Whole, a quorum is 100 Members (as compared to 218 in a fully populated House) and debate on amendments is conducted under the five-minute rule (as compared to the hour rule in the House). In addition, certain motions allowed in the House are prohibited in the Committee of the Whole including, but not limited to, motions for the previous question, to table, to adjourn, to reconsider a vote, and to refer or recommit.

Desk - The presiding officer's desk. In parliamentary parlance, a member may send an amendment or a written motion to "the desk," or a measure may be "held at the desk."

En Bloc - Several amendments offered and considered as a group. Because Members normally may offer an amendment at a time for consideration, they must obtain unanimous consent to offer amendments en bloc, or a rule providing for consideration of a measure may provide authority for a member to offer amendments en bloc.

Engrossed Bill - The official copy of a bill or joint resolution as passed by one chamber, including the text as amended by Floor action, and certified by the clerk of the House or the secretary of the Senate (as appropriate). Amendments by one house to a measure or amendments of the other also are engrossed. House engrossed documents are printed on blue paper; the Senate's are printed on white paper.

Enrolled Bill - The final official copy of a bill or joint resolution that both houses have passed in identical form. An enrolled bill is printed on parchment. After it is certified by the chief officer of the house in which it originated and signed by the House Speaker and the Senate president pro tempore, the measure is sent to the president for his signature.

Expedited Procedures - Procedures that provide a special process for the accelerated Congressional consideration of legislation. This accelerated process usually includes consideration in committee and on the Floor of the House and Senate. Furthermore, these procedures often involve a departure from the regular order of the House. Expedited procedures are provided by law, as opposed to by a special rule.

Five-Minute Rule - A debate-limiting rule of the House used when the House sits as the Committee of the Whole. A Member offering an amendment is allowed to speak for five minutes in support of each amendment and an opponent is allowed to speak for five minutes in opposition. Other Members may rise to "strike the last word" and receive five minutes to speak in favor or opposition. Additional time for speaking can be obtained through a unanimous consent request.

Free Trade Agreements - The establishment of bilateral or multilateral trade agreements establishing free-trade areas (FTAs) require changes in U.S. trade legislation. Trade law sets out procedures for the enactment of such legislation and its implementation. This law provides for expedited congressional consideration of the relevant measure and, as a rule, prohibits any amendments to it. The expedited consideration, originally called "fast track" procedure, but recently also named "trade authorities procedures (TAPs)," provides for mandatory consideration of the measure by Congress once introduced, with specific deadlines for each legislative phase, and a final up-or-down vote.

Germaneness - A rule requiring amendments pertain to the same subject as the matter under consideration. Questions of germaneness, both in committee and on the House Floor, are determined by the Chair and/or the Speaker subject to appeal to the House or the Committee.

Hopper - A box on the clerk's desk in the House chamber into which Members deposit bills and resolutions to introduce them. To "drop a bill in the hopper" is to introduce it.

House Bill (H.R.) - H.R. stands for House of Representatives and designates a measure as a bill, followed by a number assigned in the order in which bills are introduced during a two-year Congress. A bill becomes a law if passed in identical form by both houses and signed by the president, or passed over the president's veto, or if the president fails to sign it within ten days after receiving it while Congress is in session.

House Concurrent Resolution (H. Con. Res.) - H. Con. Res. stands for House Concurrent Resolution. This is a resolution that requires approval by both houses but is not sent to the president for his signature and therefore cannot have the force of law. Concurrent resolutions deal with the prerogatives or internal affairs of Congress as a whole. For example, they serve as the vehicles for agreeing to congressional budget decisions, fixing the time of congressional adjournments, agreeing to a joint session, expressing the sense of Congress on domestic and foreign issues, correcting errors in enrolled bills, authorizing the printing of documents of interest to both houses, and creating temporary joint committees.

House Joint Resolution (H. J. Res.) - H. J. Res. stands for House Joint Resolution. This is a legislative measure that Congress usually uses for purposes other than general legislation. Like a bill, it has the force of law when passed by both houses and either approved by the president or passed over the president's veto. Unlike a bill, a joint resolution enacted into law is not called an act; it retains its original title. Most often, joint resolutions deal with such relatively limited matters, such as the correction of errors in existing law, continuing appropriations, a single appropriation, or the establishment of permanent joint committees. Unlike bills, however, joint resolutions also are used to propose constitutional amendments; these do not require the president's signature and become effective only when ratified by three-fourths of the states. While a preamble is not considered appropriate in a bill, it may be included in a joint resolution to set forth the events or facts that prompted the measure, for example, a declaration of war.

House Resolution (H. Res.) - H. Res. stands for House Resolution. This type of measure is a simple resolution; that is, a nonlegislative measure that is effective only in the House and does not require concurrence with the Senate or approval by the president. Simple resolutions express nonbinding opinions on policies or issues or deal with the internal affairs or prerogatives of the House. They are used to establish select and special committees, appoint the members of standing committees, and amend the standing rules. In the House, the Rules Committee reports its special rules in the form of simple resolutions.

Lay on the Table - A motion to "lay on the table" is not debatable and is usually a method of making a final, adverse determination of a matter.

Legislative History - The documents that accompanied a bill throughout the legislative process comprise its legislative history. These include the committee report, the conference committee report and the statement of managers (if applicable), and the text of the Floor debate in both chambers. Legislative history is used by federal agencies to clarify vague provisions in the laws they are required to implement.

Marking Up a Bill - The process by which a committee or subcommittee moves through the contents of a measure, debating and voting on amendments to its provisions by revising, adding, or subtracting language prior to ordering the measure reported.

Motion to Recommit - A motion made on the Floor after the engrossment and third reading of a bill or resolution, but prior to the Chair posing the question on final passage. Preference is given to a Member who is opposed to the bill and is reserved by tradition to the minority party. The Speaker usually gives priority recognition to the bill's minority Floor manager. The motion to recommit may be without instructions, which is non-debatable and has the effect of killing the bill, or with instructions (subject to ten minutes of debate split between a proponent and opponent, and usually directs the reporting committee to amend "forthwith," meaning immediately, or rewrite the bill in a specified way). The Rules Committee's responsibility on the motion to recommit is different for simple resolutions or concurrent resolutions, but may apply to conference reports where the House acts first.

Office of the Parliamentarian - An office managed, supervised and administered by a non-partisan Parliamentarian appointed by the Speaker. This office is responsible for advising the presiding officer, Members and staff on the rules and procedures of the House, as well as for compiling and preparing the precedents of the House. All consultation with this office is confidential (if requested).

Official Reporters - Official Reporters are responsible for collecting material for printing in the *Congressional Record*. These Clerks sit in the center of the first tier of the rostrum on the House Floor. All submissions for the Record, for example, extensions of remarks, corrections to Member's Floor statements, and extraneous material, are given to the Official Reporters.

Parliamentary Inquiry - A member's question, posed to the presiding officer, about a pending procedural situation. The chair is not required to answer such questions, but usually does if they are proper inquiries and properly made. A proper inquiry deals only with questions of procedure on a pending matter, not with hypothetical situations or the interpretation or consistency of amendments.

Point of Order - An objection that the pending proposal (bill, amendment, motion, etc.) is in violation of a rule of the House. The validity of points of order is determined by the presiding officer, and if held valid, the offending bill, amendment or provision is ineligible for consideration. Points of order may be waived by special rules.

Privilege - A status relating to the rights of the House and its members and the priority of motions and actions on the Floor of the House. "Privileged questions" relate to the order of legislative business, while "questions of privilege" relate to matters affecting the safety, dignity or integrity of the House, or the rights, reputation or conduct of a Member acting as a representative.

Privileged Matters - House rules give certain House committees a "green light" to bring certain categories of legislation to the House Floor for immediate debate. The Speaker must recognize any Chairman for the purpose of calling up a privileged matter reported from his or her committee. Examples of privileged matter include special rules from the Rules Committee, conference reports from any conference committee, congressional budget resolutions from the Budget Committee, censure or expulsion resolutions from the Ethics Committee, and general appropriations bills from the Appropriations Committee.

Previous Question - A motion offered in the House to end debate and preclude further amendments from being offered. In effect, it asks, "Are we ready to vote on the issue before us?" If the previous question is ordered in the House, all debate ends and usually the House immediately votes on the pending bill or amendment. If the previous question is defeated, control of debate shifts to the leading opposition member (usually the minority Floor manager) who then manages an hour of debate and may offer a germane amendment to the pending business. The effect of defeating the previous question is to turn over control of the Floor to the minority or opposition.

Quorum - The number of Members whose presence is required for the House to conduct business. A quorum in the House is a majority of the Members (218). A quorum in the Committee of the Whole is 100 Members. A quorum is presumed to be present until its absence is demonstrated. If a quorum is not present when the question is put, a point of order can be made that a quorum is not present, at which time the Speaker (or Chair) counts for a

253

quorum. If the Speaker (or Chair) determines that a quorum is not present, Members may be summoned to the Floor. If a quorum fails to respond to the call, the only business in order is a motion to adjourn or a motion to direct the sergeant-at-arms to request the attendance of absentees.

Ramseyer Rule - A House rule requiring that committee reports contain a comparative print showing, through typographical devices such as italic print, the changes in existing law made by the proposed committee language (the "Cordon Rule" is a parallel rule of the Senate).

Reading for Amendment - In the Committee of the Whole, after a clerk has read or designated a section or paragraph of a measure, it is the House practice to complete action on all amendments to that section or paragraph before moving on to the next section or paragraph. A full reading of a section's text is often waived by unanimous consent or by a special rule from the Rules Committee, in which case the clerk reads only the section's number or designates the paragraph. Sometimes, by unanimous consent or special rule, a measure is read or designated by title rather than by section or paragraph.

Recognition - Permission by the presiding officer for a Member to speak or propose a procedural action. A Member seeking recognition must rise and address the chair, but may not do so while another Member holds the Floor unless that Member has violated a rule. Generally, recognition in the House is within the chair's discretion. Under some circumstances, the chair's discretion is absolute; under others, the chair may be required to recognize a Member eventually but not necessarily the first time the Member seeks recognition. Under still other circumstances, the chair is required to recognize certain Members for specific purposes. However, the Speaker must recognize Members for privileged business and motions, but when several Members seek recognition on business of equal privilege, the Speaker has discretion in deciding whom to recognize first. By tradition and practice, both the Speaker and the Chairman of the Committee of the Whole follow certain priorities of recognition during debate. In both houses, the chair's recognition authority is not subject to appeal.

Reconsideration - A motion to reconsider the vote by which an action was taken has, until it is disposed of, the effect of putting the action in abeyance. In essence, it is a motion to vote again on that which was just agreed to.

Re-Referral - The assignment of a measure to a committee different from the committee to which the measure was initially referred. Usually used to correct erroneous initial referrals.

Rules (Types of) - There are two specific types of Rules.

> **Standing Rules** - These are the standing Rules governing the normal order of business in the House or in a committee. These Rules are adopted by the full House and by each committee at the beginning of each Congress. These Rules generally govern such matters as the duties of officers, the code of conduct, the order of business, admission to the Floor, parliamentary procedures on handling amendments and voting, and jurisdictions of committees.

> **Special Rules** - These involve a departure from the standing rules of the House for the consideration of specified House action. They are resolutions reported by the Rules Committee, most of which govern the handling of a particular bill on the House Floor.

Senate Bill (S.) - S. stands for Senate and designates a measure introduced in the Senate as a bill, followed by a number assigned in the order in which bills are introduced during a two-year Congress. A bill becomes a law if passed in identical form by both houses and signed by the president, or passed over the president's veto, or if the president fails to sign it within ten days after receiving it while Congress is in session.

Senate Concurrent Resolution (S. Con. Res.) - S. Con. Res. is an abbreviation for Senate Concurrent Resolution. This is a resolution that requires approval by both houses but is not sent to the president for his signature and therefore cannot have the force of law. Concurrent resolutions deal with the prerogatives or internal affairs of Congress as a whole. For example, they serve as the vehicles for agreeing to congressional budget decisions, fixing the time of congressional adjournments, agreeing to a joint session, expressing the sense of Congress on domestic and foreign issues, correcting errors in enrolled bills, authorizing the printing of documents of interest to both houses, and creating temporary joint committees.

Senate Joint Resolution (S. J. Res.) - S. J. Res. is an abbreviation for Senate Joint Resolution. This is a legislative measure that Congress usually uses for purposes other than general legislation. Like a bill, it has the force of law when passed by both houses and either approved by the president or passed over the president's veto. Unlike a bill, a joint resolution enacted into law is not called an act; it retains its original title. Most often, joint resolutions deal with such relatively limited matters, such as the correction of errors in existing

255

law, continuing appropriations, a single appropriation, or the establishment of permanent joint committees. Unlike bills, however, joint resolutions also are used to propose constitutional amendments; these do not require the president's signature and become effective only when ratified by three-fourths of the states. While a preamble is not considered appropriate in a bill, it may be included in a joint resolution to set forth the events or facts that prompted the measure, for example, a declaration of war.

Senate Resolution (S. Res.) - S. Res. stands for Senate Resolution. This type of measure is a simple resolution; that is, a non-legislative measure that is effective only in the Senate and does not require concurrence with the Senate or approval by the president. Simple resolutions express nonbinding opinions on policies or issues or deal with the internal affairs or prerogatives of the Senate. They are used to establish select and special committees, appoint the members of standing committees, and amend the standing rules.

Sergeant-at-Arms - The Sergeant-at-Arms is the chief law enforcement officer for the House of Representatives. The officer is responsible for maintaining security, order, and decorum in the House Chamber, House wing of the Capitol and the House office buildings.

Standing Committees - These permanent House panels are identified in House Rule X, which also lists the jurisdiction of each committee. Because they have legislative jurisdiction, standing committees consider bills and issues and recommend measures for consideration by the full House. They also have oversight responsibility to monitor agencies, programs, and activities within their jurisdictions, and, in some cases, in areas that cut across committee jurisdictions.

Suspension of the Rules - A timesaving method used to consider legislation. By suspending the rules and passing a measure, this procedure has the effect of preventing any points of order from being raised against a measure for violation of a rule. Under this procedure, the bill is un-amendable (except for one amendment by the Floor manager if offered as part of the motion) and debate on the motion and the measure is limited to forty minutes equally divided between a proponent and an opponent. A motion to recommit is not in order under this procedure. However, a favorable vote of two-thirds of those present is necessary for passage. This procedure is in order every Monday, Tuesday, and Wednesday and is intended to be reserved for relatively non-controversial bills. Both the Republican Conference and Democratic

Caucus have their own internal rules for determining whether legislation is eligible for suspension consideration.

Unanimous Consent - A method used to expedite consideration of non-controversial measures on the House Floor. Proceedings of the House or actions on legislation often take place by unanimous consent of the House (i.e., without objection by any Member), whether or not a rule of the House is being violated.

Unanimous Consent Agreements - Agreements negotiated among Senators by the Majority and Minority Leaders to limit debate on a specified measure, to restrict amendments to it, and to waive points of order. Requires the consent of every Senator and may be denied by a single objection. These agreements, also called "time agreements," are the Senate parallel to "special rules" from the House Rules Committee.

Waiver - A temporary setting aside of one or more rules by prohibiting points of order that might be raised to enforce those rules. The House uses special rules from the Rules Committee for this purpose. In addition, the House procedure for suspending the rules and passing a measure implicitly imposes a blanket waiver because it suspends all rules, including statutory rules that might conflict with the suspension procedure or the measure's passage.

Yielding Time - Once a Member has been recognized by the Speaker (or Chair) to speak, he controls the Floor; in general, no other Member may speak without being granted permission to do so by the Member recognized. Another Member who wishes to speak will ask the recognized Member to yield by saying, "Will the gentleman yield to me?"

Index

D

E

F

L

M

Q

R

S

About the Authors

Mark Strand is the President of the Congressional Institute. Starting in 1982, Strand spent nearly 24 years on Capitol Hill, most recently as chief of staff to Senator James M. Talent of Missouri. From 2001-2002, Strand was Vice-President of Government Affairs for the American Water Works Company – the largest publicly held water utility in the United States. Prior to that, Strand served as Staff Director of the House Committee on Small Business when Talent was Chairman. He has served as Chief of Staff to Talent, Bill Lowery of California and Stan Parris of Virginia. He has also been a Legislative Director and a Press Secretary. Strand obtained a B.S. in Political Science and History from the Regents College of the University of New York and an MBA in Marketing from the University of Phoenix in 2003, and is pursuing his Masters in Legislative Affairs at George Washington University. He completed the Stennis Congressional Fellowship in 2000 and has been a frequent participant in seminars on Congressional ethics as well as strategic planning and Congressional office management. He is married and has three daughters.

Michael S. Johnson served 14 years in the Executive and Legislative branches of government, first on the White House communications staff of President Gerald R. Ford. He served first as press secretary and later as Chief of Staff for former House Republican Leader Bob Michel of Illinois. Johnson entered the private sector in 1990, serving as a lobbyist with Texas and Ohio law firms. He served as a senior vice president of APCO Worldwide, an international public affairs firm for five years, before joining the OB-C Group in 2001. Johnson has participated in every Republican national convention since 1980, has taught policy and public affairs, serves as a political and communications adviser, and is the current Chairman of the Congressional Institute. A native of Illinois who was reared and educated in South Dakota, Johnson began his career in journalism as a reporter and eventually executive editor of a small Illinois daily newspaper. He is married and has five children.

Jerome F. (Jerry) Climer arrived on Capitol Hill in 1967 where he served as the legislative staff (offices had fewer personnel in those days) to a freshman Member of the US House who managed to stay in office for another 20 years. After taking time out to manage an unsuccessful US Senate campaign, he spent a number of years in the Executive Branch and then returned to the House as Chief Legislative Assistant to another Congressman and then for six years as Chief of Staff to yet another House Member. His final five, official, years on Capitol Hill were served as Leadership Assistant to a Member of the House Republican Leadership. Then Climer co-founded the Congressional Institute, which he served as President for 20 years until his retirement in 2008. He now serves as President of the Public Governance Institute, a 501 (c)(3) organization and heads Policy Implementations Consultants, LLC, a private consulting endeavor.